Individualism
and
Economic Order

FRIEDRICH A. HAYEK

Individualism
and
Economic
Order

THE UNIVERSITY OF CHICAGO PRESS

Chicago and London

THE UNIVERSITY OF CHICAGO PRESS, CHICAGO 60637
THE UNIVERSITY OF CHICAGO PRESS, LTD., LONDON

ISBN: 0-226-32093-6
LCN: 48-4149

Preface

ALTHOUGH the essays collected in this volume may at first appear to be concerned with a great variety of topics, I hope that
the reader will soon discover that most of them treat of closely connected problems. While they range from discussions of moral philosophy to the methods of the social sciences and from problems of economic policy to pure economic theory, these questions are treated
in most of the essays as different aspects of the same central issue. This
connection will be seen most readily in the first six essays, yet in some
measure the three on the problem of socialist calculation which follow them may be regarded as an application of the same ideas to a
particular problem, although when I wrote these I did not yet quite
see it in that light. Only the last three essays deal with somewhat different points of theory or policy; but, since I believe that the problems
with which they are concerned will be discussed even more in the
future than they have been in the past, I have taken this opportunity
to make them available in a more convenient form.

Since I published not long ago a more popular book on problems
related to some of those discussed here, I should in fairness warn the
reader that the present volume is not intended for popular consumption. Only a few of the essays collected here (chaps. i and vi, and possibly iv and v) may in a sense be regarded as supplementary to that
advance sketch of certain practical conclusions which a sense of ur-
gency has tempted me to publish under the title *The Road to Serfdom*.
The rest are definitely addressed to fellow-students and are fairly
technical in character. All are admittedly fragments, products which
have emerged in the pursuit of a distant goal, which for the time being
must serve in place of the finished product. I should perhaps add that
from my recent publications in the field with which most of the essays
in this volume deal I have not included two series of articles on
"Scientism and the Study of Society" and the "Counterrevolution of

Preface

Science" because they are intended to form part of a larger and more systematic work; in the meantime they can be found in the volumes of *Economica* for 1941–45 and 1940, respectively.

My thanks are due to the editors of the *American Economic Review*, *Economica*, the *Economic Journal*, *Ethics*, and the *New Commonwealth Quarterly* for permission to reprint articles which first appeared in these journals, and to Messrs. George Routledge & Sons, Ltd., London, for permission to reproduce the two essays originally contributed to the volume on *Collectivist Economic Planning* published by them in 1935.

F. A. HAYEK

LONDON SCHOOL OF ECONOMICS

Contents

I. Individualism: *True and False**

> Du dix-huitième siècle et de la révolution, comme d'une source commune,
> étaient sortis deux fleuves: le premier conduisait les hommes aux institutions
> libres, tandis que le second les menait au pouvoir absolu.
>
> —ALEXIS DE TOCQUEVILLE.

1

TO ADVOCATE any clear-cut principles of social order is today an almost certain way to incur the stigma of being an unpractical doctrinaire. It has come to be regarded as the sign of the judicious mind that in social matters one does not adhere to fixed principles but decides each question "on its merits"; that one is generally guided by expediency and is ready to compromise between opposed views. Principles, however, have a way of asserting themselves even if they are not explicitly recognized but are only implied in particular decisions, or if they are present only as vague ideas of what is or is not being done. Thus it has come about that under the sign of "neither individualism nor socialism" we are in fact rapidly moving from a society of free individuals toward one of a completely collectivist character.

I propose not only to undertake to defend a general principle of social organization but shall also try to show that the aversion to general principles, and the preference for proceeding from particular instance to particular instance, is the product of the movement which with the "inevitability of gradualness" leads us back from a social order resting on the general recognition of certain principles to a system in which order is created by direct commands.

After the experience of the last thirty years, there is perhaps not

* The twelfth Finlay Lecture, delivered at University College, Dublin, on December 17, 1945. Published by Hodges, Figgis & Co., Ltd., Dublin, and B. H. Blackwell, Ltd., Oxford, 1946.

much need to emphasize that without principles we drift. The pragmatic attitude which has been dominant during that period, far from increasing our command over developments, has in fact led us to a state of affairs which nobody wanted; and the only result of our disregard of principles seems to be that we are governed by a logic of events which we are vainly attempting to ignore. The question now is not whether we need principles to guide us but rather whether there still exists a body of principles capable of general application which we could follow if we wished. Where can we still find a set of precepts which will give us definite guidance in the solution of the problems of our time? Is there anywhere a consistent philosophy to be found which supplies us not merely with the moral aims but with an adequate method for their achievement?

That religion itself does not give us definite guidance in these matters is shown by the efforts of the church to elaborate a complete social philosophy and by the entirely opposite results at which many arrive who start from the same Christian foundations. Though the declining influence of religion is undoubtedly one major cause of our present lack of intellectual and moral orientation, its revival would not much lessen the need for a generally accepted principle of social order. We still should require a political philosophy which goes beyond the fundamental but general precepts which religion or morals provide.

The title which I have chosen for this chapter shows that to me there still seems to exist such a philosophy—a set of principles which, indeed, is implicit in most of Western or Christian political tradition but which can no longer be unambiguously described by any readily understood term. It is therefore necessary to restate these principles fully before we can decide whether they can still serve us as practical guides.

The difficulty which we encounter is not merely the familiar fact that the current political terms are notoriously ambiguous or even that the same term often means nearly the opposite to different groups. There is the much more serious fact that the same word frequently appears to unite people who in fact believe in contradictory and irreconcilable ideals. Terms like "liberalism" or "democracy," "capitalism" or "socialism," today no longer stand for coherent systems of ideas. They have come to describe aggregations of quite heterogeneous principles and facts which historical accident has associated with these words but which have little in common beyond having been advocated at different times by the same people or even merely under the same name.

No political term has suffered worse in this respect than "individualism." It not only has been distorted by its opponents into an unrecognizable caricature—and we should always remember that the political concepts which are today out of fashion are known to most of our contemporaries only through the picture drawn of them by their enemies—but has been used to describe several attitudes toward society which have as little in common among themselves as they have with those traditionally regarded as their opposites. Indeed, when in the preparation of this paper I examined some of the standard descriptions of "individualism," I almost began to regret that I had ever connected the ideals in which I believe with a term which has been so abused and so misunderstood. Yet, whatever else "individualism" may have come to mean in addition to these ideals, there are two good reasons for retaining the term for the view I mean to defend: this view has always been known by that term, whatever else it may also have meant at different times, and the term has the distinction that the word "socialism" was deliberately coined to express its opposition to individualism.[1] It is with the system which forms the alternative to socialism that I shall be concerned.

2

Before I explain what I mean by true individualism, it may be useful if I give some indication of the intellectual tradition to which it

1. Both the term "individualism" and the term "socialism" are originally the creation of the Saint-Simonians, the founders of modern socialism. They first coined the term "individualism" to describe the competitive society to which they were opposed and then invented the word "socialism" to describe the centrally planned society in which all activity was directed on the same principle that applied within a single factory. See on the origin of these terms the present author's article on "The Counter-Revolution of Science," *Economica*, VIII (new ser., 1941), 146.

belongs. The true individualism which I shall try to defend began its modern development with John Locke, and particularly with Bernard Mandeville and David Hume, and achieved full stature for the first time in the work of Josiah Tucker, Adam Ferguson, and Adam Smith and in that of their great contemporary, Edmund Burke—the man whom Smith described as the only person he ever knew who thought on economic subjects exactly as he did without any previous communication having passed between them.[2] In the nineteenth century I find it represented most perfectly in the work of two of its greatest historians and political philosophers: Alexis de Tocqueville and Lord Acton. These two men seem to me to have more successfully developed what was best in the political philosophy of the Scottish philosophers, Burke, and the English Whigs than any other writers I know; while the classical economists of the nineteenth century, or at least the Benthamites or philosophical radicals among them, came increasingly under the influence of another kind of individualism of different origin.

This second and altogether different strand of thought, also known as individualism, is represented mainly by French and other Continental writers—a fact due, I believe, to the dominant role which Cartesian rationalism plays in its composition. The outstanding representatives of this tradition are the Encyclopedists, Rousseau, and the physiocrats; and, for reasons we shall presently consider, this rationalistic individualism always tends to develop into the opposite of individualism, namely, socialism or collectivism. It is because only the first kind of individualism is consistent that I claim for it the name of true individualism, while the second kind must probably be regarded as a source of modern socialism as important as the properly collectivist theories.[3]

2. R. Bisset, *Life of Edmund Burke* (2d ed., 1800), II, 429. Cf. also W. C. Dunn, "Adam Smith and Edmund Burke: Complimentary Contemporaries," *Southern Economic Journal* (University of North Carolina), Vol. VII, No. 3 (January, 1941).

3. Carl Menger, who was among the first in modern times consciously to revive the methodical individualism of Adam Smith and his school, was probably also the first to point out the connection between the design theory of social institutions and

Individualism: True and False

I can give no better illustration of the prevailing confusion about the meaning of individualism than the fact that the man who to me seems to be one of the greatest representatives of true individualism, Edmund Burke, is commonly (and rightly) represented as the main opponent of the so-called "individualism" of Rousseau, whose theories he feared would rapidly dissolve the commonwealth "into the dust and powder of individuality,"[4] and that the term "individualism" itself was first introduced into the English language through the translation of one of the works of another of the great representatives of true individualism, De Tocqueville, who uses it in his *Democracy in America* to describe an attitude which he deplores and rejects.[5] Yet there can no doubt that both Burke and De Tocqueville stand in all essentials close to Adam Smith, to whom nobody will deny the title of individualist, and that the "individualism" to which they are opposed is something altogether different from that of Smith.

---

socialism. See his *Untersuchungen über die Methode der Sozialwissenschaften* (1883), esp. Book IV, chap. 2, toward the end of which (p. 208) he speaks of "a pragmatism which, against the intention of its representatives, leads inevitably to socialism."

It is significant that the physiocrats already were led from the rationalistic individualism from which they started, not only close to socialism (fully developed in their contemporary Morelly's *Le Code de la nature* [1755], but to advocate the worst depotism. "L'État fait des hommes tout ce qu'il veut," wrote Bodeau.

4. Edmund Burke, *Reflections on the Revolution in France* (1790), in *Works* (World's Classics ed.), IV, 105: "Thus the commonwealth itself would, in a few generations, be disconnected into the dust and powder of individuality, and at length dispersed to all winds of heaven." That Burke (as A. M. Osborn points out in her book on *Rousseau and Burke* [Oxford, 1940], p. 23), after he had first attacked Rousseau for his extreme "individualism," later attacked him for his extreme collectivism was far from inconsistent but merely the result of the fact that in the case of Rousseau, as in that of all others, the rationalistic individualism which they preached inevitably led to collectivism.

5. Alexis de Tocqueville, *Democracy in America,* trans. Henry Reeve (London, 1864), Vol. II, Book II, chap. 2, where De Tocqueville defines individualism as "a mature and calm feeling, which disposes each member of the community to sever himself from the mass of his fellows, and to draw apart with his family and friends; so that, after he has thus formed a little circle of his own, he willingly leaves society at large to itself." The translator in a note to this passage apologizes for introducing the French term "individualism" into English and explains that he knows "no English word exactly equivalent to the expression." As Albert Schatz pointed out in the book mentioned below, De Tocqueville's use of the well-established French term in this peculiar sense is entirely arbitrary and leads to serious confusion with the established meaning.

5

What, then, are the essential characteristics of true individualism? The first thing that should be said is that it is primarily a *theory* of society, an attempt to understand the forces which determine the social life of man, and only in the second instance a set of political maxims derived from this view of society. This fact should by itself be sufficient to refute the silliest of the common misunderstandings: the belief that individualism postulates (or bases its arguments on the assumption of) the existence of isolated or self-contained individuals, instead of starting from men whose whole nature and character is determined by their existence in society.[6] If that were true, it would indeed have nothing to contribute to our understanding of society. But its basic contention is quite a different one; it is that there is no other way toward an understanding of social phenomena but through our understanding of individual actions directed toward other people and guided by their expected behavior.[7] This argument is directed primarily against the properly collectivist theories of society which pretend to be able directly to comprehend social wholes like society, etc., as entities *sui generis* which exist independently of the individuals which compose them. The next step in the individualistic analysis of society, however, is directed against the rationalistic pseudo-individualism which also leads to practical collectivism. It is the contention that, by tracing the combined effects of individual actions, we discover

6. In his excellent survey of the history of individualist theories the late Albert Schatz rightly concludes that "nous voyons tout d'abord avec évidence ce que l'individualisme n'est pas. C'est précisément ce qu'on croit communément qu'il est: un système d'isolè-ment dans l'existence et une apologie de l'égoisme" (*L'Individualisme économique et social* [Paris, 1907], p. 558). This book, to which I am much indebted, deserves to be much more widely known as a contribution not only to the subject indicated by its title but to the history of economic theory in general.

7. In this respect, as Karl Pribram has made clear, individualism is a necessary result of philosophical nominalism, while the collectivist theories have their roots in the "realist" or (as K. R. Popper now more appropriately calls it) "essentialist" tradition (Pribram, *Die Entstehung der individualistischen Sozialphilosophie* [Leipzig, 1912]). But this "nominalist" approach is characteristic only of true individualism, while the false individualism of Rousseau and the physiocrats, in accordance with the Cartesian origin, is strongly "realist" or "essentialist."

that many of the institutions on which human achievements rest have arisen and are functioning without a designing and directing mind; that, as Adam Ferguson expressed it, "nations stumble upon establishments, which are indeed the result of human action but not the result of human design";[8] and that the spontaneous collaboration of free men often creates things which are greater than their individual minds can ever fully comprehend. This is the great theme of Josiah Tucker and Adam Smith, of Adam Ferguson and Edmund Burke,

8. Adam Ferguson, *An Essay on the History of Civil Society* (1st ed., 1767), p. 187. Cf. also *ibid.*: "The forms of society are derived from an obscure and distant origin; they arise, long before the date of philosophy, from the instincts, not from the speculations of man.... We ascribe to a previous design, what came to be known only by experience, what no human wisdom could foresee, and what, without the concurring humour and disposition of his age, no authority could enable an individual to execute" (pp. 187 and 188).

It may be of interest to compare these passages with the similar statements in which Ferguson's contemporaries expressed the same basic idea of the eighteenth-century British economists:

Josiah Tucker, *Elements of Commerce* (1756), reprinted in *Josiah Tucker: A Selection from His Economic and Political Writings*, ed. R. L. Schuyler (New York, 1931), pp. 31 and 92: "The main point is neither to extinguish nor to enfeeble self-love, but to give it such a direction that it may promote the public interest by promoting its own.... The proper design of this chapter is to show that the universal mover in human nature, self-love, may receive such a direction in this case (as in all others) as to promote the public interest by those efforts it shall make towards pursuing its own."

Adam Smith, *Wealth of Nations* (1776), ed. Cannan, I, 421: "By directing that industry in such a manner as its produce may be of the greatest value, he intends only his own gain, and he is in this, as in many other cases, led by an invisible hand to promote an end which was no part of his intention. Nor is it always the worse for the society that it was no part of it. By pursuing his own interest he frequently promotes that of the society more effectually than when he really intends to promote it." Cf. also *The Theory of Moral Sentiments* (1759), Part IV (9th ed., 1801), chap. i, p. 386.

Edmund Burke, *Thoughts and Details on Scarcity* (1795), in *Works* (World's Classics ed.), VI, 9: "The benign and wise disposer of all things, who obliges men, whether they will or not, in pursuing their own selfish interests, to connect the general good with their own individual success."

After these statements have been held up for scorn and ridicule by the majority of writers for the last hundred years (C. E. Raven not long ago called the last-quoted statement by Burke a "sinister sentence"—see his *Christian Socialism* [1920], p. 34), it is interesting now to find one of the leading theorists of modern socialism adopting Adam Smith's conclusions. According to A. P. Lerner (*The Economics of Control* [New York, 1944], p. 67), the essential social utility of the price mechanism is that "if it is appropriately used it induces each member of society, while seeking his own benefit, to do that which is in the general social interest. Fundamentally this is the great discovery of Adam Smith and the Physiocrats."

7

the great discovery of classical political economy which has become the basis of our understanding not only of economic life but of most truly social phenomena.

The difference between this view, which accounts for most of the order which we find in human affairs as the unforeseen result of individual actions, and the view which traces all discoverable order to deliberate design is the first great contrast between the true individualism of the British thinkers of the eighteenth century and the so-called "individualism" of the Cartesian school.[9] But it is merely one aspect of an even wider difference between a view which in general rates rather low the place which reason plays in human affairs, which contends that man has achieved what he has in spite of the fact that he is only partly guided by reason, and that his individual reason is very limited and imperfect, and a view which assumes that Reason, with a capital *R*, is always fully and equally available to all humans and that everything which man achieves is the direct result of, and therefore subject to, the control of individual reason. One might even say that the former is a product of an acute consciousness of the limitations of the individual mind which induces an attitude of humility toward the impersonal and anonymous social processes by which individuals help to create things greater than they know, while the latter is the product of an exaggerated belief in the powers of individual reason and of a consequent contempt for anything which has not been consciously designed by it or is not fully intelligible to it.

The antirationalistic approach, which regards man not as a highly rational and intelligent but as a very irrational and fallible being, whose individual errors are corrected only in the course of a social

9. Cf. Schatz, *op. cit.*, pp. 41–42, 81, 378, 568–69, esp. the passage quoted by him (p. 41, n. 1) from an article by Albert Sorel ("Comment j'ai lu la 'Réforme sociale,'" in *Réforme sociale*, November 1, 1906, p. 614): "Quel que fut mon respect, assez commandé et indirect encore pour le *Discours de la méthode*, je savais déja que de ce fameux discours il était sorti autant de déraison sociale et d'aberrations métaphysiques, d'abstractions et d'utopies, que de données positives, que s'il menait à Comte il avait aussie mené à Rousseau." On the influence of Descartes on Rousseau see further P. Janet, *Histoire de la science politique* (3d ed., 1887), p. 423; F. Bouillier, *Histoire de la philosophie cartésienne* (3d ed., 1868), p. 643; and H. Michel, *L'Idée de l'état* (3d ed., 1898), p. 68.

process, and which aims at making the best of a very imperfect material, is probably the most characteristic feature of English individualism. Its predominance in English thought seems to me due largely to the profound influence exercised by Bernard Mandeville, by whom the central idea was for the first time clearly formulated.[10]

I cannot better illustrate the contrast in which Cartesian or rationalistic "individualism" stands to this view than by quoting a famous passage from Part II of the *Discourse on Method*. Descartes argues that "there is seldom so much perfection in works composed of many separate parts, upon which different hands had been employed, as in those completed by a single master." He then goes on to suggest (after, significantly, quoting the instance of the engineer drawing up his plans) that "those nations which, starting from a semi-barbarous state and advancing to civilization by slow degrees, have had their laws successively determined, and, as it were, forced upon them simply by experience of the hurtfulness of particular crimes and disputes, would by this process come to be possessed of less perfect institutions than those which, from the commencement of their association as communities, have followed the appointment of some wise legislator." To drive this point home, Descartes adds that in his opin-

10. The decisive importance of Mandeville in the history of economics, long overlooked or appreciated only by a few authors (particularly Edwin Cannan and Albert Schatz), is now beginning to be recognized, thanks mainly to the magnificent edition of the *Fable of the Bees* which we owe to the late F. B. Kaye. Although the fundamental ideas of Mandeville's work are already implied in the original poem of 1705, the decisive elaboration and especially his full account of the origin of the division of labor, of money, and of language occur only in Part II of the *Fable* which was published in 1728 (see Bernard Mandeville, *The Fable of the Bees*, ed. F. B. Kaye [Oxford, 1924], II, 142, 287–88, 349–50). There is space here to quote only the crucial passage from his account of the development of the division of labor where he observes that "we often ascribe to the excellency of man's genius, and the depth of his penetration, what is in reality owing to the length of time, and the experience of many generations, all of them very little differing from one another in natural parts and sagacity" (*ibid.*, p. 142).

It has become usual to describe Giambattista Vico and his (usually wrongly quoted) formula, *homo non intelligendo fit omnia* (*Opere*, ed. G. Ferrari [2d ed.; Milan, 1854], V, 183), as the beginning of the antirationalistic theory of social phenomena, but it would appear that he has been both preceded and surpassed by Mandeville.,

Perhaps it also deserves mention that not only Mandeville but also Adam Smith occupy honorable places in the development of the theory of language which in so many ways raises problems of a nature kindred to those of the other social sciences.

ion "the past pre-eminence of Sparta was due not to the pre-eminence of each of its laws in particular ... but to the circumstance that, originated by a single individual, they all tended to a single end."[11]

It would be interesting to trace further the development of this social contract individualism or the "design" theories of social institutions, from Descartes through Rousseau and the French Revolution down to what is still the characteristic attitude of the engineers to social problems.[12] Such a sketch would show how Cartesian rationalism has persistently proved a grave obstacle to an understanding of historical phenomena and that it is largely responsible for the belief in inevitable laws of historical development and the modern fatalism derived from this belief.[13]

All we are here concerned with, however, is that this view, though also known as "individualism," stands in complete contrast to true individualism on two decisive points. While it is perfectly true of this pseudo-individualism that "belief in spontaneous social products was logically impossible to any philosophers who regarded individual man as the starting point and supposed him to form societies by the union of his particular will with another in a formal contract,"[14] true individualism is the only theory which can claim to make the formation of spontaneous social products intelligible. And, while the design theories necessarily lead to the conclusion that social processes can be made to serve human ends only if they are subjected to the control of individual human reason, and thus lead directly to socialism, true

11. Réné Descartes, *A Discourse on Method* (Everyman's ed.), pp. 10–11.
12. On the characteristic approach of the engineer type of mind to economic phenomena compare the present author's study on "Scientism and the Study of Society," *Economica*, Vols. IX–XI (new ser., 1942–44), esp. XI, 34 ff.
13. Since this lecture was first published I have become acquainted with an instructive article by Jerome Rosenthal on "Attitudes of Some Modern Rationalists to History" (*Journal of the History of Ideas*, IV, No. 4 [October, 1943], 429–56), which shows in considerable detail the antihistorical attitude of Descartes and particularly his disciple Malebranche and gives interesting examples of the contempt expressed by Descartes in his *Recherche de la vérité par la lumière naturelle* for the study of history, languages, geography, and especially the classics.
14. James Bonar, *Philosophy and Political Economy* (1893), p. 85.

Individualism: True and False

individualism believes on the contrary that, if left free, men will often achieve more than individual human reason could design or foresee.

This contrast between the true, antirationalistic and the false, rationalistic individualism permeates all social thought. But because both theories have become known by the same name, and partly because the classical economists of the nineteenth century, and particularly John Stuart Mill and Herbert Spencer, were almost as much influenced by the French as by the English tradition, all sorts of conceptions and assumptions completely alien to true individualism have come to be regarded as essential parts of its doctrine.

Perhaps the best illustration of the current misconceptions of the individualism of Adam Smith and his group is the common belief that they have invented the bogey of the "economic man" and that their conclusions are vitiated by their assumption of a strictly rational behavior or generally by a false rationalistic psychology. They were, of course, very far from assuming anything of the kind. It would be nearer the truth to say that in their view man was by nature lazy and indolent, improvident and wasteful, and that it was only by the force of circumstances that he could be made to behave economically or carefully to adjust his means to his ends. But even this would be unjust to the very complex and realistic view which these men took of human nature. Since it has become fashionable to deride Smith and his contemporaries for their supposedly erroneous psychology, I may perhaps venture the opinion that for all practical purposes we can still learn more about the behavior of men from the *Wealth of Nations* than from most of the more pretentious modern treatises on "social psychology."

However that may be, the main point about which there can be little doubt is that Smith's chief concern was not so much with what man might occasionally achieve when he was at his best but that he should have as little opportunity as possible to do harm when he was at his worst. It would scarcely be too much to claim that the main merit of the individualism which he and his contemporaries advocated is that it is a system under which bad men can do least harm. It

11

is a social system which does not depend for its functioning on our finding good men for running it, or on all men becoming better than they now are, but which makes use of men in all their given variety and complexity, sometimes good and sometimes bad, sometimes intelligent and more often stupid. Their aim was a system under which it should be possible to grant freedom to all, instead of restricting it, as their French contemporaries wished, to "the good and the wise."[15]

The chief concern of the great individualist writers was indeed to

15. A. W. Benn, in his *History of English Rationalism in the Nineteenth Century* (1906), says rightly: "With Quesnay, following nature meant ascertaining by a study of the world about us and of its laws what conduct is most conducive to health and happiness; and the natural rights meant liberty to pursue the course so ascertained. Such liberty only belongs to the wise and good, and can only be granted to those whom the tutelary authority in the state is pleased to regard as such. With Adam Smith and his disciples, on the other hand, nature means the totality of impulses and instincts by which the individual members of society are animated; and their contention is that the best arrangements result from giving free play to those forces in the confidence that partial failure will be more than compensated by successes elsewhere, and that the pursuit of his own interest by each will work out in the greatest happiness of all" (I, 289).

On this whole question see Elie Halévy, *The Growth of Philosophic Radicalism* (1928), esp. pp. 266–70.

The contrast of the Scottish philosophers of the eighteenth century with their French contemporaries is also brought out in Gladys Bryson's recent study on *Man and Society: The Scottish Enquiry of the Eighteenth Century* (Princeton, 1945), p. 145. She emphasizes that the Scottish philosophers "all wanted to break away from Cartesian rationalism, with its emphasis on abstract intellectualism and innate ideas," and repeatedly stresses the "anti-individualistic" tendencies of David Hume (pp. 106, 155)—using "individualistic" in what we call here the false, rationalistic sense. But she occasionally falls back into the common mistake of regarding them as "representative and typical of the thought of the century" (p. 176). There is still, largely as a result of an acceptance of the German conception of "the Enlightenment," too much inclination to regard the views of all the eighteenth-century philosophers as similar, whereas in many respects the differences between the English and the French philosophers of the period are much more important than the similarities. The common habit of lumping Adam Smith and Quesnay together, caused by the former belief that Smith was greatly indebted to the physiocrats, should certainly cease, now that this belief has been disproved by W. R. Scott's recent discoveries (see his *Adam Smith as Student and Professor* [Glasgow, 1937], p. 124). It is also significant that both Hume and Smith are reported to have been stimulated to their work by their opposition to Montesquieu.

Some suggestive discussion of the differences between the British and the French social philosophers of the eighteenth century, somewhat distorted, however, by the author's hostility toward the "economic liberalism" of the former, will be found in Rudolf Goldscheid, *Grundlinien zu einer Kritik der Willenskraft* (Vienna, 1905), pp. 32–37.

find a set of institutions by which man could be induced, by his own choice and from the motives which determined his ordinary conduct, to contribute as much as possible to the need of all others; and their discovery was that the system of private property did provide such inducements to a much greater extent than had yet been understood. They did not contend, however, that this system was incapable of further improvement and, still less, as another of the current distortions of their arguments will have it, that there existed a "natural harmony of interests" irrespective of the positive institutions. They were more than merely aware of the conflicts of individual interests and stressed the necessity of "well-constructed institutions" where the "rules and principles of contending interests and compromised advantages"[16] would reconcile conflicting interests without giving any one group power to make their views and interests always prevail over those of all others.

4

There is one point in these basic psychological assumptions which it is necessary to consider somewhat more fully. As the belief that individualism approves and encourages human selfishness is one of the main reasons why so many people dislike it, and as the confusion which exists in this respect is caused by a real intellectual difficulty, we must carefully examine the meaning of the assumptions it makes. There can be no doubt, of course, that in the language of the great writers of the eighteenth century it was man's "self-love," or even his "selfish interests," which they represented as the "universal mover," and that by these terms they were referring primarily to a moral attitude, which they thought to be widely prevalent. These terms, however, did not mean egotism in the narrow sense of concern with only the immediate needs of one's proper person. The "self," for which alone people were supposed to care, did as a matter of course include their family and friends; and it would have made no difference to the argument if it had included anything for which people in fact did care.

16. Edmund Burke, *Thoughts and Details on Scarcity* (1795), in *Works* (World's Classics ed.), VI, 15.

Far more important than this moral attitude, which might be regarded as changeable, is an indisputable intellectual fact which nobody can hope to alter and which by itself is a sufficient basis for the conclusions which the individualist philosophers drew. This is the constitutional limitation of man's knowledge and interests, the fact that he *cannot* know more than a tiny part of the whole of society and that therefore all that can enter into his motives are the immediate effects which his actions will have in the sphere he knows. All the possible differences in men's moral attitudes amount to little, so far as their significance for social organization is concerned, compared with the fact that all man's mind can effectively comprehend are the facts of the narrow circle of which he is the center; that, whether he is completely selfish or the most perfect altruist, the human needs for which he *can* effectively care are an almost negligible fraction of the needs of all members of society. The real question, therefore, is not whether man is, or ought to be, guided by selfish motives but whether we can allow him to be guided in his actions by those immediate consequences which he can know and care for or whether he ought to be made to do what seems appropriate to somebody else who is supposed to possess a fuller comprehension of the significance of these actions to society as a whole.

To the accepted Christian tradition that man must be free to follow *his* conscience in moral matters if his actions are to be of any merit, the economists added the further argument that he should be free to make full use of *his* knowledge and skill, that he must be allowed to be guided by his concern for the particular things of which *he* knows and for which *he* cares, if he is to make as great a contribution to the common purposes of society as he is capable of making. Their main problem was how these limited concerns, which did in fact determine people's actions, could be made effective inducements to cause them voluntarily to contribute as much as possible to needs which lay outside the range of their vision. What the economists understood for the first time was that the market as it had grown up was an effective way of making man take part in a process more complex and extended than he could comprehend and that it was through the market that he was made to contribute "to ends which were no part of his purpose."

It was almost inevitable that the classical writers in explaining their contention should use language which was bound to be misunderstood and that they thus earned the reputation of having extolled selfishness. We rapidly discover the reason when we try to restate the correct argument in simple language. If we put it concisely by saying that people are and ought to be guided in their actions by *their* interests and desires, this will at once be misunderstood or distorted into the false contention that they are or ought to be exclusively guided by their personal needs or selfish interests, while what we mean is that they ought to be allowed to strive for whatever *they* think desirable.

Another misleading phrase, used to stress an important point, is the famous presumption that each man knows his interests best. In this form the contention is neither plausible nor necessary for the individualist's conclusions. The true basis of his argument is that nobody can know *who* knows best and that the only way by which we can find out is through a social process in which everybody is allowed to try and see what he can do. The fundamental assumption, here as elsewhere, is the unlimited variety of human gifts and skills and the consequent ignorance of any single individual of most of what is known to all the other members of society taken together. Or, to put this fundamental contention differently, human Reason, with a capital R, does not exist in the singular, as given or available to any particular person, as the rationalist approach seems to assume, but must be conceived as an interpersonal process in which anyone's contribution is tested and corrected by others. This argument does not assume that all men are equal in their natural endowments and capacities but only that no man is qualified to pass final judgment on the capacities which another possesses or is to be allowed to exercise.

Here I may perhaps mention that only because men are in fact unequal can we treat them equally. If all men were completely equal in their gifts and inclinations, we should have to treat them differently in order to achieve any sort of social organization. Fortunately, they are not equal; and it is only owing to this that the differentiation of functions need not be determined by the arbitrary decision of some organizing will but that, after creating formal equality of the rules applying in the same manner to all, we can leave each individual to find his own level.

There is all the difference in the world between treating people equally and attempting to make them equal. While the first is the condition of a free society, the second means, as De Tocqueville described it, "a new form of servitude."[17]

5

From the awareness of the limitations of individual knowledge and from the fact that no person or small group of persons can know all that is known to somebody, individualism also derives its main practical conclusion: its demand for a strict limitation of all coercive or exclusive power. Its opposition, however, is directed only against the use of *coercion* to bring about organization or association, and not against association as such. Far from being opposed to voluntary association, the case of the individualist rests, on the contrary, on the contention that much of what in the opinion of many can be brought about only by conscious direction, can be better achieved by the voluntary and spontaneous collaboration of individuals. The consistent individualist ought therefore to be an enthusiast for voluntary collaboration—wherever and whenever it does not degenerate into coercion of others or lead to the assumption of exclusive powers.

True individualism is, of course, not anarchism, which is but another product of the rationalistic pseudo-individualism to which it is opposed. It does not deny the necessity of coercive power but wishes

17. This phrase is used over and over again by De Tocqueville to describe the effects of socialism, but see particularly *Oeuvres complètes*, IX (1886), 541, where he says: "Si, en définitive, j'avais à trouver une formule générale pour exprimer ce que m'apparait le socialisme dans son ensemble, je dirais que c'est une nouvelle formule de la servitude." Perhaps I may be allowed to add that it was this phrase of De Tocqueville's which suggested to me the title of a recent book of mine.

to limit it—to limit it to those fields where it is indispensable to prevent coercion by others and in order to reduce the total of coercion to a minimum. While all the individualist philosophers are probably agreed on this general formula, it must be admitted that they are not always very informative on its application in specific cases. Neither the much abused and much misunderstood phrase of "laissez faire" nor the still older formula of "the protection of life, liberty, and property" are of much help. In fact, in so far as both tend to suggest that we can just leave things as they are, they may be worse than no answer; they certainly do not tell us what are and what are not desirable or necessary fields of government activity. Yet the decision whether individualist philosophy can serve us as a practical guide must ultimately depend on whether it will enable us to distinguish between the agenda and the nonagenda of government.

Some general rules of this kind which are of very wide applicability seem to me to follow directly from the basic tenets of individualism: If each man is to use *his* peculiar knowledge and skill with the aim of furthering the aims for which *he* cares, and if, in so doing, he is to make as large a contribution as possible to needs which are beyond his ken, it is clearly necessary, first, that he should have a clearly delimited area of responsibility and, second, that the relative importance to him of the different results he can achieve must correspond to the relative importance to others of the more remote and to him unknown effects of his action.

Let us first take the problem of the determination of a sphere of responsibility and leave the second problem for later. If man is to remain free to make full use of his knowledge or skill, the delimitation of spheres of responsibility must not take the form of an assignation to him of particular ends which he must try to achieve. This would be imposing a specific duty rather than delimiting a sphere of responsibility. Nor must it take the form of allocating to him specific resources selected by some authority, which would take the choice almost as much out of his hands as the imposition of specific tasks. If man is to exercise his own gifts, it must be as a result of his activities

17

and planning that his sphere of responsibility is determined. The solution to this problem which men have gradually developed and which antedates government in the modern sense of the word is the acceptance of formal principles, "a standing rule to live by, common to every one of that society"[18]—of rules which, above all, enable man to distinguish between mine and thine, and from which he and his fellows can ascertain what is his and what is somebody else's sphere of responsibility.

The fundamental contrast between government by rules, whose main purpose is to inform the individual what is his sphere of responsibility within which he must shape his own life, and government by orders which impose specific duties has become so blurred in recent years that it is necessary to consider it a little further. It involves nothing less than the distinction between freedom under the law and the use of the legislative machinery, whether democratic or not, to abolish freedom. The essential point is not that there should be some kind of guiding principle behind the actions of the government but that government should be confined to making the individuals observe principles which *they* know and can take into account in *their* decisions. It means, further, that what the individual may or may not do, or what he can expect his fellows to do or not to do, must depend not on some remote and indirect consequences which his actions may have but on the immediate and readily recognizable circumstances which he can be supposed to know. He must have rules referring to typical situations, defined in terms of what can be known to the acting persons and without regard to the distant effects in the particular instance—rules which, if they are regularly observed, will in the majority of cases operate beneficially—even if they do not do so in the proverbial "hard cases which make bad law."

The most general principle on which an individualist system is

---

18. John Locke, *Two Treatises of Government* (1690), Book II, chap. 4, § 22: "Freedom of men under government is to have a standing rule to live by, common to every one of that society and made by the legislative power erected in it."

based is that it uses the universal acceptance of general principles as the means to create order in social affairs. It is the opposite of such government by principles when, for example, a recent blueprint for a controlled economy suggests as "the fundamental principle of organisation ... that in any particular instance the means that serves society best should be the one that prevails."[19] It is a serious confusion thus to speak of principle when all that is meant is that no principle but only expediency should rule; when everything depends on what authority decrees to be "the interests of society." Principles are a means to prevent clashes between conflicting aims and not a set of fixed ends. Our submission to general principles is necessary because we cannot be guided in our practical action by full knowledge and evaluation of all the consequences. So long as men are not omniscient, the only way in which freedom can be given to the individual is by such general rules to delimit the sphere in which the decision is his. There can be no freedom if the government is not limited to particular kinds of action but can use its powers in any ways which serve particular ends. As Lord Acton pointed out long ago: "Whenever a single definite object is made the supreme end of the State, be it the advantage of a class, the safety or the power of the country, the greatest happiness of the greatest number or the support of any speculative idea, the State becomes for the time inevitably absolute."[20]

6

But, if our main conclusion is that an individualist order must rest on the enforcement of abstract principles rather than on the enforcement of specific orders, this still leaves open the question of the kind of general rules which we want. It confines the exercise of coercive powers in the main to one method, but it still allows almost unlimited scope to human ingenuity in the designing of the most effective set

19. Lerner, *op. cit.*, p. 5.
20. Lord Acton, "Nationality" (1862), reprinted in *The History of Freedom and Other Essays* (1907), p. 288.

of rules; and, though the best solutions of the concrete problems will in most instances have to be discovered by experience, there is a good deal more that we can learn from the general principles of individualism with regard to the desirable nature and contents of these rules. There is, in the first instance, one important corollary of what has already been said, namely, that the rules, because they are to serve as signposts to the individuals in making their own plans, should be designed to remain valid for long periods. Liberal or individualist policy must be essentially long-run policy; the present fashion to concentrate on short-run effects, and to justify this by the argument that "in the long run we are all dead," leads inevitably to the reliance on orders adjusted to the particular circumstances of the moment in the place of rules couched in terms of typical situations.

We need, and get from the basic principles of individualism, however, much more definite aid than this for the construction of a suitable legal system. The endeavor to make man by the pursuit of his interests contribute as much as possible to the needs of other men leads not merely to the general principle of "private property"; it also assists us in determining what the contents of property rights ought to be with respect to different kinds of things. In order that the individual in his decisions should take account of all the physical effects caused by these decisions, it is necessary that the "sphere of responsibility" of which I have been speaking be made to comprise as fully as possible all the direct effects which his actions have on the satisfactions which other people derive from the things under his control. This is achieved on the whole by the simple conception of property as the exclusive right to use a particular thing where mobile effects, or what the lawyer calls "chattels," are concerned. But it raises much more difficult problems in connection with land, where the recognition of the principle of private property helps us very little until we know precisely what rights and obligations ownership includes. And when we turn to such problems of more recent origin as the control of the air or of electric power, or of inventions and of literary or artistic creations, nothing short of going back to *rationale* of property will help us to decide what should be in the particular instance the sphere of control or responsibility of the individual.

I cannot here go further into the fascinating subject of a suitable legal framework for an effective individualist system or enter into discussion of the many supplementary functions, such as assistance in the spreading of information and in the elimination of genuinely avoidable uncertainty,[21] by which the government might greatly increase the efficiency of individual action. I mention them merely in order to stress that there are further (and noncoercive!) functions of government beyond the mere enforcement of civil and criminal law which can be fully justified on individualist principles.

There is still, however, one point left, to which I have already referred, but which is so important that I must give it further attention. It is that any workable individualist order must be so framed not only that the relative remunerations the individual can expect from the different uses of his abilities and resources correspond to the relative utility of the result of his efforts to others but also that these remunerations correspond to the objective results of his efforts rather than to their subjective merits. An effectively competitive market satisfies both these conditions. But it is in connection with the second that our personal sense of justice so frequently revolts against the impersonal decisions of the market. Yet, if the individual is to be free to choose, it is inevitable that he should bear the risk attaching to that choice and

21. The actions a government can expediently take to reduce really *avoidable* uncertainty for the individuals are a subject which has given rise to so many confusions that I am afraid to let the brief allusion to it in the text stand without some further explanation. The point is that, while it is easy to protect a particular person or group against the loss which might be caused by an unforseen change, by preventing people from taking notice of the change after it has occurred, this merely shifts the loss onto other shoulders but does not prevent it. If, e.g., capital invested in very expensive plant is protected against obsolescence by new inventions by prohibiting the introduction of such new inventions, this increases the security of the owners of the existing plant but deprives the public of the benefit of the new inventions. Or, in other words, it does not really reduce uncertainty for society as a whole if we make the behavior of the people more predictable by preventing them from adapting themselves to an unforeseen change in their knowledge of the world. The only genuine reduction of uncertainty consists in increasing its knowledge, but never in preventing people from making use of new knowledge.

21

that in consequence he be rewarded, not according to the goodness or badness of his intentions, but solely on the basis of the value of the results to others. We must face the fact that the preservation of individual freedom is incompatible with a full satisfaction of our views of distributive justice.

7

While the theory of individualism has thus a definite contribution to make to the technique of constructing a suitable legal framework and of improving the institutions which have grown up spontaneously, its emphasis, of course, is on the fact that the part of our social order which can or ought to be made a conscious product of human reason is only a small part of all the forces of society. In other words, that the state, the embodiment of deliberately organized and consciously directed power, ought to be only a small part of the much richer organism which we call "society," and that the former ought to provide merely a framework within which free (and therefore not "consciously directed") collaboration of men has the maximum of scope.

This entails certain corollaries on which true individualism once more stands in sharp opposition to the false individualism of the rationalistic type. The first is that the deliberately organized state on the one side, and the individual on the other, far from being regarded as the only realities, while all the intermediate formations and associations are to be deliberately suppressed, as was the aim of the French Revolution, the noncompulsory conventions of social intercourse are considered as essential factors in preserving the orderly working of human society. The second is that the individual, in participating in the social processes, must be ready and willing to adjust himself to changes and to submit to conventions which are not the result of intelligent design, whose justification in the particular instance may not be recognizable, and which to him will often appear unintelligible and irrational.

Individualism: True and False

I need not say much on the first point. That true individualism affirms the value of the family and all the common efforts of the small community and group, that it believes in local autonomy and voluntary associations, and that indeed its case rests largely on the contention that much for which the coercive action of the state is usually invoked can be done better by voluntary collaboration need not be stressed further. There can be no greater contrast to this than the false individualism which wants to dissolve all these smaller groups into atoms which have no cohesion other than the coercive rules imposed by the state, and which tries to make all social ties prescriptive, instead of using the state mainly as a protection of the individual against the arrogation of coercive powers by the smaller groups.

Quite as important for the functioning of an individualist society as these smaller groupings of men are the traditions and conventions which evolve in a free society and which, without being enforceable, establish flexible but normally observed rules that make the behavior of other people predictable in a high degree. The willingness to submit to such rules, not merely so long as one understands the reason for them but so long as one has no definite reasons to the contrary, is an essential condition for the gradual evolution and improvement of rules of social intercourse; and the readiness ordinarily to submit to the products of a social process which nobody has designed and the reasons for which nobody may understand is also an indispensable condition if it is to be possible to dispense with compulsion.[22] That the existence of common conventions and traditions among a group of people will enable them to work together smoothly and efficiently with much less formal organization and compulsion than a group

22. The difference between the rationalistic and the true individualistic approach is well shown in the different views expressed by French observers on the apparent irrationality of English social institutions. While Henri de Saint-Simon, e.g., complains that "cent volumes *in folio*, du caractère plus fin, ne suffiraient pas pour rendre compte de toutes les inconséquences organiques qui existent en Angleterre" (*Oeuvres de Saint-Simon et d'Enfantin* [Paris, 1865–78], XXXVIII, 179), De Tocqueville retorts "que ces bizarreries des Anglais pussent avoir quelques rapports avec leurs libertés, c'est ce qui ne lui tombe point dans l'esprit" (*L'Ancien régime et la révolution* [7th ed.; Paris, 1866], p. 103).

without such common background, is, of course, a commonplace. But the reverse of this, while less familiar, is probably not less true: that coercion can probably only be kept to a minimum in a society where conventions and tradition have made the behavior of man to a large extent predictable.[23]

This brings me to my second point: the necessity, in any complex society in which the effects of anyone's action reach far beyond his possible range of vision, of the individual submitting to the anonymous and seemingly irrational forces of society—a submission which must include not only the acceptance of rules of behavior as valid without examining what depends in the particular instance on their being observed but also a readiness to adjust himself to changes which may profoundly affect his fortunes and opportunities and the causes of which may be altogether unintelligible to him. It is against these that modern man tends to revolt unless their necessity can be shown to rest upon "reason made clear and demonstrable to every individual." Yet it is just here that the understandable craving for intelligibility produces illusory demands which no system can satisfy. Man in a complex society can have no choice but between adjusting himself to what to him must seem the blind forces of the social process and obeying the orders of a superior. So long as he knows only the hard discipline of the market, he may well think the direction by some other intelligent human brain preferable; but, when he tries it, he soon discovers that the former still leaves him at least some choice, while the latter leaves him none, and that it is better to have a choice between several unpleasant alternatives than being coerced into one.

The unwillingness to tolerate or respect any social forces which are

23. Is it necessary to quote Edmund Burke once more to remind the reader how essential a condition for the possibbility of a free society was to him the strength of moral rules? "Men are qualified for civil liberty," he wrote, "in exact proportion to their disposition to put moral chains upon their own appetites; in proportion as their love of justice is above their rapacity; in proportion as their own soundness and sobriety of understanding is above their vanity and presumption; in proportion as they are more disposed to listen to the councils of the wise and good, in preference to the flattery of knaves" (*A Letter to a Member of the National Assembly* [1791], in *Works* [World's Classics ed.], IV, 319).

not recognizable as the product of intelligent design, which is so important a cause of the present desire for comprehensive economic planning, is indeed only one aspect of a more general movement. We meet the same tendency in the field of morals and conventions, in the desire to substitute an artificial for the existing languages, and in the whole modern attitude toward processes which govern the growth of knowledge. The belief that only a synthetic system of morals, an artificial language, or even an artificial society can be justified in an age of science, as well as the increasing unwillingness to bow before any moral rules whose utility is not rationally demonstrated, or to conform with conventions whose rationale is not known, are all manifestations of the same basic view which wants all social activity to be recognizably part of a single coherent plan. They are the results of that same rationalistic "individualism" which wants to see in everything the product of conscious individual reason. They are certainly not, however, a result of true individualism and may even make the working of a free and truly individualistic system difficult or impossible. Indeed, the great lesson which the individualist philosophy teaches us on this score is that, while it may not be difficult to destroy the spontaneous formations which are the indispensable bases of a free civilization, it may be beyond our power deliberately to reconstruct such a civilization once these foundations are destroyed.

8

The point I am trying to make is well illustrated by the apparent paradox that the Germans, though commonly regarded as very docile, are also often described as being particularly individualistic. With some truth this so-called German individualism is frequently represented as one of the causes why the Germans have never succeeded in developing free political institutions. In the rationalistic sense of the term, in their insistence on the development of "original" personalities which in every respect are the product of the conscious choice of the individual, the German intellectual tradition indeed favors a kind of "individualism" little known elsewhere. I remember well how surprised and even shocked I was myself when as a young student, on my first contact with English and American contemporaries, I discovered how much they were disposed to conform in all externals to common usage rather than, as seemed natural to me, to be proud to be different and original in most respects. If you doubt the significance of such an individual experience, you will find it fully confirmed in most German discussions of, for example, the English public school system, such as you will find in Dibelius' well-known book on England.[24] Again and again you will find the same surprise about this tendency toward voluntary conformity and see it contrasted with the ambition of the young German to develop an "original personality," which in every respect expresses what he has come to regard as right and true. This cult of the distinct and different individuality has, of course, deep roots in the German intellectual tradition and, through the influence of some of its greatest exponents, especially Goethe and Wilhelm von Humboldt, has made itself felt far beyond Germany and is clearly seen in J. S. Mill's *Liberty*.

This sort of "individualism" not only has nothing to do with true individualism but may indeed prove a grave obstacle to the smooth working of an individualist system. It must remain an open question whether a free or individualistic society can be worked successfully if people are too "individualistic" in the false sense, if they are too unwilling voluntarily to conform to traditions and conventions, and if they refuse to recognize anything which is not consciously designed or which cannot be demonstrated as rational to every individual. It is at least understandable that the prevalence of this kind of "individualism" has often made people of good will despair of the possibility of achieving order in a free society and even made them ask for a dictatorial government with the power to impose on society the order which it will not produce itself.

In Germany, in particular, this preference for the deliberate organization and the corresponding contempt for the spontaneous and un-

24. W. Dibelius, *England* (1923), pp. 464–68 of 1934 English translation.

controlled, was strongly supported by the tendency toward centralization which the struggle for national unity produced. In a country where what traditions it possessed were essentially local, the striving for unity implied a systematic opposition to almost everything which was a spontaneous growth and its consistent replacement by artificial creations. That, in what a recent historian has well described as a "desperate search for a tradition which they did not possess,"[25] the Germans should have ended by creating a totalitarian state which forced upon them what they felt they lacked should perhaps not have surprised us as much as it did.

9

If it is true that the progressive tendency toward central control of all social processes is the inevitable result of an approach which insists that everything must be tidily planned and made to show a recognizable order, it is also true that this tendency tends to create conditions in which nothing but an all-powerful central government can preserve order and stability. The concentration of all decisions in the hands of authority itself produces a state of affairs in which what structure society still possesses is imposed upon it by government and in which the individuals have become interchangeable units with no other definite or durable relations to one another than those determined by the all-comprehensive organization. In the jargon of the modern sociologists this type of society has come to be known as "mass society"—a somewhat misleading name, because the characteristic attributes of this kind of society are not so much the result of mere numbers as they are of the lack of any spontaneous structure other than that impressed upon it by deliberate organization, an incapacity to evolve its own differentiations, and a consequent dependence on a power which deliberately molds and shapes it. It is connected with numbers only in so far as in large nations the process of centralization will much sooner reach a point where deliberate organization from the top smothers those spontaneous formations which

25. E. Vermeil, *Germany's Three Reichs* (London, 1944), p. 224.

are founded on contacts closer and more intimate than those that can exist in the large unit.

It is not surprising that in the nineteenth century, when these tendencies first became clearly visible, the opposition to centralization became one of the main concerns of the individualist philosophers. This opposition is particularly marked in the writings of the two great historians whose names I have before singled out as the leading representatives of true individualism in the nineteenth century, De Tocqueville and Lord Acton; and it finds expression in their strong sympathies for the small countries and for the federal organization of large units. There is even more reason now to think that the small countries may before long become the last oases that will preserve a free society. It may already be too late to stop the fatal course of progressive centralization in the bigger countries which are well on the way to produce those mass societies in which despotism in the end comes to appear as the only salvation. Whether even the small countries will escape will depend on whether they keep free from the poison of nationalism, which is both an inducement to, and a result of, that same striving for a society which is consciously organized from the top.

The attitude of individualism to nationalism, which intellectually is but a twin brother of socialism, would deserve special discussion. Here I can only point out that the fundamental difference between what in the nineteenth century was regarded as liberalism in the English-speaking world and what was so called on the Continent is closely connected with their descent from true individualism and the false rationalistic individualism, respectively. It was only liberalism in the English sense that was generally opposed to centralization, to nationalism and to socialism, while the liberalism prevalent on the Continent favored all three. I should add, however, that, in this as in so many other respects, John Stuart Mill, and the later English liberalism derived from him, belong at least as much to the Continental as to the English tradition; and I know no discussion more illuminating of these basic differences than Lord Acton's criticism of the concessions Mill had made to the nationalistic tendencies of Continental liberalism.[26]

10

There are two more points of difference between the two kinds of individualism which are also best illustrated by the stand taken by Lord Acton and De Tocqueville by their views on democracy and equality toward trends which became prominent in their time. True individualism not only believes in democracy but can claim that democratic ideals spring from the basic principles of individualism. Yet, while individualism affirms that all government should be democratic, it has no superstitious belief in the omnicompetence of majority decisions, and in particular it refuses to admit that "absolute power may, by the hypothesis of popular origin, be as legitimate as constitutional freedom."[27] It believes that under a democracy, no less than under any other form of government, "the sphere of enforced command ought to be restricted within fixed limits";[28] and it is particularly opposed to the most fateful and dangerous of all current misconceptions of democracy—the belief that we must accept as true and binding for future development the views of the majority. While democracy is founded on the convention that the majority view decides on common action, it does not mean that what is today the majority view ought to become the generally accepted view—even if that were necessary to achieve the aims of the majority. On the contrary, the whole justification of democracy rests on the fact that in course of time what is today the view of a small minority may become the majority view. I believe, indeed, that one of the most important questions on which political theory will have to discover an answer in the near future is that of finding a line of demarcation between the fields in which the majority views must be binding for all and

26. Lord Acton, "Nationality" (1862), reprinted in *The History of Freedom*, pp. 270–300.
27. Lord Acton, "Sir Erskine May's Democracy in Europe" (1878), reprinted in *The History of Freedom*, p. 78.
28. Lord Acton, *Lectures on Modern History* (1906), p. 10.

the fields in which, on the contrary, the minority view ought to be allowed to prevail if it can produce results which better satisfy a demand of the public. I am, above all, convinced that, where the interests of a particular branch of trade are concerned, the majority view will always be the reactionary, stationary view and that the merit of competition is precisely that it gives the minority a chance to prevail. Where it can do so without any coercive powers, it ought always to have the right.

I cannot better sum up this attitude of true individualism toward democracy than by once more quoting Lord Acton: "The true democratic principle," he wrote, "that none shall have power over the people, is taken to mean that none shall be able to restrain or to elude its power. The true democratic principle, that the people shall not be made to do what it does not like, is taken to mean that it shall never be required to tolerate what it does not like. The true democratic principle, that every man's will shall be as unfettered as possible, is taken to mean that the free will of the collective people shall be fettered in nothing."[29]

When we turn to equality, however, it should be said at once that true individualism is not equalitarian in the modern sense of the word. It can see no reason for trying to make people equal as distinct from treating them equally. While individualism is profoundly opposed to all prescriptive privilege, to all protection, by law or force, of any rights not based on rules equally applicable to all persons, it also denies government the right to limit what the able or fortunate may achieve. It is equally opposed to any rigid limitation of the position individuals may achieve, whether this power is used to perpetuate inequality or to create equality. Its main principle is that no man or group of men should have power to decide what another man's status ought to be, and it regards this as a condition of freedom so essential that it must not be sacrificed to the gratification of our sense of justice or of our envy.

29. Lord Acton, "Sir Erskine May's Democracy in Europe," reprinted in *The History of Freedom*, pp. 93–94.

30

Individualism: True and False

From the point of view of individualism there would not appear to exist even any justification for making all individuals start on the same level by preventing them from profiting by advantages which they have in no way earned, such as being born to parents who are more intelligent or more conscientious than the average. Here individualism is indeed less "individualistic" than socialism, because it recognizes the family as a legitimate unit as much as the individual; and the same is true with respect to other groups, such as linguistic or religious communities, which by their common efforts may succeed for long periods in preserving for their members material or moral standards different from those of the rest of the population. De Tocqueville and Lord Acton speak with one voice on this subject. "Democracy and socialism," De Tocqueville wrote, "have nothing in common but one word, equality. But notice the difference: while democracy seeks equality in liberty, socialism seeks equality in restraint and servitude."[30] And Acton joined him in believing that "the deepest cause which made the French revolution so disastrous to liberty was its theory of equality"[31] and that "the finest opportunity ever given to the world was thrown away, because the passion for equality made vain the hope for freedom."[32]

11

It would be possible to continue for a long time discussing further differences separating the two traditions of thought which, while bearing the same name, are divided by fundamentally opposed principles. But I must not allow myself to be diverted too far from my task of tracing to its source the confusion which has resulted from this and of showing that there is one consistent tradition which, whether you agree with me or not that it is "true" individualism, is at any rate the only kind of individualism which I am prepared to de-

30. Alexis de Tocqueville, *Oeuvres complètes*, IX, 546.

31. Lord Acton, "Sir Erskine May's Democracy in Europe," reprinted in *The History of Freedom*, p. 88.

32. Lord Acton, "The History of Freedom in Christianity" (1877), reprinted in *The History of Freedom*, p. 57.

fend and, indeed, I believe, the only kind which can be defended consistently. So let me return, in conclusion, to what I said in the beginning: that the fundamental attitude of true individualism is one of humility toward the processes by which mankind has achieved things which have not been designed or understood by any individual and are indeed greater than individual minds. The great question at this moment is whether man's mind will be allowed to continue to grow as part of this process or whether human reason is to place itself in chains of its own making.

What individualism teaches us is that society is greater than the individual only in so far as it is free. In so far as it is controlled or directed, it is limited to the powers of the individual minds which control or direct it. If the presumption of the modern mind, which will not respect anything that is not consciously controlled by individual reason, does not learn in time where to stop, we may, as Edmund Burke warned us, "be well assured that everything about us will dwindle by degrees, until at length our concerns are shrunk to the dimensions of our minds."

II. Economics and Knowledge[*]

1

THE ambiguity of the title of this paper is not accidental. Its main subject is, of course, the role which assumptions and propositions about the knowledge possessed by the different members of society play in economic analysis. But this is by no means unconnected with the other question which might be discussed under the same title—the question to what extent formal economic analysis conveys any knowledge about what happens in the real world. Indeed, my main contention will be that the tautologies, of which formal equilibrium analysis in economics essentially consists, can be turned into propositions which tell us anything about causation in the real world only in so far as we are able to fill those formal propositions with definite statements about how knowledge is acquired and communicated. In short, I shall contend that the empirical element in economic theory—the only part which is concerned not merely with implications but with causes and effects and which leads therefore to conclusions which, at any rate in principle, are capable of verification[1] —consists of propositions about the acquisition of knowledge.

Perhaps I should begin by reminding you of the interesting fact that in quite a number of the more recent attempts made in different fields to push theoretical investigation beyond the limits of traditional equilibrium analysis, the answer has soon proved to turn on the assumptions which we make with regard to a point which, if not identical with mine, is at least part of it, namely, with regard to foresight. I think that the field in which, as one would expect, the discus-

* Presidential address delivered before the London Economic Club, November 10, 1936. Reprinted from *Economica*, IV (new ser., 1937), 33–54.
1. Or rather falsification (cf. K. R. Popper, *Logik der Foschung* [Vienna, 1935], *passim*).

33

sion of the assumptions concerning foresight first attracted wider attention was the theory of risk.[2] The stimulus which was exercised in this connection by the work of Frank H. Knight may yet prove to have a profound influence far beyond its special field. Not much later the assumptions to be made concerning foresight proved to be of fundamental importance for the solution of the puzzles of the theory of imperfect competition, the questions of duopoly and oligopoly. Since then, it has become more and more obvious that, in the treatment of the more "dynamic" questions of money and industrial fluctuations, the assumptions to be made about foresight and "anticipations" play an equally central role and that in particular the concepts which were taken over into these fields from pure equilibrium analysis, like those of an equilibrium rate of interest, could be properly defined only in terms of assumptions concerning foresight. The situation seems here to be that, before we can explain why people commit mistakes, we must first explain why they should ever be right.

In general, it seems that we have come to a point where we all realize that the concept of equilibrium itself can be made definite and clear only in terms of assumptions concerning foresight, although we may not yet all agree what exactly these essential assumptions are. This question will occupy me later in this essay. At the moment I am concerned only to show that at the present juncture, whether we want to define the boundaries of economic statics or whether we want to go beyond it, we cannot escape the vexed problem of the exact position which assumptions about foresight are to have in our reasoning. Can this be merely an accident?

As I have already suggested, the reason for this seems to me to be that we have to deal here only with a special aspect of a much wider question which we ought to have faced at a much earlier stage. Questions essentially similar to those mentioned arise in fact as soon as we try to apply the system of tautologies—those series of propositions

2. A more complete survey of the process by which the significance of anticipations was gradually introduced into economic analysis would probably have to begin with Irving Fisher's *Appreciation and Interest* (1896).

which are necessarily true because they are merely transformations of the assumptions from which we start and which constitute the main content of equilibrium analysis—to the situation of a society consisting of several independent persons. I have long felt that the concept of equilibrium itself and the methods which we employ in pure analysis have a clear meaning only when confined to the analysis of the action of a single person and that we are really passing into a different sphere and silently introducing a new element of altogether different character when we apply it to the explanation of the interactions of a number of different individuals.

I am certain that there are many who regard with impatience and distrust the whole tendency, which is inherent in all modern equilibrium analysis, to turn economics into a branch of pure logic, a set of self-evident propositions which, like mathematics or geometry, are subject to no other test but internal consistency. But it seems that, if only this process is carried far enough, it carries its own remedy with it. In distilling from our reasoning about the facts of economic life those parts which are truly a priori, we not only isolate one element of our reasoning as a sort of Pure Logic of Choice in all its purity but we also isolate, and emphasize the importance of, another element which has been too much neglected. My criticism of the recent tendencies to make economic theory more and more formal is not that they have gone too far but that they have not yet been carried far enough to complete the isolation of this branch of logic and to restore to its rightful place the investigation of causal processes, using formal economic theory as a tool in the same way as mathematics.

2

But before I can prove my contention that the tautological propositions of pure equilibrium analysis as such are not directly applicable to the explanation of social relations, I must first show that the concept of equilibrium *has* a clear meaning if applied to the actions of a single individual and what this meaning is. Against my contention it might be argued that it is precisely here that the concept of equilibrium is of no significance, because, if one wanted to apply it, all one could say would be that an isolated person was always in equilibrium. But this last statement, although a truism, shows nothing but the way in which the concept of equilibrium is typically misused. What is relevant is not whether a person as such is or is not in equilibrium but which of his actions stand in equilibrium relationships to each other. All propositions of equilibrium analysis, such as the proposition that relative values will correspond to relative costs, or that a person will equalize the marginal returns of any one factor in its different uses, are propositions about the relations between actions. Actions of a person can be said to be in equilibrium in so far as they can be understood as part of one plan. Only if this is the case, only if all these actions have been decided upon at one and the same moment, and in consideration of the same set of circumstances, have our statements about their interconnections, which we deduce from our assumptions about the knowledge and the preferences of the person, any application. It is important to remember that the so-called "data," from which we set out in this sort of analysis, are (apart from his tastes) all facts given to the person in question, the things as they are known to (or believed by) him to exist, and not, strictly speaking, objective facts. It is only because of this that the propositions we deduce are necessarily a priori valid and that we preserve the consistency of the argument.[3]

The two main conclusions from these considerations are, first, that, since equilibrium relations exist between the successive actions of a person only in so far as they are part of the execution of the same plan, any change in the relevant knowledge of the person, that is, any change which leads him to alter his plan, disrupts the equilibrium relation between his actions taken before and those taken after the change in his knowledge. In other words, the equilibrium relationship comprises only his actions during the period in which his anticipations prove correct. Second, that, since equilibrium is a relationship

3. Cf., on this point particularly, Ludwig von Mises, *Grundprobleme der Nationalökonomie* (Jena, 1933), pp. 22 ff., 160 ff.

between actions, and since the actions of one person must necessarily take place successively in time, it is obvious that the passage of time is essential to give the concept of equilibrium any meaning. This deserves mention, since many economists appear to have been unable to find a place for time in equilibrium analysis and consequently have suggested that equilibrium must be conceived as timeless. This seems to me to be a meaningless statement.

3

Now, in spite of what I have said before about the doubtful meaning of equilibrium analysis in this sense if applied to the conditions of a competitive society, I do not, of course, want to deny that the concept was originally introduced precisely to describe the idea of some sort of balance between the actions of different individuals. All I have argued so far is that the sense in which we use the concept of equilibrium to describe the interdependence of the different actions of one person does not immediately admit of application to the relations between actions of different people. The question really is what use we make of it when we speak of equilibrium with reference to a competitive system.

The first answer which would seem to follow from our approach is that equilibrium in this connection exists if the actions of all members of the society over a period are all executions of their respective individual plans on which each decided at the beginning of the period. But, when we inquire further what exactly this implies, it appears that this answer raises more difficulties than it solves. There is no special difficulty about the concept of an isolated person (or a group of persons directed by one of them) acting over a period according to a preconceived plan. In this case, the plan need not satisfy any special criteria in order that its execution be conceivable. It may, of course, be based on wrong assumptions concerning the external facts and on this account may have to be changed. But there will always be a conceivable set of external events which would make it possible to execute the plan as originally conceived.

The situation is, however, different with plans determined upon simultaneously but independently by a number of persons. In the first instance, in order that all these plans can be carried out, it is necessary for them to be based on the expectation of the same set of external events, since, if different people were to base their plans on conflicting expectations, no set of external events could make the execution of all these plans possible. And, second, in a society based on exchange their plans will to a considerable extent provide for actions which require corresponding actions on the part of other individuals. This means that the plans of different individuals must in a special sense be compatible if it is to be even conceivable that they should be able to carry all of them out.[4] Or, to put the same thing in different words, since some of the data on which any one person will base his plans will be the expectation that other people will act in a particular way, it is essential for the compatibility of the different plans that the plans of the one contain exactly those actions which form the data for the plans of the other.

In the traditional treatment of equilibrium analysis part of this difficulty is apparently avoided by the assumption that the data, in the form of demand schedules representing individual tastes and technical facts, are equally given to all individuals and that their acting on the same premises will somehow lead to their plans becoming adapted to each other. That this does not really overcome the difficulty created by the fact that one person's actions are the other person's data, and that it involves to some degree circular reasoning, has often been pointed out. What, however, seems so far to have escaped notice is that this whole procedure involves a confusion of a much more general character, of which the point just mentioned is merely a special instance, and which is due to an equivocation of the term "datum." The data which here are supposed to be objective facts and the same for all people are evidently no longer the same thing as the

4. It has long been a subject of wonder to me why there should, to my knowledge, have been no systematic attempts in sociology to analyze social relations in terms of correspondence and noncorrespondence, or compatibility and noncompatibility, of individual aims and desires.

data which formed the starting-point for the tautological transformations of the Pure Logic of Choice. There "data" meant those facts, and only those facts, which were present in the mind of the acting person, and only this subjective interpretation of the term "datum" made those propositions necessary truths. "Datum" meant given, known, to the person under consideration. But in the transition from the analysis of the action of an individual to the analysis of the situation in a society the concept has undergone an insidious change of meaning.

4

The confusion about the concept of a datum is at the bottom of so many of our difficulties in this field that it is necessary to consider it in somewhat more detail. Datum means, of course, something given, but the question which is left open, and which in the social sciences is capable of two different answers, is to *whom* the facts are supposed to be given. Economists appear subconsciously always to have been somewhat uneasy about this point and to have reassured themselves against the feeling that they did not quite know to whom the facts were given by underlining the fact that they *were* given—even by using such pleonastic expressions as "given data." But this does not answer the question whether the facts referred to are supposed to be given to the observing economist or to the persons whose actions he wants to explain, and, if to the latter, whether it is assumed that the same facts are known to all the different persons in the system or whether the "data" for the different persons may be different.

There seems to be no possible doubt that these two concepts of "data," on the one hand, in the sense of the objective real facts, as the observing economist is supposed to know them, and, on the other, in the subjective sense, as things known to the persons whose behavior we try to explain, are really fundamentally different and ought to be carefully distinguished. And, as we shall see, the question why the data in the subjective sense of the term should ever come to correspond to the objective data is one of the main problems we have to answer.

The usefulness of the distinction becomes immediately apparent when we apply it to the question of what we can mean by the concept of a society being at any one moment in a state of equilibrium. There are evidently two senses in which it can be said that the subjective data, given to the different persons, and the individual plans, which necessarily follow from them, are in agreement. We may mean merely that these plans are mutually compatible and that there is consequently a conceivable set of external events which will allow all people to carry out their plans and not cause any disappointments. If this mutual compatibility of intentions were not given, and if in consequence no set of external events could satisfy all expectations, we could clearly say that this is not a state of equilibrium. We have a situation where a revision of the plans on the part of at least some people is inevitable, or, to use a phrase which in the past has had a rather vague meaning, but which seems to fit this case perfectly, where "endogenous" disturbances are inevitable.

There still remains, however, the other question of whether the individual sets of subjective data correspond to the objective data and whether, in consequence, the expectations on which plans were based are borne out by the facts. If correspondence between data in this sense were required for equilibrium, it would never be possible to decide otherwise than retrospectively, at the end of the period for which people have planned, whether at the beginning the society has been in equilibrium. It seems to be more in conformity with established usage to say in such a case that the equilibrium, as defined in the first sense, may be disturbed by an unforeseen development of the (objective) data and to describe this as an exogenous disturbance. In fact, it seems hardly possible to attach any definite meaning to the much used concept of a change in the (objective) data unless we distinguish between external developments in conformity with, and those different from, what has been expected, and define as a "change" any divergence of the actual from the expected development, irrespective of whether it means a "change" in some absolute sense. If, for example, the alternations of the seasons suddenly ceased and the weather remained constant from a certain day onward, this would certainly represent a change of data in our sense, that is, a change relative to expectations, although in an absolute sense it would not represent a change but rather an absence of change. But all this means that we can speak of a change in data only if equilibrium in the first sense exists, that is, if expectations coincide. If they conflicted, any development of the external facts might bear out somebody's expectations and disappoint those of others, and there would be no possibility of deciding what was a change in the objective data.[5]

5

For a society, then, we *can* speak of a *state* of equilibrium at a point of time—but it means only that the different plans which the individuals composing it have made for action in time are mutually compatible. And equilibrium will continue, once it exists, so long as the external data correspond to the common expectations of all the members of the society. The continuance of a state of equilibrium in this sense is then not dependent on the objective data being constant in an absolute sense and is not necessarily confined to a stationary process. Equilibrium analysis becomes in principle applicable to a progressive society and to those intertemporal price relationships which have given us so much trouble in recent times.[6]

5. Cf. the present author's article, "The Maintenance of Capital," *Economica*, II (new ser., 1935), 265, reprinted in *Profits, Interest, and Investment* (London, 1939).

6. This separation of the concept of equilibrium from that of a stationary state seems to me to be no more than the necessary outcome of a process which has been going on for a fairly long time. That this association of the two concepts is not essential but only due to historical reasons is today probably generally felt. If complete separation has not yet been effected, it is apparently only because no alternative definition of a state of equilibrium has yet been suggested which has made it possible to state in a general form those propositions of equilibrium analysis which are essentially independent of the concept of a stationary state. Yet it is evident that most of the propositions of equilibrium analysis are not supposed to be applicable only in that stationary state which will probably never be reached. The process of separation seems to have begun with Marshall and his distinction between long- and short-run equilibriums. Cf. statements like this: "For the nature of equilibrium itself, and that of the causes by which it is determined, depend on the length of the period over which the market is taken to extend" (*Principles* [7th ed.], I, 330). The idea of a state of equilibrium which was

Individualism and Economic Order

These considerations seem to throw considerable light on the relationship between equilibrium and foresight, which has been somewhat hotly debated in recent times.[7] It appears that the concept of equilibrium merely means that the foresight of the different members of the society is in a special sense correct. It must be correct in the sense that every person's plan is based on the expectation of just those actions of other people which those other people intend to perform and that all these plans are based on the expectation of the same set of external facts, so that under certain conditions nobody will have any reason to change his plans. Correct foresight is then not, as it has sometimes been understood, a precondition which must exist in order that equilibrium may be arrived at. It is rather the defining characteristic of a state of equilibrium. Nor need foresight for this purpose be perfect in the sense that it need extend into the indefinite future or that everybody must foresee everything correctly. We should rather say that equilibrium will last so long as the anticipations prove correct and that they need to be correct only on those points which are relevant for the decisions of the individuals. But on this question of what is relevant foresight or knowledge, more later.

Before I proceed further I should probably stop for a moment to illustrate by a concrete example what I have just said about the meaning of a state of equilibrium and how it can be disturbed. Consider the preparations which will be going on at any moment for the production of houses. Brickmakers, plumbers, and others will all be producing materials which in each case will correspond to a certain

---

not a stationary state was already inherent in my "Das intertemporale Gleichgewichtssystem der Preise und die Bewegungen des Geldwerters," *Weltwirtschaftliches Archiv,* Vol. XXVIII (June, 1928), and is, of course, essential if we want to use the equilibrium apparatus for the explanation of any of the phenomena connected with "investment." On the whole matter much historical information will be found in E. Schams, "Komparative Statik," *Zeitschrift für Nationalökonomie,* Vol. II, No. 1 (1930). See also F. H. Knight, *The Ethics of Competition* (London, 1935), p. 175 n.; and for some further developments since this essay was first published, the present author's *Pure Theory of Capital* (London, 1941), chap. ii.

7. Cf. particularly Oskar Morgenstern, "Vollkommene Voraussicht und wirtschaftliches Gleichgewicht," *Zeitschrift für Nationalökonomie,* VI (1934), 3.

quantity of houses for which just this quantity of the particular material will be required. Similarly we may conceive of prospective buyers as accumulating savings which will enable them at certain dates to buy a certain number of houses. If all these activities represent preparations for the production (and acquisition) of the same amount of houses, we can say that there is equilibrium between them in the sense that all the people engaged in them may find that they can carry out their plans.[8] This need not be so, because other circumstances which are not part of their plan of action may turn out to be different from what they expected. Part of the materials may be destroyed by an accident, weather conditions may make building impossible, or an invention may alter the proportions in which the different factors are wanted. This is what we call a change in the (external) data, which disturbs the equilibrium which has existed. But if the different plans were from the beginning incompatible, it is inevitable, whatever happens, that somebody's plans will be upset and have to be altered and that in consequence the whole complex of actions over the period will not show those characteristics which apply if all the actions of each individual can be understood as part of a single individual plan, which he has made at the beginning.[9]

8. Another example of more general importance would, of course, be the correspondence between "investment" and "saving" in the sense of the proportion (in terms of relative cost) in which entrepreneurs provide producers' goods and consumers' goods for a particular date, and the proportion in which consumers in general will at this date distribute their resources between producers' goods and consumers' goods (cf. my essays, "Price Expectations, Monetary Disturbances, and Malinvestment" [1933], reprinted in *Profits, Interest, and Investment* [London, 1939], pp. 135–56, and "The Maintenance of Capital," in the same volume, pp. 83–134). It may be of interest in this connection to mention that in the course of investigations of the same field, which led the present author to these speculations, that of the theory of crises, the great French sociologist G. Tarde stressed the "contradiction de croyances" or "contradiction de jugements" or "contradictions d'espérances" as the main cause of these phenomena (*Psychologie économique* [Paris, 1902], II, 128–29; cf. also N. Pinkus, *Das Problem des Normalen in der Nationalökonomie* [Leipzig, 1906], pp. 252 and 275).

9. It is an interesting question, but one which I cannot discuss here, whether, in order that we can speak of equilibrium, every single individual must be right, or whether it would not be sufficient if, in consequence of a compensation of errors in different directions, quantities of the different commodities coming on the market were the same as if every individual had been right. It seems to me as if equilibrium

6

When in all this I emphazise the distinction between mere inter-compatibility of the individual plans[10] and the correspondence between them and the actual external facts or objective data, I do not, of course, mean to suggest that the subjective interagreement is not in some way brought about by the external facts. There would, of course, be no reason why the subjective data of different people should ever correspond unless they were due to the experience of the same objective facts. But the point is that pure equilibrium analysis is not concerned with the way in which this correspondence is brought about. In the description of an existing state of equilibrium which it provides, it is simply assumed that the subjective data coincide with the objective facts. The equilibrium relationships cannot be deduced merely from the objective facts, since the analysis of what people will do can start only from what is known to them. Nor can equilibrium analysis start merely from a given set of subjective data, since the subjective data of different people would be either compatible or incompatible, that is, they would already determine whether equilibrium did or did not exist.

We shall not get much further here unless we ask for the reasons for our concern with the admittedly fictitious state of equilibrium. Whatever may occasionally have been said by overpure economists, there seems to be no possible doubt that the only justification for this is the supposed existence of a tendency toward equilibrium. It is only by this assertion that such a tendency exists that economics ceases to be an exercise in pure logic and becomes an empirical science; and it is to economics as an empirical science that we must now turn.

---

in the strict sense would require the first condition to be satisfied, but I can conceive that a wider concept, requiring only the second condition, might occasionally be useful. A fuller discussion of this problem would have to consider the whole question of the significance which some economists (including Pareto) attach to the law of great numbers in this connection. On the general point see P. N. Rosenstein-Rodan, "The Coordination of the General Theories of Money and Price," *Economica*, August, 1936.

10. Or, since in view of the tautological character of the Pure Logic of Choice "individual plans" and "subjective data" can be used interchangeably, the agreement between the subjective data of the different individuals.

Economics and Knowledge

In the light of our analysis of the meaning of a state of equilibrium it should be easy to say what is the real content of the assertion that a tendency toward equilibrium exists. It can hardly mean anything but that, under certain conditions, the knowledge and intentions of the different members of society are supposed to come more and more into agreement or, to put the same thing in less general and less exact but more concrete terms, that the expectations of the people and particularly of the entrepreneurs will become more and more correct. In this form the assertion of the existence of a tendency toward equilibrium is clearly an empirical proposition, that is, an assertion about what happens in the real world which ought, at least in principle, to be capable of verification. And it gives our somewhat abstract statement a rather plausible common-sense meaning. The only trouble is that we are still pretty much in the dark about (*a*) the *conditions* under which this tendency is supposed to exist and (*b*) the nature of the *process* by which individual knowledge is changed.

7

In the usual presentations of equilibrium analysis it is generally made to appear as if these questions of how the equilibrium comes about were solved. But, if we look closer, it soon becomes evident that these apparent demonstrations amount to no more than the apparent proof of what is already assumed.[11] The device generally adopted for this purpose is the assumption of a perfect market where every event becomes known instantaneously to every member. It is necessary to remember here that the perfect market which is required to satisfy the assumptions of equilibrium analysis must not be confined to the particular markets of all the individual commodities; the whole economic system must be assumed to be one perfect market in which everybody knows everything. The assumption of a perfect market,

11. This seems to be implicitly admitted, although hardly consciously recognized, when in recent times it is frequently stressed that equilibrium analysis only describes the conditions of equilibrium without attempting to derive the position of equilibrium from the data. Equilibrium analysis in this sense would, of course, be pure logic and contain no assertions about the real world.

then, means nothing less than that all the members of the community, even if they are not supposed to be strictly omniscient, are at least supposed to know automatically all that is relevant for their decisions. It seems that that skeleton in our cupboard, the "economic man," whom we have exorcised with prayer and fasting, has returned through the back door in the form of a quasi-omniscient individual.

The statement that, if people know everything, they are in equilibrium is true simply because that is how we define equilibrium. The assumption of a perfect market in this sense is just another way of saying that equilibrium exists but does not get us any nearer an explanation of when and how such a state will come about. It is clear that, if we want to make the assertion that, under certain conditions, people will approach that state, we must explain by what process they will acquire the necessary knowledge. Of course, any assumption about the actual acquisition of knowledge in the course of this process will also be of a hypothetical character. But this does not mean that all such assumptions are equally justified. We have to deal here with assumptions about causation, so that what we assume must not only be regarded as possible (which is certainly not the case if we just regard people as omniscient) but must also be regarded as likely to be true; and it must be possible, at least in principle, to demonstrate that it is true in particular cases.

The significant point here is that it is these apparently subsidiary hypotheses or assumptions that people do learn from experience, and about how they acquire knowledge, which constitute the empirical content of our propositions about what happens in the real world. They usually appear disguised and incomplete as a description of the type of market to which our proposition refers; but this is only one, though perhaps the most important, aspect of the more general problem of how knowledge is acquired and communicated. The important point of which economists frequently do not seem to be aware is that the nature of these hypotheses is in many respects rather different from the more general assumptions from which the Pure Logic of Choice starts. The main differences seem to me to be two:

Economics and Knowledge

First, the assumptions from which the Pure Logic of Choice starts are facts which we know to be common to all human thought. They may be regarded as axioms which define or delimit the field within which we are able to understand or mentally to reconstruct the processes of thought of other people. They are therefore universally applicable to the field in which we are interested—although, of course, where *in concreto* the limits of this field are is an empirical question. They refer to a type of human action (what we commonly call "rational," or even merely "conscious," as distinguished from "instinctive" action) rather than to the particular conditions under which this action is undertaken. But the assumptions or hypotheses, which we have to introduce when we want to explain the social processes, concern the relation of the thought of an individual to the outside world, the question to what extent and how his knowledge corresponds to the external facts. And the hypotheses must necessarily run in terms of assertions about causal connections, about how experience creates knowledge.

Second, while in the field of the Pure Logic of Choice our analysis can be made exhaustive, that is, while we can here develop a formal apparatus which covers all conceivable situations, the supplementary hypotheses must of necessity be selective, that is, we must select from the infinite variety of possible situations such ideal types as for some reason we regard as specially relevant to conditions in the real world.[12] Of course, we could also develop a separate science, the subject mattter of which was *per definitionem* confined to a "perfect market" or some similarly defined object, just as the Logic of Choice applies only to persons who have to allot limited means among a variety of ends. For

12. The distinction drawn here may help to solve the old difference between economists and sociologists about the role which "ideal types" play in the reasoning of economic theory. The sociologists used to emphasize that the usual procedure of economic theory involved the assumption of particular ideal types, while the economic theorist pointed out that his reasoning was of such generality that he need not make use of any "ideal types." The truth seems to be that within the field of the Pure Logic of Choice, in which the economist was largely interested, he was right in his assertion but that, as soon as he wanted to use it for the explanation of a social process, he had to use "ideal types" of one sort or another.

the field so defined our propositions would again become a priori true, but for such a procedure we should lack the justification which consists in the assumption that the situation in the real world is similar to what we assume it to be.

8

I must now turn to the question of what are the concrete hypotheses concerning the conditions under which people are supposed to acquire the relevant knowledge and the process by which they are supposed to acquire it. If it were at all clear what the hypotheses usually employed in this respect were, we should have to scrutinize them in two respects: we should have to investigate whether they were necessary and sufficient to explain a movement toward equilibrium, and we should have to show to what extent they were borne out by reality. But I am afraid that I am now getting to a stage where it becomes exceedingly difficult to say what exactly are the assumptions on the basis of which we assert that there will be a tendency toward equilibrium and to claim that our analysis has an application to the real world.[13] I cannot pretend that I have as yet got much further on this point. Consequently, all I can do is to ask a number of questions to which we shall have to find an answer if we want to be clear about the significance of our argument.

The only condition about the necessity of which for the establishment of an equilibrium economists seem to be fairly agreed is the "constancy of the data." But after what we have seen about the vagueness of the concept of "datum" we shall suspect, and rightly, that this does not get us much further. Even if we assume—as we probably

13. The older economists were often more explicit on this point than their successors. See, e.g., Adam Smith (*Wealth of Nations,* ed. Cannan, I, 116): "In order, however, that this equality [of wages] may take place in the whole of their advantages or disadvantages, three things are required even when there is perfect freedom. First, the employment must be well known and long established in the neighbourhood ..."; or David Ricardo (*Letters to Malthus,* October 22, 1811, p. 18): "It would be no answer to me to say that men were ignorant of the best and cheapest mode of conducting their business and paying their debts, because that is a question of fact, not of science, and might be argued against almost every proposition in Political Economy."

must—that here the term is used in its objective sense (which includes, it will be remembered, the preferences of the different individuals), it is by no means clear that this is either required or sufficient in order that people shall actually acquire the necessary knowledge or that it was meant as a statement of the conditions under which they will do so. It is rather significant that, at any rate, some authors feel it necessary to add "perfect knowledge" as an additional and separate condition.[14] Indeed, we shall see that constancy of the objective data is neither a necessary nor a sufficient condition. That it cannot be a necessary condition follows from the facts, first, that nobody would want to interpret it in the absolute sense that nothing must ever happen in the world, and, second, that, as we have seen, as soon as we want to include changes which occur periodically or perhaps even changes which proceed at a constant rate, the only way in which we can define constancy is with reference to expectations. All that this condition amounts to, then, is that there must be some discernible regularity in the world which makes it possible to predict events correctly. But, while this is clearly not sufficient to prove that people will learn to foresee events correctly, the same is true to a hardly less degree even about constancy of data in an absolute sense. For any one individual, constancy of the data does in no way mean constancy of all the facts independent of himself, since, of course, only the tastes and not the actions of the other people can in this sense be assumed to be constant. As all those other people will change their decisions as they gain experience about the external facts and about other people's actions, there is no reason why these processes of successive changes should ever come to an end. These difficulties are well known,[15] and I mention them here only to remind you how little we actually know about the conditions under which an equilibrium will ever be reached. But I do not propose to follow this line of approach further, though not because this question of the empirical probability that people will learn (that is, that their subjective data will come to correspond with

14. See N. Kaldor, "A Classificatory Note on the Determinateness of Equilibrium," *Review of Economic Studies*, I, No. 2 (1934), 123.

15. *Ibid., passim.*

each other and with the objective facts) is lacking in unsolved and highly interesting problems. The reason is rather that there seems to me to be another and more fruitful way of approach to the central problem.

9

The questions I have just discussed concerning the conditions under which people are likely to acquire the necessary knowledge, and the process by which they will acquire it, have at least received some attention in past discussions. But there is a further question which seems to me to be at least equally important but which appears to have received no attention at all, and that is how much knowledge and what sort of knowledge the different individuals must possess in order that we may be able to speak of equilibrium. It is clear that, if the concept is to have any empirical significance, it cannot presuppose that everybody knows everything. I have already had to use the undefined term "relevant knowledge," that is, the knowledge which is relevant to a particular person. But what is this relevant knowledge? It can hardly mean simply the knowledge which actually influenced his actions, because his decisions might have been different not only if, for instance, the knowledge he possessed had been correct instead of incorrect but also if he had possessed knowledge about altogether different fields.

Clearly there is here a problem of the *division of knowledge*[16] which is quite analogous to, and at least as important as, the problem of the division of labor. But, while the latter has been one of the main subjects of investigation ever since the beginning of our science, the former has been as completely neglected, although it seems to me to be the really central problem of economics as a social science. The problem which we pretend to solve is how the spontaneous interaction of a number of people, each possessing only bits of knowledge, brings

16. Cf. L. v. Mises, *Gemeinwirtschaft* (2d ed.; Jena, 1932), p. 96: "Die Verteilung der Verfügungsgewalt über die wirtschaftlichen Güter der arbeitsteilig wirtschaftenden Sozialwirtschaft auf viele Individuen bewirkt eine Art geistige Arbeitsteilung, ohne die Produktionsrechnung und Wirtschaft nicht möglich wäre."

about a state of affairs in which prices correspond to costs, etc., and which could be brought about by deliberate direction only by somebody who possessed the combined knowledge of all those individuals. Experience shows us that something of this sort does happen, since the empirical observation that prices do tend to correspond to costs was the beginning of our science. But in our analysis, instead of showing what bits of information the different persons must possess in order to bring about that result, we fall in effect back on the assumption that everybody knows everything and so evade any real solution of the problem.

Before, however, I can proceed further to consider this division of knowledge among different persons, it is necessary to become more specific about the sort of knowledge which is relevant in this connection. It has become customary among economists to stress only the need of knowledge of prices, apparently because—as a consequence of the confusions between objective and subjective data—the complete knowledge of the objective facts was taken for granted. In recent times even the knowledge of current prices has been taken so much for granted that the only connection in which the question of knowledge has been regarded as problematic has been the anticipation of future prices. But, as I have already indicated at the beginning of this essay, price expectations and even the knowledge of current prices are only a very small section of the problem of knowledge as I see it. The wider aspect of the problem of knowledge with which I am concerned is the knowledge of the basic fact of how the different commodities can be obtained and used,[17] and under what conditions they are actually obtained and used, that is, the general question of why the subjective data to the different persons correspond to the objec-

17. Knowledge in this sense is more than what is usually described as skill, and the division of knowledge of which we here speak more than is meant by the division of labor. To put it shortly, "skill" refers only to the knowledge of which a person makes use in his trade, while the further knowledge about which we must know something in order to be able to say anything about the processes in society is the knowledge of alternative possibilities of action of which he makes no direct use. It may be added that knowledge, in the sense in which the term is here used, is identical with foresight only in the sense in which all knowledge is capacity to predict.

tive facts. Our problem of knowledge here is just the existence of this correspondence which in much of current equilibrium analysis is simply assumed to exist, but which we have to explain if we want to show why the propositions, which are necessarily true about the attitude of a person toward things which he believes to have certain properties, should come to be true of the actions of society with regard to things which either do possess these properties, or which, for some reason which we shall have to explain, are commonly believed by the members of society to possess these properties.[18]

But, to revert to the special problem I have been discussing, the amount of knowledge different individuals must possess in order that equilibrium may prevail (or the "relevant" knowledge they must possess): we shall get nearer to an answer if we remember how it can become apparent either that equilibrium did not exist or that it is being disturbed. We have seen that the equilibrium connections will be severed if any person changes his plans, either because his tastes change (which does not concern us here) or because new facts become known to him. But there are evidently two different ways in which he may learn of new facts that make him change his plans, which for our purposes are of altogether different significance. He may learn of the new facts as it were by accident, that is, in a way which is not a necessary consequence of his attempt to execute his original plan, or it may be inevitable that in the course of his attempt he will find that the facts are different from what he expected. It is obvious that, in order that he may proceed according to plan, his knowledge needs to be correct

18. That all propositions of economic theory refer to things which are defined in terms of human attitudes toward them, that is, that the "sugar" about which economic theory may occasionally speak is defined not by its "objective" qualities but by the fact that people believe that it will serve certain needs of theirs in a certain way, is the source of all sorts of difficulties and confusions, particularly in connection with the problem of "verification." It is, of course, also in this connection that the contrast between the *verstehende* social science and the behaviorist approach becomes so glaring. I am not certain that the behaviorists in the social sciences are quite aware of *how* much of the traditional approach they would have to abandon if they wanted to be consistent or that they would want to adhere to it consistently if they were aware of this. It would, for instance, imply that propositions of the theory of money would have to refer exclusively to, say, "round disks of metal, bearing a certain stamp," or some similarly defined physical object or group of objects.

only on the points on which it will necessarily be confirmed or corrected in the course of the execution of the plan. But he may have no knowledge of things which, if he possessed it, would certainly affect his plan.

The conclusion, then, which we must draw is that the relevant knowledge which he must possess in order that equilibrium may prevail is the knowledge which he is bound to acquire in view of the position in which he originally is, and the plans which he then makes. It is certainly not all the knowledge which, if he acquired it by accident, would be useful to him and lead to a change in his plan. We may therefore very well have a position of equilibrium only because some people have no chance of learning about facts which, if they knew them, would induce them to alter their plans. Or, in other words, it is only relative to the knowledge which a person is bound to acquire in the course of the attempt to carry out his original plan that an equilibrium is likely to be reached.

While such a position represents in one sense a position of equilibrium, it is clear that it is not an equilibrium in the special sense in which equilibrium is regarded as a sort of optimum position. In order that the results of the combination of individual bits of knowledge should be comparable to the results of direction by an omniscient dictator, further conditions must apparently be introduced.[19] While it should be possible to define the amount of knowledge which individuals must possess in order that his result should follow, I know of no real attempt in this direction. One condition would probably be that each of the alternative uses of any sort of resources is known to the owner of some such resources actually used for another purpose and that in this way all the different uses of these resources are connected, either directly or indirectly.[20] But I mention this condition

19. These conditions are usually described as absence of "frictions." In a recently published article ("Quantity of Capital and the Rate of Interest," *Journal of Political Economy*, XLIV, No. 5 [1936], 638) Frank H. Knight rightly points out that " 'error' is the usual meaning of friction in economic discussion."

20. This would be one, but probably not yet a sufficient, condition to insure that, with a given state of demand, the marginal productivity of the different factors of production in their different uses should be equalized and that in this sense an equilibrium of production should be brought about. That it is not necessary, as one might

only as an instance of how it will in most cases be sufficient that in each field there is a certain margin of people who possess among them all the relevant knowledge. To elaborate this further would be an interesting and a very important task but a task that would far exceed the limits of this paper.

Although what I have said on this point has been largely in the form of a criticism, I do not want to appear unduly despondent about what we have already achieved. Even if we have jumped over an essential link in our argument, I still believe that, by what is implicit in its reasoning, economics has come nearer than any other social science to an answer to that central question of all social sciences: How can the combination of fragments of knowledge existing in different minds bring about results which, if they were to be brought about deliberately, would require a knowledge on the part of the directing mind which no single person can possess? To show that in this sense the spontaneous actions of individuals will, under conditions which we can define, bring about a distribution of resources which can be understood as if it were made according to a single plan, although nobody has planned it, seems to me indeed an answer to the problem which has sometimes been metaphorically described as that of the "social mind." But we must not be surprised that such claims have usually been rejected, since we have not based them on the right grounds.

---

think, that every possible alternative use of any kind of resources should be known to at least one among the owners of each group of such resources which are used for one particular purpose is due to the fact that the alternatives known to the owners of the resources in a particular use are reflected in the prices of these resources. In this way it may be a sufficient distribution of knowledge of the alternative uses, $m, n, o, \ldots y, z$, of a commodity, if A, who uses the quantity of these resources in his possession for m, knows of n, and B, who uses his for n, knows of m, while C, who uses his for o, knows of n, etc., until we get to L, who uses his for z, but knows only of y. I am not clear to what extent in addition to this a particular distribution of the knowledge of the different proportions is required in which different factors can be combined in the production of any one commodity. For complete equilibrium additional assumptions will be required about the knowledge which consumers possess about the serviceability of the commodities for the satisfaction of their wants.

Economics and Knowledge

There is only one more point in this connection which I should like to mention. This is that, if the tendency toward equilibrium, which on empirical grounds we have reason to believe to exist, is only toward an equilibrium relative to that knowledge which people will acquire in the course of their economic activity, and if any other change of knowledge must be regarded as a "change in the data" in the usual sense of the term, which falls outside the sphere of equilibrium analysis, this would mean that equilibrium analysis can really tell us nothing about the significance of such changes in knowledge, and it would also go far to account for the fact that pure analysis seems to have so extraordinarily little to say about institutions, such as the press, the purpose of which is to communicate knowledge. It might even explain why the preoccupation with pure analysis should so frequently create a peculiar blindness to the role played in real life by such institutions as advertising.

10

With these rather desultory remarks on topics which would deserve much more careful examination I must conclude my survey of these problems. There are only one or two further remarks which I want to add.

One is that, in stressing the nature of the empirical propositions of which we must make use if the formal apparatus of equilibrium analysis is to serve for an explanation of the real world, and in emphasizing that the propositions about how people will learn, which are relevant in this connection, are of a fundamentally different nature from those of formal analysis, I do not mean to suggest that there opens here and now a wide field for empirical research. I very much doubt whether such investigation would teach us anything new. The important point is rather that we should become aware of what the questions of fact are on which the applicability of our argument to the real world depends, or, to put the same thing in other words, at what point our argument, when it is applied to phenomena of the real world, becomes subject to verification.

The second point is that I do of course not want to suggest that the sorts of problems I have been discussing were foreign to the arguments of the economists of the older generations. The only objection that can be made against them is that they have so mixed up the two sorts of propositions, the a priori and the empirical, of which every realistic economist makes constant use, that it is frequently quite impossible to see what sort of validity they claimed for a particular statement. More recent work has been free from this fault—but only at the price of leaving more and more obscure what sort of relevance their arguments had to the phenomena of the real world. All I have tried to do has been to find the way back to the common-sense meaning of our analysis, of which, I am afraid, we are likely to lose sight as our analysis becomes more elaborate. You may even feel that most of what I have said has been commonplace. But from time to time it is probably necessary to detach one's self from the technicalities of the argument and to ask quite naïvely what it is all about. If I have only shown not only that in some respects the answer to this question is not obvious but that occasionally we even do not quite know what it is, I have succeeded in my purpose.

III. The Facts of the Social Sciences*

1

THERE exists today no commonly accepted term to describe the group of disciplines with which we shall be concerned in this paper. The term "moral sciences," in the sense in which John Stuart Mill used it, did approximately cover the field, but it has long been out of fashion and would now carry inappropriate connotations to most readers. While it is for that reason necessary to use the familiar "social sciences" in the title, I must begin by emphasizing that by no means all the disciplines concerned with the phenomena of social life present the particular problems we shall discuss. Vital statistics, for example, or the study of the spreading of contagious diseases, undoubtedly deal with social phenomena but raise none of the specific questions to be considered here. They are, if I may call them so, true natural sciences of society and differ in no important respect from the other natural sciences. But it is different with the study of language or the market, of law and most other human institutions. It is this group of disciplines which alone I propose to consider and for which I am compelled to use the somewhat misleading term "social sciences."

Since I shall contend that the role of experience in these fields of knowledge is fundamentally different from that which it plays in the natural sciences, I had, perhaps, better explain that I myself originally approached my subject thoroughly imbued with a belief in the universal validity of the methods of the natural sciences. Not only was my first technical training largely scientific in the narrow sense of the word but also what little training I had in philosophy or scientific

* Read before the Cambridge University Moral Science Club, November 19, 1942. Reprinted from *Ethics*, LIV, No. 1 (October, 1943), 1–13. Some of the issues raised in this essay are discussed at greater length in the author's article on "Scientism and the Study of Society," which appeared in three instalments in *Economica*, 1942–45.

method was entirely in the school of Ernst Mach and later of the logical positivists. Yet all this had the effect only of creating an awareness, which became more and more definite as time went on, that, certainly in economics, all the people who are universally regarded as talking sense are constantly infringing the accepted canons of scientific method evolved from the practice of the natural sciences; that even the natural scientists, when they begin to discuss social phenomena, as a rule —at least in so far as they preserve any common sense—do the same; but that, in the not infrequent instances when a natural scientist seriously tries to apply his professional habits of thought to social problems, the result has almost invariably been disastrous—that is, of a sort which to all professional students of these fields seems utter nonsense. But, while it is easy to show the absurdity of most concrete attempts to make the social sciences "scientific," it is much less easy to put up a convincing defense of our own methods, which, though satisfying to most people in particular applications, are, if looked at with a critical eye, suspiciously similar to what is popularly known as "medieval scholasticism."

2

But enough of introduction. Let me plunge directly to the middle of my subject and ask with what kind of facts we have to deal in the social sciences. This question immediately raises another which is in many ways crucial for my problem: What do we mean when we speak of "a certain *kind* of facts"? Are they given to us as facts of a certain kind, or do we make them such by looking at them in a certain way? Of course all our knowledge of the external world is in a way derived from sense perception and therefore from our knowledge of physical facts. But does this mean that all our knowledge is of physical facts only? This depends on what we mean by "a kind of facts."

An analogy from the physical sciences will make the position clear. All levers or pendulums which we can conceive have chemical and optical properties. But, when we talk about levers or pendulums, we do not talk about chemical or optical facts. What makes a number of individual things facts of a kind are the attributes which we select in order to treat them as members of a class. This is, of course, commonplace. But it means that, though all the social phenomena with which we can possibly deal may have physical attributes, they need not be physical facts for our purpose. That depends on how we shall find it convenient to classify them for the discussion of our problems. Are the human actions which we observe, and the objects of these actions, things of the same or a different kind because they appear as physically the same or different to us, the observers—or for some other reason?

Now the social sciences are without exception concerned with the way in which men behave toward their environment—other men or things—or I should say rather that these are the elements from which the social sciences build patterns of relationships between many men. How must we define or classify the objects of their activity if we want to explain or understand their actions? Is it the physical attributes of the objects—what *we* can find out about these objects by studying them—or is it by something else that we must classify the objects when we attempt to explain what men do about them? Let me first consider a few examples.

Take such things as tools, food, medicine, weapons, words, sentences, communications, and acts of production—or any one particular instance of any of these. I believe these to be fair samples of the kind of objects of human activity which constantly occur in the social sciences. It is easily seen that all these concepts (and the same is true of more concrete instances) refer not to some objective properties possessed by the things, or which the observer can find out about them, but to views which some other person holds about the things. These objects cannot even be defined in physical terms, because there is no single physical property which any one member of a class must possess. These concepts are also not merely abstractions of the kind we use in all physical sciences; they abstract from *all* the physical properties of the things themselves. They are all intsances of what are sometimes called "teleological concepts," that is, they can be defined only by indicating relations between three terms: a purpose, somebody who holds that purpose, and an object which that person thinks to be a suitable means for that purpose. If we wish, we could say that all these objects are defined not in terms of their "real" properties but in terms of opinions people hold about them. In short, in the social sciences the things are what people think they are. Money is money, a word is a word, a cosmetic is a cosmetic, if and because somebody thinks they are.

That this is not more obvious is due to the historical accident that in the world in which we live the knowledge of most people is approximately similar to our own. It stands out much more strongly when we think of men with a knowledge different from our own, for example, people who believe in magic. That a charm believed to protect the wearer's life, or a ritual intended to secure good harvests, can be defined only in terms of people's beliefs about them is obvious. But the logical character of the concepts we have to use in attempts to interpret people's actions is the same whether our beliefs coincide with theirs or not. Whether a medicine is a medicine, for the purpose of understanding a person's actions, depends solely on whether that person believes it to be one, irrespective of whether we, the observers, agree or not. Sometimes it is somewhat difficult to keep this distinction clearly in mind. We are likely, for example, to think of the relationship between parent and child as an "objective" fact. But, when we use this concept in studying family life, what is relevant is not that x is the natural offspring of y but that either or both believe this to be the case. The relevant character is not different from the case where x and y believe some spiritual tie to exist between them in the existence of which we do not believe. Perhaps the relevant distinction comes out most clearly in the general and obvious statement that no superior knowledge the observer may possess about the object, but which is not possessed by the acting person, can help us in understanding the motives of their actions.

The objects of human activity, then, for the purposes of the social sciences are of the same or of a different kind, or belong to the same or different classes, not according to what we, the observers, know about the objects, but according to what we think the observed person knows about it. We somehow, and for reasons which I shall presently consider, impute knowledge to the observed person. Before I go on to ask on what grounds such an imputation to the acting person of knowledge about the object is based, what this means, and what follows from the fact that we define the objects of human action in such a way, I must turn for a moment to consider the second kind of elements with which we have to deal in the social sciences: not the environment toward which the human beings behave but human action itself. When we examine the classification of different kinds of actions which we must use when we discuss intelligible human behavior, we meet precisely the same situation as we did in analyzing the classification of objects of human actions. Of the examples I have given before, the last four fall into this category: words, sentences, communications, and acts of production are instances of human actions of this kind. Now, what makes two instances of the same word or the same act of production actions of the same kind, in the sense that is relevant when we discuss intelligible behavior? Surely not any physical properties they have in common. It is not because I know explicitly what physical properties the sound of the word "sycamore" pronounced at different times by different people has in common but because I know that x or y intend all these different sounds or signs to mean the same word, or that they understand them all as the same word, that I treat them as instances of the same class. It is not because of any objective or physical similarity but because of the (imputed) intention of the acting person that I regard the various ways in which in different circumstances he may make, say, a spindle, as instances of the same act of production.

Please note that neither with respect to the objects of human activity nor with respect to the different kinds of human activity themselves do I argue that their physical properties do not come into the process of classification. What I am arguing is that no physical properties can enter into the explicit definition of any of these classes, because the elements of these classes need not possess common physical attributes, and we do not even consciously or explicitly know which are the various physical properties of which an object would have to possess at least one to be a member of a class. The situation may be described schematically by saying that we know that the objects *a, b, c, . . .* , which may be physically completely dissimilar and which we can never exhaustively enumerate, are objects of the same kind because the attitude of X toward them all is similar. But the fact that X's attitude toward them is similar can again be defined only by saying that he will react toward them by any one of the actions *a, β, γ, . . .* , which again may be physically dissimilar and which we will not be able to enumerate exhaustively, but which we just know to "mean" the same thing.

This result of reflecting about what we are actually doing is no doubt a little disturbing. Yet there seems to me no possible doubt that this not only is precisely what we are doing, in ordinary life as well as in the social sciences, when we talk about other people's intelligible action, but that it is the *only* way in which we can ever "understand" what other people do; and that, therefore, we *must* rely on this sort of reasoning whenever we discuss what we all know as specifically human or intelligible activities. We all know what we mean when we say that we see a person "playing" or "working," a man doing this or that "deliberately," or when we say that a face looks "friendly" or a man "frightened." But, though we might be able to explain how we recognize any one of these things in a particular case, I am certain none of us can enumerate, and no science can—at least as yet—tell us all the different physical symptoms by which we recognize the presence of these things. The common attributes which the elements of any of these classes possess are not physical attributes but must be something else.

From the fact that whenever we interpret human action as in any sense purposive or meaningful, whether we do so in ordinary life or for the purposes of the social sciences, we have to define both the objects of human activity and the different kinds of actions themselves, not in physical terms but in terms of the opinions or intentions of the acting persons, there follow some very important consequences; namely, nothing less than that we can, from the concepts of the objects, analytically conclude something about what the actions will be. If we define an object in terms of a person's attitude toward it, it follows, of course, that the definition of the object implies a statement about the attitude of the person toward the thing. When we say that a person possesses food or money, or that he utters a word, we imply that he knows that the first can be eaten, that the second can be used to buy something with, and that the third can be understood—and perhaps many other things. Whether this implication is in any way significant, that is, whether to make it explicit adds in any way to our knowledge, depends on whether, when we say to a person that this or that thing is food or money, we state thereby merely the observed facts from which we derive this knowledge or whether we imply more than that.

How can we ever know that a person holds certain beliefs about his environment? What do we mean when we say that we know he holds certain beliefs—when we say that we know that he uses this thing as a tool or that gesture or sound as a means of communication? Do we mean merely what we actually observe in the particular case, for example, that we see him chewing and swallowing his food, swinging a hammer, or making noises? Or do we not always when we say we "understand" a person's action, when we talk about "why" he is doing this or that, impute to him something beyond what we can observe—at least beyond what we can observe in the particular case?

If we consider for a moment the simplest kinds of actions where this problem arises, it becomes, of course, rapidly obvious that, in discussing what we regard as other people's conscious actions, we invariably interpret their action on the analogy of our own mind: that is, that we group their actions, and the objects of their actions, into classes or categories which we know solely from the knowledge of our own mind. We assume that the idea of a purpose or a tool, a weapon or food, is common to them with us, just as we assume that they can see the difference between different colors or shapes as well as we. We thus always supplement what we actually see of another person's action by projecting into that person a system of classification of objects which we know, not from observing other people, but because it is in terms of these classes that we think ourselves. If, for example, we watch a person cross a square full of traffic, dodging some cars and pausing to let others pass, we know (or we believe we know) much more than we actually perceive with our eyes. This would be equally true if we saw a man behave in a physical environment quite unlike anything we have ever seen before. If I see for the first time a big boulder or an avalanche coming down the side of a mountain toward a man and see him run for his life, I know the meaning of this action because I know what I would or might have done in similar circumstances.

There can be no doubt that we all constantly act on the assumption that we can in this way interpret other people's actions on the analogy of our own mind and that in the great majority of instances this procedure *works*. The trouble is that we can never be sure. On watching a few movements or hearing a few words of a man, we decide that he is sane and not a lunatic and thereby exclude the possibility of his behaving in an infinite number of "odd" ways which none of us could ever enumerate and which just do not fit into what we know to be reasonable behavior—which means nothing else than that those actions cannot be interpreted by analogy of our own mind. We can neither explain precisely how, for practical purposes, we know that a man is sane and not a lunatic, nor can we exclude the possibility that in one case in a thousand we may be wrong. Similarly, I shall, from a few observations, be able rapidly to conclude that a man is signaling or hunting, making love to or punishing another person, though I may never have seen these things done in this particular way; and yet my conclusion will be sufficiently certain for all practical purposes.

The important question which arises is whether it is legitimate to employ in scientific analysis such concepts as these, which refer to a state of affairs which we all recognize "intuitively" and which we not only unhesitatingly use in daily life but on which all social intercourse, all communication between men, is based; or whether we should be precluded from doing so because we cannot state any physical conditions from which we can derive with certainty that the postulated conditions are really present in any particular case, and because for this reason we can never be certain whether any particular instance is really a member of the class about which we talk—although we all agree that

The Facts of the Social Sciences

in the great majority of cases our diagnosis will be correct. The hesitation which we at first feel about this is probably due to the fact that the retention of such a procedure in the social sciences seems to be in conflict with the most marked tendency of the development of scientific thought in modern times. But is there really such a conflict? The tendency to which I refer has been correctly described as one toward the progressive elimination of all "anthropomorphic" explanations from the physical sciences. Does this really mean that we must refrain from treating man "anthropomorphically"—or is it not rather obvious, as soon as we put it in this way, that such an extrapolation of past tendencies is absurd?

I do not wish, of course, in this connection to raise all the problems connected with the behaviorist program, though a more systematic survey of my subject could hardly avoid doing so. Indeed, the question with which we are here concerned is nothing else than whether the social sciences could possibly discuss the kind of problems with which they are concerned in purely behavioristic terms—or even whether consistent behaviorism is possible.

Perhaps the relation between the strictly empirical factor and the part which we add from the knowledge of our own mind in interpreting another person's action can be stated with the help of a (somewhat questionable) use of the distinction between the denotation and the connotation of a concept. What I shall in particular circumstances recognize as a "friendly face," the denotation of the concept, is largely a matter of experience. But what I mean when I say that this is a "friendly face," no experience in the ordinary sense of the term can tell me. What I mean by a "friendly face" does not depend on the physical properties of different concrete instances, which may conceivably have nothing in common. Yet I learn to recognize them as members of the same class—and what makes them members of the same class is not any of their physical properties but an imputed meaning.

The importance of this distinction grows as we move outside the familiar surroundings. As long as I move among my own kind of people, it is probably the physical properties of a bank note or a revolver from which I conclude that they are money or a weapon to the person holding them. When I see a savage holding cowrie shells or a long, thin tube, the physical properties of the thing will probably tell me nothing. But the observations which suggest to me that the cowrie shells are money to him and the blowpipe a weapon will throw much light on the object—much more light than these same observations could possibly give if I were not familiar with the conception of money or a weapon. In recognizing the things as such, I begin to understand the people's behavior. I am able to fit into a scheme of actions which "make sense" just because I have come to regard it not as a thing with certain physical properties but as the kind of thing which fits into the pattern of my own purposive action.

If what we do when we speak about understanding a person's action is to fit what we actually observe into patterns we find ready in our own mind, it follows, of course, that we can understand less and less as we turn to beings more and more different from ourselves. But it also follows that it is not only impossible to recognize, but meaningless to speak of, a mind different from our own. What we mean when we speak of another mind is that we can connect what we observe because the things we observe fit into the way of our own thinking. But where this possibility of interpreting in terms of analogies from our own mind ceases, where we can no longer "understand"—there is no sense in speaking of mind at all; there are then only physical facts which we can group and classify solely according to the physical properties which we observe.

An interesting point in this connection is that, as we go from interpreting the actions of men very much like ourselves to men who live in a very different environment, it is the most concrete concepts which first lose their usefulness for interpreting the people's actions and the most general or abstract which remain helpful longest. My knowledge of the everyday things around me, of the particular ways in which we express ideas or emotions, will be of little use in interpreting the behavior of the inhabitants of Tierra del Fuego. But my understanding of what I mean by a means to an end, by food or a weapon, a word or a sign, and probably even an exchange or a gift, will still be useful and even essential in my attempt to understand what they do.

3

So far the discussion has been limited to the question of how we classify individual actions and their objects in the discussion of social phenomena. I must now turn to the question of the purpose for which we use this classification. Even though concern with classifications takes up a great deal of our energies in the social sciences—so much, indeed, in economics, for example, that one of the best-known modern critics of the discipline has described it as a purely "taxonomic" science —this is not our ultimate purpose. Like all classifications, it is merely a convenient way of arranging our facts for whatever we want to explain. But before I can turn to this, I must, first, clear a common misunderstanding from our way and, second, explain a claim frequently made on behalf of this process of classification—a claim which to anyone brought up in the natural sciences sounds highly suspicious but which nevertheless follows merely from the nature of our object.

The misunderstanding is that the social sciences aim at *explaining* individual behavior and particularly that the elaborate process of classification which we use either is, or serves, such an explanation. The social sciences do in fact nothing of the sort. If conscious action can be "explained," this is a task for psychology but not for economics or linguistics, jurisprudence or any other social science. What we do is merely to classify types of individual behavior which we can understand, to develop their classification—in short, to provide an orderly arrangement of the material which we have to use in our further task. Economists, and the same is probably also true in the other social sciences, are usually a little ashamed to admit that this part of their task is "only" a kind of logic. I think that they would be wise frankly to recognize and to face this fact.

The claim to which I have referred follows directly from this character of the first part of our task as a branch of applied logic. But it sounds startling enough at first. It is that we can derive from the knowledge of our own mind in an "a priori" or "deductive" or "analytic" fashion, an (at least in principle) *exhaustive* classification of all the possible forms of intelligible behavior. It is against this claim, rarely openly made, but always implied, that all the taunts against the economists are directed, when we are accused of spinning knowledge out of our inner consciousness and what other similar abusive epithets there are. Yet when we reflect that, whenever we discuss intelligible behavior, we discuss actions which we can interpret in terms of our own mind, the claim loses its startling character and in fact becomes no more than a truism. If we can understand only what is similar to our own mind, it necessarily follows that we must be able to find all that we can understand in our own mind. Of course, when I say that we can *in principle* achieve an exhaustive classification of all possible forms of intelligible behavior, this does not mean that we may not discover that, in interpreting human actions, we do use processes of thought which we have not yet analyzed or made explicit. We constantly do. What I meant is that when we discuss any particular class of intelligible action which we have defined as actions of one kind, in the sense in which I have used that term, then we can, within that field, provide a completely exhaustive classification of the forms of action which fall within it. If, for example, we define as economic actions all acts of choice which are made necessary by the scarcity of means available for our ends, we can, step by step, proceed to subdivide the possible situations into alternatives so that at each step there is no third possibility: a given means may be useful only for one or for many ends, a given end can be achieved by one or by several different means, different means may be wanted for a given end either alternatively or cumulatively, etc.

But I must leave what I have called the first part of my task and turn to the question of the use we make of these elaborate classifications in the social sciences. The answer is, briefly, that we use the different kinds of individual behavior thus classified as elements from which we construct hypothetical models in an attempt to reproduce the patterns of social relationships which we know in the world around us.

The Facts of the Social Sciences

But this still leaves us with the question whether this is the right way to study social phenomena. Have we not in these social structures at last definite tangible social facts which we ought to observe and measure, as we observe and measure physical facts? Should we not here at least derive all our knowledge by observing and experiencing, instead of by "constructing models" from the elements found in our own thought?

The belief that, when we turn from the action of the individual to the observation of social collectivities, we move from the realm of vague and subjective speculation to the realm of objective fact is very widespread. It is the belief held by all who think that they may make the social sciences more "scientific" by imitating the model of the natural sciences. Its intellectual basis has been most clearly expressed by the founder of "sociology," Auguste Comte, when in a famous statement he asserted that in the field of social phenomena, as in biology, "the whole of the object is certainly much better known and more immediately accessible" than the constituent parts.[1] Most of the science he attempted to create is still based on this or similar beliefs.

I believe that this view which regards social collectivities such as "society" or the "state," or any particular social institution or phenomenon, as in any sense more objective than the intelligible actions of the individuals is sheer illusion. I shall argue that what we call "social facts" are no more facts in the specific sense in which this term is used in the physical sciences than are individual actions or their objects; that these so-called "facts" are rather precisely the same kind of mental models constructed by us from elements which we find in our own minds as those which we construct in the theoretical social sciences; so that what we do in those sciences is in a logical sense exactly the same thing as what we always do when we talk about a state or a community, a language or a market, only that we make explicit what in everyday speech is concealed and vague.

I cannot attempt here to explain this in connection with any one of the theoretical social disciplines—or, rather, in connection with the

1. *Cours*, IV, 258.

only one among them where I should be competent to do this, economics. To do so, I should have to spend far more time than I have on technicalities. But it will perhaps be even more helpful if I attempt to do so with respect to the pre-eminently descriptive and, in a sense, pre-eminently empirical discipline in the social field, namely, history. To consider the nature of "historical facts" will be particularly appropriate, since the social scientists are constantly advised, by those who want to make the social sciences more "scientific," to turn to history for their facts and to use the "historical method" as a substitute for the experimental. Indeed, outside the social sciences themselves (and, it seems, particularly among logicians)[2] it appears to have become almost accepted doctrine that the historical method is the legitimate path toward generalizations about social phenomena.[3]

What do we mean by a "fact" of history? Are the facts with which human history is concerned significant to us as physical facts or in some other sense? What sort of things are the Battle of Waterloo, the French government under Louis XIV, or the feudal system? Perhaps we shall get further if, instead of tackling this question directly, we ask how we decide whether any particular bit of information we have constitutes part of the "fact" "Battle of Waterloo." Was the man plowing his field just beyond the extreme wing of Napoleon's guards part of the Battle of Waterloo? Or the chevalier who dropped his snuffbox on hearing the news of the storming of the Bastille part of the French Revolution? To follow up this kind of question will show at least one thing: that we cannot define a historical fact in terms of spatiotemporal co-ordinates. Neither is everything which takes place at one time and in one place part of the same historical fact, nor must all parts of the

2. C.f., e.g., L. S. Stebbing, *A Modern Introduction to Logic* (2d ed., 1933), p. 383.

3. I am sure that I need not here especially guard myself against the misunderstanding that what I shall have to say about the relation between history and theory is meant in any sense to diminish the importance of history. I should like even to emphasize that the whole purpose of theory is to help our understanding of historical phenomena and that the most perfect knowledge of theory will be of very little use indeed without a most extensive knowledge of a historical character. But this has really nothing to do with my present subject, which is the nature of "historical facts" and the respective roles which history and theory play in their discussion.

same historical fact belong to the same time and place. The classical Greek language or the organization of the Roman legions, the Baltic trade of the eighteenth century or the evolution of common law, or any move of any army—these are all historical facts where no physical criterion can tell us what are the parts of the fact and how they hang together. Any attempt to define them must take the form of a mental reconstruction, of a model, in which intelligible individual attitudes form the elements. In most instances, no doubt, the model will be so simple that the interconnection of its parts are readily visible; and there will consequently be little justification for dignifying the model with the name of a "theory." But, if our historical fact is such a complex as a language or a market, a social system or a method of land cultivation, what we call a fact is either a recurrent process or a complex pattern of persistent relationships which is not "given" to our observation but which we can only laboriously reconstruct—and which we can reconstruct only because the parts (the relations from which we build up the structure) are familiar and intelligible to us. To put it paradoxically, what we call historical facts are really theories which, in a methodological sense, are of precisely the same character as the more abstract or general models which the theoretical sciences of society construct. The situation is not that we first study the "given" historical facts and then perhaps can generalize about them. We rather use a theory when we select from the knowledge we have about a period certain parts as intelligibly connected and forming part of the same historical fact. We never observe states or governments, battles or commercial activities, or a people as a whole. When we use any of these terms, we always refer to a scheme which connects individual activities by intelligible relations; that is, we use a theory which tells us what is and what is not part of our subject. It does not alter the position that the theorizing is usually done for us by our informant or source who, in reporting the fact, will use terms like "state" or "town" which cannot be defined in physical terms but which refer to a complex of relationships which, made explicit, constitute a "theory" of the subject.

71

Individualism and Economic Order

Social theory, in the sense in which I use the term, is, then, logically prior to history. It explains the terms which history must use. This is, of course, not inconsistent with the fact that historical study frequently forces the theorist to revise the constructions or to provide new ones in terms of which he can arrange the information which he finds. But in so far as the historian talks, not merely about the individual actions of particular people but about what, in some sense, we can call social phenomena, his facts can be explained as facts of a certain kind only in terms of a theory about how its elements hang together. The social complexes, the social wholes which the historian discusses, are never found ready given as are the persistent structures in the organic (animal or vegetable) world. They are created by him by an act of construction or interpretation—a construction which for most purposes is done spontaneously and without any elaborate apparatus. But in some connections where, for example, we deal with such things as languages, economic systems, or bodies of law, these structures are so complicated that, without the help of an elaborate technique, they can no longer be reconstructed without the danger of going wrong and being led into contradictions.

This is all the theories of the social sciences aim to do. They are not *about* the social wholes as wholes; they do not pretend to discover by empirical observation laws of behavior or change of these wholes. Their task is rather, if I may so call it, to *constitute* these wholes, to provide schemes of structural relationships which the historian can use when he has to attempt to fit together into a meaningful whole the elements which he actually finds. The historian cannot avoid constantly using social theories in this sense. He may do so unconsciously, and in fields in which the relationships are not too complex his instinct may guide him aright. When he turns to more complex phenomena such as those of language, law, or economics, and still disdains to make use of the models worked out for him by the theorists, he is almost certain to come to grief. And this "coming to grief" will significantly show itself by the theoretician either demonstrating to him that he has involved himself in contradictions or showing him that in his explanations he has asserted a sequence of "causation" which, as soon as his assumptions are made explicit, he will have to admit does not follow from his assumptions.

There are two important consequences which follow from this and which can here be only briefly stated. The first is that the theories of the social sciences do not consist of "laws" in the sense of empirical rules about the behavior of objects definable in physical terms. All that the theory of the social sciences attempts is to provide a technique of reasoning which assists us in connecting individual facts, but which, like logic or mathematics, is not about the facts. It can, therefore, and this is the second point, never be verified or falsified by reference to facts. All that we can and must verify is the presence of our assumptions in the particular case. We have already referred to the special problems and difficulties which this raises. In this connection a genuine "question of fact" arises—though one it will often not be possible to answer with the same certainty as is the case in the natural sciences. But the theory itself, the mental scheme for the interpretation, can never be "verified" but only tested for its consistency. It may be irrelevant because the conditions to which it refers never occur; or it may prove inadequate because it does not take account of a sufficient number of conditions. But it can no more be disproved by facts than can logic or mathematics.

There still remains, however, the question whether this kind of "compositive" theory, as I like to call it, which "constitutes" the social "wholes" by constructing models from intelligible elements, is the *only* kind of social theory, or whether we might not also aim at empirical generalizations about the behavior of these wholes as wholes, at laws of the changes of languages or institutions—the kind of laws which are the aim of "historical method."

I shall not enlarge here on the curious contradiction into which the defendants of this method usually involve themselves when they first emphasize that all historical phenomena are unique or singular and then proced to claim that their study can arrive at generalizations. The point I wish to make is rather that if, of the infinite variety of phenomena which we can find in any concrete situation, only those can be regarded as part of one object which we can connect by means of our mental models, the object can possess no attributes beyond those which can be derived from our model. Of course, we can go on constructing models which fit concrete situations more and more closely—concepts of states or languages which possess an ever richer connotation. But as members of a class, as similar units about which we can make generalizations, these models can never possess any properties which we have not given to them or which do not derive deductively from the assumptions on which we have built them. Experience can never teach us that any particular kind of structure has properties which do not follow from the definition (or the way we construct it). The reason for this is simply that these wholes or social structures are never given to us as natural units, are not definite objects given to observation, that we never deal with the whole of reality but always only with a selection made with the help of our models.[4]

I have not space to discuss more fully the nature of "historical facts" or the objects of history, but I should like briefly to refer to one question which, though not strictly germane to my subject, is yet not quite irrelevant. It is the very fashionable doctrine of "historical relativism," the belief that different generations or ages must of necessity hold different views about the same historical facts. It seems to me that this doctrine is the result of the same illusion that historical facts are definitely given to us and not the result of a deliberate selection of what we regard as a connected set of events relevant to the answer of a particular question—an illusion which seems to me to be due to the belief that we can define a historical fact in physical terms by its spatiotemporal co-ordinates. But a thing so defined, say, "Germany between

4. Incidentally, I am not convinced that this last point really constitutes a difference between the social and the natural sciences. But, if it does not, I think that it is the natural scientists who are mistaken in believing that they ever deal with the *whole* of reality and not merely with selected "aspects" of it. But this whole problem whether we can ever talk about, or perceive, an object which is indicated to us in a purely demonstrative manner, and which in this sense is an individual as distinguished from a "unit class" (which is really concrete and not an abstraction), would lead too far beyond my present subject.

1618 and 1648," just is not *one* historical object. Within the space-time continuum thus defined we can find any number of interesting social phenomena which to the historian are altogether different objects: the history of Family X, the development of printing, the change of legal institutions, etc., which may or may not be connected but which are no more part of one social fact than any other two events in human history. This particular period, or any other period, is, as such, no definite "historical fact," no single historical object. According to our interests we can ask any number of different questions referring to this period and accordingly shall have to give different answers and shall have to construct different models of connected events. And this is what historians *do* at different times because they are interested in different questions. But as it is only the question that we ask which singles out, from the infinite variety of social events which we can find at any given time and place, a definite set of connected events which can be termed one historical fact, the experience that people give different answers to different questions does, of course, not prove that they hold different views about the same historical fact. There is no reason whatever, on the other hand, why historians at different times, but possessing the same information, should answer the same question differently. This alone, however, would justify the thesis about an inevitable relativity of historical knowledge.

I mention this because this historical relativism is a typical product of that so-called "historicism" which is, in fact, a product of the misapplication of the scientistic prejudice to historical phenomena—of the belief that social phenomena are ever given to us as the facts of nature are given to us. They are accessible to us only because we can understand what other people tell us and can be understood only by interpreting other people's intentions and plans. They are not physical facts, but the elements from which we reproduce them are always familiar categories of our own mind. Where we could no longer interpret what we know about other people by the analogy of our own mind, history would cease to be human history; it would then, indeed, have to run in purely behavioristic terms such as the history we might

75

write of an ant heap or the history an observer from Mars might write of the human race.

If this account of what the social sciences are actually doing appears to you as a description of a topsy-turvy world in which everything is in the wrong place, I beg you to remember that these disciplines deal with a world at which from our position we necessarily look in a different manner from that in which we look at the world of nature. To employ a useful metaphor: while at the world of nature we look from the outside, we look at the world of society from the inside; while, as far as nature is concerned, our concepts are about the facts and have to be adapted to the facts, in the world of society at least some of the most familiar concepts are the stuff from which that world is made. Just as the existence of a common structure of thought is the condition of the possibility of our communicating with one another, of your understanding what I say, so it is also the basis on which we all interpret such complicated social structures as those which we find in economic life or law, in language, and in customs.

IV. The Use of Knowledge in Society[*]

1

WHAT is the problem we wish to solve when we try to construct
a rational economic order? On certain familiar assumptions
the answer is simple enough. *If* we possess all the relevant information,
if we can start out from a given system of preferences, and *if* we command complete knowledge of available means, the problem which remains is purely one of logic. That is, the answer to the question of what
is the best use of the available means is implicit in our assumptions.
The conditions which the solution of this optimum problem must
satisfy have been fully worked out and can be stated best in mathematical form: put at their briefest, they are that the marginal rates of
substitution between any two commodities or factors must be the same
in all their different uses.

This, however, is emphatically *not* the economic problem which
society faces. And the economic calculus which we have developed to
solve this logical problem, though an important step toward the solution of the economic problem of society, does not yet provide an answer
to it. The reason for this is that the "data" from which the economic
calculus starts are never for the whole society "given" to a single mind
which could work out the implications and can never be so given.

The peculiar character of the problem of a rational economic order
is determined precisely by the fact that the knowledge of the circumstances of which we must make use never exists in concentrated or
integrated form but solely as the dispersed bits of incomplete and frequently contradictory knowledge which all the separate individuals
possess. The economic problem of society is thus not merely a problem
of how to allocate "given" resources—if "given" is taken to mean given

[*] Reprinted from the *American Economic Review*, XXXV, No. 4 (September,
1945), 519–30.

to a single mind which deliberately solves the problem set by these "data." It is rather a problem of how to secure the best use of resources known to any of the members of society, for ends whose relative importance only these individuals know. Or, to put it briefly, it is a problem of the utilization of knowledge which is not given to anyone in its totality.

This character of the fundamental problem has, I am afraid, been obscured rather than illuminated by many of the recent refinements of economic theory, particularly by many of the uses made of mathematics. Though the problem with which I want primarily to deal in this paper is the problem of a rational economic organization, I shall in its course be led again and again to point to its close connections with certain methodological questions. Many of the points I wish to make are indeed conclusions toward which diverse paths of reasoning have unexpectedly converged. But, as I now see these problems, this is no accident. It seems to me that many of the current disputes with regard to both economic theory and economic policy have their common origin in a misconception about the nature of the economic problem of society. This misconception in turn is due to an erroneous transfer to social phenomena of the habits of thought we have developed in dealing with the phenomena of nature.

2

In ordinary language we describe by the word "planning" the complex of interrelated decisions about the allocation of our available resources. All economic activity is in this sense planning; and in any society in which many people collaborate, this planning, whoever does it, will in some measure have to be based on knowledge which, in the first instance, is not given to the planner but to somebody else, which somehow will have to be conveyed to the planner. The various ways in which the knowledge on which people base their plans is communicated to them is the crucial problem for any theory explaining the economic process, and the problem of what is the best way of utilizing knowledge initially dispersed among all the people is at least one of the main problems of economic policy—or of designing an efficient economic system.

The answer to this question is closely connected with that other question which arises here, that of *who* is to do the planning. It is about this question that all the dispute about "economic planning" centers. This is not a dispute about whether planning is to be done or not. It is a dispute as to whether planning is to be done centrally, by one authority for the whole economic system, or is to be divided among many individuals. Planning in the specific sense in which the term is used in contemporary controversy necessarily means central planning—direction of the whole economic system according to one unified plan. Competition, on the other hand, means decentralized planning by many separate persons. The halfway house between the two, about which many people talk but which few like when they see it, is the delegation of planning to organized industries, or, in other words, monopolies.

Which of these systems is likely to be more efficient depends mainly on the question under which of them we can expect that fuller use will be made of the existing knowledge. This, in turn, depends on whether we are more likely to succeed in putting at the disposal of a single central authority all the knowledge which ought to be used but which is initially dispersed among many different individuals, or in conveying to the individuals such additional knowledge as they need in order to enable them to dovetail their plans with those of others.

3

It will at once be evident that on this point the position will be different with respect to different kinds of knowledge. The answer to our question will therefore largely turn on the relative importance of the different kinds of knowledge: those more likely to be at the disposal of particular individuals and those which we should with greater confidence expect to find in the possession of an authority made up of suitably chosen experts. If it is today so widely assumed that the latter will be in a better position, this is because one kind of knowledge, namely, scientific knowledge, occupies now so prominent a place in public imagination that we tend to forget that it is not the only kind that is relevant. It may be admitted that, as far as scientific knowledge is concerned, a body of suitably chosen experts may be in the best position to command all the best knowledge available—though this is of course merely shifting the difficulty to the problem of selecting the experts. What I wish to point out is that, even assuming that this problem can be readily solved, it is only a small part of the wider problem.

Today it is almost heresy to suggest that scientific knowledge is not the sum of all knowledge. But a little reflection will show that there is beyond question a body of very important but unorganized knowledge which cannot possibly be called scientific in the sense of knowledge of general rules: the knowledge of the particular circumstances of time and place. It is with respect to this that practically every individual has some advantage over all others because he possesses unique information of which beneficial use might be made, but of which use can be made only if the decisions depending on it are left to him or are made with his active co-operation. We need to remember only how much we have to learn in any occupation after we have completed our theoretical training, how big a part of our working life we spend learning particular jobs, and how valuable an asset in all walks of life is knowledge of people, of local conditions, and of special circumstances. To know of and put to use a machine not fully employed, or somebody's skill which could be better utilized, or to be aware of a surplus stock which can be drawn upon during an interruption of supplies, is socially quite as useful as the knowledge of better alternative techniques. The shipper who earns his living from using otherwise empty or half-filled journeys of tramp-steamers, or the estate agent whose whole knowledge is almost exclusively one of temporary opportunities, or the *arbitrageur* who gains from local differences of commodity prices—are all performing eminently useful functions based on special knowledge of circumstances of the fleeting moment not known to others.

The Use of Knowledge in Society

It is a curious fact that this sort of knowledge should today be generally regarded with a kind of contempt and that anyone who by such knowledge gains an advantage over somebody better equipped with theoretical or technical knowledge is thought to have acted almost disreputably. To gain an advantage from better knowledge of facilities of communication or transport is sometimes regarded as almost dishonest, although it is quite as important that society make use of the best opportunities in this respect as in using the latest scientific discoveries. This prejudice has in a considerable measure affected the attitude toward commerce in general compared with that toward production. Even economists who regard themselves as definitely immune to the crud ematerialist fallacies of the past constantly commit the same mistake where activities directed toward the acquisition of such practical knowledge are concerned—apparently because in their scheme of things all such knowledge is supposed to be "given." The common idea now seems to be that all such knowledge should as a matter of course be readily at the command of everybody, and the reproach of irrationality leveled against the existing economic order is frequently based on the fact that it is not so available. This view disregards the fact that the method by which such knowledge can be made as widely available as possible is precisely the problem to which we have to find an answer.

4

If it is fashionable today to minimize the importance of the knowledge of the particular circumstances of time and place, this is closely connected with the smaller importance which is now attached to change as such. Indeed, there are few points on which the assumptions made (usually only implicitly) by the "planners" differ from those of their opponents as much as with regard to the significance and frequency of changes which will make substantial alterations of production plans necessary. Of course, if detailed economic plans could be laid down for fairly long periods in advance and then closely adhered to, so that no further economic decisions of importance would be required, the task of drawing up a comprehensive plan governing all economic activity would be much less formidable.

It is, perhaps, worth stressing that economic problems arise always and only in consequence of change. As long as things continue as before, or at least as they were expected to, there arise no new problems requiring a decision, no need to form a new plan. The belief that changes, or at least day-to-day adjustments, have become less important in modern times implies the contention that economic problems also have become less important. This belief in the decreasing importance of change is, for that reason, usually held by the same people who argue that the importance of economic considerations has been driven into the background by the growing importance of technological knowledge.

Is it true that, with the elaborate apparatus of modern production, economic decisions are required only at long intervals, as when a new factory is to be erected or a new process to be introduced? Is it true that, once a plant has been built, the rest is all more or less mechanical, determined by the character of the plant, and leaving little to be changed in adapting to the ever changing circumstances of the moment?

The fairly widespread belief in the affirmative is not, as far as I can ascertain, borne out by the practical experience of the businessman. In a competitive industry at any rate—and such an industry alone can serve as a test—the task of keeping cost from rising requires constant struggle, absorbing a great part of the energy of the manager. How easy it is for an inefficient manager to dissipate the differentials on which profitability rests and that it is possible, with the same technical facilities, to produce with a great variety of costs are among the commonplaces of business experience which do not seem to be equally familiar in the study of the economist. The very strength of the desire, constantly voiced by producers and engineers, to be allowed to proceed untrammeled by considerations of money costs, is eloquent testimony to the extent to which these factors enter into their daily work.

One reason why economists are increasingly apt to forget about the constant small changes which make up the whole economic picture is probably their growing preoccupation with statistical aggregates, which show a very much greater stability than the movements of the detail. The comparative stability of the aggregates cannot, however, be accounted for—as the statisticians occasionally seem to be inclined to do—by the "law of large numbers" or the mutual compensation of random changes. The number of elements with which we have to deal is not large enough for such accidental forces to produce stability. The continuous flow of goods and services is maintained by constant deliberate adjustments, by new dispositions made every day in the light of circumstances not known the day before, by B stepping in at once when A fails to deliver. Even the large and highly mechanized plant keeps going largely because of an environment upon which it can draw for all sorts of unexpected needs: tiles for its roof, stationery or its forms, and all the thousand and one kinds of equipment in which it cannot be self-contained and which the plans for the operation of the plant require to be readily available in the market.

This is, perhaps, also the point where I should briefly mention the fact that the sort of knowledge with which I have been concerned is knowledge of the kind which by its nature cannot enter into statistics and therefore cannot be conveyed to any central authority in statistical form. The statistics which such a central authority would have to use would have to be arrived at precisely by abstracting from minor differences between the things, by lumping together, as resources of one kind, items which differ as regards location, quality, and other particulars, in a way which may be very significant for the specific decision. It follows from this that central planning based on statistical information by its nature cannot take direct account of these circumstances of time and place and that the central planner will have to find some way or other in which the decisions depending on them can be left to the "man on the spot."

5

If we can agree that the economic problem of society is mainly one of rapid adaptation to changes in the particular circumstances of time and place, it would seem to follow that the ultimate decisions must be left to the people who are familiar with these circumstances, who know directly of the relevant changes and of the resources immediately available to meet them. We cannot expect that this problem will be solved by first communicating all this knowledge to a central board which, after integrating all knowledge, issues its orders. We must solve it by some form of decentralization. But this answers only part of our problem. We need decentralization because only thus can we insure that the knowledge of the particular circumstances of time and place will be promptly used. But the "man on the spot" cannot decide solely on the basis of his limited but intimate knowledge of the facts of his immediate surroundings. There still remains the problem of communicating to him such further information as he needs to fit his decisions into the whole pattern of changes of the larger economic system.

How much knowledge does he need to do so successfully? Which of the events which happen beyond the horizon of his immediate knowledge are of relevance to his immediate decision, and how much of them need he know?

There is hardly anything that happens anywhere in the world that *might* not have an effect on the decision he ought to make. But he need not know of these events as such, nor of *all* their effects. It does not matter for him *why* at the particular moment more screws of one size than of another are wanted, *why* paper bags are more readily available than canvas bags, or *why* skilled labor, or particular machine tools, have for the moment become more difficult to obtain. All that is significant for him is *how much more or less* difficult to procure they have become compared with other things with which he is also concerned, or how much more or less urgently wanted are the alternative things he produces or uses. It is always a question of the relative importance of the particular things with which he is concerned, and the causes which alter their relative importance are of no interest to him beyond the effect on those concrete things of his own environment.

It is in this connection that what I have called the "economic calculus" (or the Pure Logic of Choice) helps us, at least by analogy, to see how this problem can be solved, and in fact is being solved, by the price system. Even the single controlling mind, in possession of all the data for some small, self-contained economic system, would not—every time some small adjustment in the allocation of resources had to be made—go explicitly through all the relations between ends and means which might possibly be affected. It is indeed the great contribution of the Pure Logic of Choice that it has demonstrated conclusively that even such a single mind could solve this kind of problem only by constructing and constantly using rates of equivalence (or "values," or "marginal rates of substitution"), that is, by attaching to each kind of scarce resource a numerical index which cannot be derived from any property possessed by that particular thing, but which reflects, or in which is condensed, its significance in view of the whole means-end structure. In any small change he will have to consider only these quantitative indices (or "values") in which all the relevant information is concentrated; and, by adjusting the quantities one by one, he can appropriately rearrange his dispositions without having to solve the whole puzzle *ab initio* or without needing at any stage to survey it at once in all its ramifications.

Fundamentally, in a system in which the knowledge of the relevant facts is dispersed among many people, prices can act to co-ordinate the separate actions of different people in the same way as subjective values help the individual to co-ordinate the parts of his plan. It is worth contemplating for a moment a very simple and commonplace instance of the action of the price system to see what precisely it accomplishes. Assume that somewhere in the world a new opportunity for the use of some raw material, say, tin, has arisen, or that one of the sources of supply of tin has been eliminated. It does not matter for our purpose—and it is significant that it does not matter—which of these two causes has made tin more scarce. All that the users of tin need to know is that some of the tin they used to consume is now more profitably employed elsewhere and that, in consequence, they must economize tin. There is no need for the great majority of them even to know where the more urgent need has arisen, or in favor of what other needs they ought to husband the supply. If only some of them know directly of the new demand, and switch resources over to it, and if the people who are aware of the new gap thus created in turn fill it from still other sources, the effect will rapidly spread throughout the whole economic system and influence not only all the uses of tin but also those of its substitutes and the substitutes of these substitutes, the supply of all the things made of tin, and their substitutes, and so on; and all his without the great majority of those instrumental in bringing about these substitutions knowing anything at all about the original cause of these changes. The whole acts as one market, not because any of its members survey the whole field, but because their limited individual fields of vision sufficiently overlap so that through many intermediaries the relevant information is communicated to all. The mere fact that there is one price for any commodity—or rather that local prices are connected in a manner determined by the cost of transport, etc.—brings about the solution which (it is just conceptually possible) might have been arrived at by one single mind possessing all the information which is in fact dispersed among all the people involved in the process.

6

We must look at the price system as such a mechanism for communicating information if we want to understand its real function—a function which, of course, it fulfils less perfectly as prices grow more rigid. (Even when quoted prices have become quite rigid, however, the forces which would operate through changes in price still operate to a considerable extent through changes in the other terms of the contract.) The most significant fact about this system is the economy of knowledge with which it operates, or how little the individual participants need to know in order to be able to take the right action. In abbreviated form, by a kind of symbol, only the most essential information is passed on and passed on only to those concerned. It is more than a metaphor to describe the price system as a kind of machinery for registering change, or a system of telecommunications which enables individual producers to watch merely the movement of a few pointers, as an engineer might watch the hands of a few dials, in order to adjust their activities to changes of which they may never know more than is reflected in the price movement.

Of course, these adjustments are probably never "perfect" in the sense in which the economist conceives of them in his equilibrium analysis. But I fear that our theoretical habits of approaching the problem with the assumption of more or less perfect knowledge on the part of almost everyone has made us somewhat blind to the true function of the price mechanism and led us to apply rather misleading standards in judging its efficiency. The marvel is that in a case like that of a scarcity of one raw material, without an order being issued, without more than perhaps a handful of people knowing the cause, tens of thousands of people whose identity could not be ascertained by months of investigation, are made to use the material or its products more sparingly; that is, they move in the right direction. This is enough of a marvel even if, in a constantly changing world, not all will hit it off so perfectly that their profit rates will always be maintained at the same even or "normal" level.

I have deliberately used the word "marvel" to shock the reader out of the complacency with which we often take the working of this mechanism for granted. I am convinced that if it were the result of deliberate human design, and if the people guided by the price changes understood that their decisions have significance far beyond their immediate aim, this mechanism would have been acclaimed as one of the greatest triumphs of the human mind. Its misfortune is the double one that it is not the product of human design and that the people guided by it usually do not know why they are made to do what they do. But those who clamor for "conscious direction"—and who cannot believe that anything which has evolved without design (and even without our understanding it) should solve problems which we should not be able to solve consciously—should remember this: The problem is precisely how to extend the span of our utilization of resources beyond the span of the control of any one mind; and, therefore, how to dispense with the need of conscious control and how to provide inducements which will make the individuals do the desirable things without anyone having to tell them what to do.

The problem which we meet here is by no means peculiar to economics but arises in connection with nearly all truly social phenomena, with language and with most of our cultural inheritance, and constitutes really the central theoretical problem of all social science. As Alfred Whitehead has said in another connection, "It is a profoundly erroneous truism, repeated by all copy-books and by eminent people when they are making speeches, that we should cultivate the habit of thinking what we are doing. The precise opposite is the case. Civilization advances by extending the number of important operations which we can perform without thinking about them." This is of profound significance in the social field. We make constant use of formulas, symbols, and rules whose meaning we do not understand and through the use of which we avail ourselves of the assistance of knowledge which individually we do not possess. We have developed these practices and institutions by building upon habits and institutions which have proved successful in their own sphere and which have in turn become the foundation of the civilization we have built up.

The price system is just one of those formations which man has learned to use (though he is still very far from having learned to make the best use of it) after he had stumbled upon it without understanding it. Through it not only a division of labor but also a co-ordinated utilization of resources based on an equally divided knowledge has become possible. The people who like to deride any suggestion that this may be so usually distort the argument by insinuating that it asserts that by some miracle just that sort of system has spontaneously grown up which is best suited to modern civilization. It is the other way round: man has been able to develop that division of labor on which our civilization is based because he happened to stumble upon a method which made it possible. Had he not done so, he might still have developed some other, altogether different, type of civilization, something like the "state" of the termite ants, or some other altogether unimaginable type. All that we can say is that nobody has yet succeeded in designing an alternative system in which certain features of the existing one can be preserved which are dear even to those who most violently assail it—such as particularly the extent to which the individual can choose his pursuits and consequently freely use his own knowledge and skill.

7

It is in many ways fortunate that the dispute about the indispensability of the price system for any rational calculation in a complex society is now no longer conducted entirely between camps holding different political views. The thesis that without the price system we could not preserve a society based on such extensive division of labor as ours was greeted with a howl of derision when it was first advanced by Von Mises twenty-five years ago. Today the difficulties which some still find in accepting it are no longer mainly political, and this makes for an atmosphere much more conducive to reasonable discussion. When we find Leon Trotsky arguing that "economic accounting is unthinkable without market relations"; when Professor Oscar Lange promises Professor von Mises a statue in the marble halls of the future Central Planning Board; and when Professor Abba P. Lerner rediscovers Adam Smith and emphasizes that the essential utility of the price system consists in inducing the individual, while seeking his own interest, to do what is in the general interest, the differences can indeed no longer be ascribed to political prejudice. The remaining dissent seems clearly to be due to purely intellectual, and more particularly methodological, differences.

A recent statement by Joseph Schumpeter in his *Capitalism, Socialism, and Democracy* provides a clear illustration of one of the methodological differences which I have in mind. Its author is pre-eminent

89

among those economists who approach economic phenomena in the light of a certain branch of positivism. To him these phenomena accordingly appear as objectively given quantities of commodities impinging directly upon each other, almost, it would seem, without any intervention of human minds. Only against this background can I account for the following (to me startling) pronouncement. Professor Schumpeter argues that the possibility of a rational calculation in the absence of markets for the factors of production follows for the theorist "from the elementary proposition that consumers in evaluating ('demanding') consumers' goods *ipso facto* also evaluate the means of production which enter into the production of these goods."[1]

Taken literally, this statement is simply untrue. The consumers do nothing of the kind. What Professor Schumpeter's *"ipso facto"* presumably means is that the valuation of the factors of production is implied in, or follows necessarily from, the valuation of consumers' goods. But this, too, is not correct. Implication is a logical relationship which can be meaningfully asserted only of propositions simultaneously present to one and the same mind. It is evident, however, that the values of the factors of production do not depend solely on the valuation of the consumers' goods but also on the conditions of supply of the various factors of production. Only to a mind to which all these facts were simultaneously known would the answer necessarily follow from the facts given to it. The practical problem, however, arises precisely because these facts are never so given to a single mind, and

1. *Capitalism, Socialism, and Democracy* (New York: Harper & Bros., 1942), p. 175. Professor Schumpeter is, I believe, also the original author of the myth that Pareto and Barone have "solved" the problem of socialist calculation. What they, and many others, did was merely to state the conditions which a rational allocation of resources would have to satisfy and to point out that these were essentially the same as the conditions of equilibrium of a competitive market. This is something altogether different from showing how the allocation of resources satisfying these conditions can be found in practice. Pareto himself (from whom Barone has taken practically everything he has to say), far from claiming to have solved the practical problem, in fact explicitly denies that it can be solved without the help of the market. See his *Manuel d'économie pure* (2d ed., 1927), pp. 233–34. The relevant passage is quoted in an English translation at the beginning of my article on "Socialist Calculation: The Competitive 'Solution,' " in *Economica*, VIII, No. 26 (new ser., 1940), 125; reprinted below as chapter viii.

because, in consequence, it is necessary that in the solution of the problem knowledge should be used that is dispersed among many people.

The problem is thus in no way solved if we can show that all the facts, *if* they were known to a single mind (as we hypothetically assume them to be given to the observing economist), would uniquely determine the solution; instead we must show how a solution is produced by the interactions of people each of whom possesses only partial knowledge. To assume all the knowledge to be given to a single mind in the same manner in which we assume it to be given to us as the explaining economists is to assume the problem away and to disregard everything that is important and significant in the real world.

That an economist of Professor Schumpeter's standing should thus have fallen into a trap which the ambiguity of the term "datum" sets to the unwary can hardly be explained as a simple error. It suggests rather that there is something fundamentally wrong with an approach which habitually disregards an essential part of the phenomena with which we have to deal: the unavoidable imperfection of man's knowledge and the consequent need for a process by which knowledge is constantly communicated and acquired. Any approach, such as that of much of mathematical economics with its simultaneous equations, which in effect starts from the assumption that people's *knowledge* corresponds with the objective *facts* of the situation, systematically leaves out what is our main task to explain. I am far from denying that in our system equilibrium analysis has a useful function to perform. But when it comes to the point where it misleads some of our leading thinkers into believing that the situation which it describes has direct relevance to the solution of practical problems, it is high time that we remember that it does not deal with the social process at all and that it is no more than a useful preliminary to the study of the main problem.

V. The Meaning of Competition*

1

THERE are signs of increasing awareness among economists that what they have been discussing in recent years under the name of "competition" is not the same thing as what is thus called in ordinary language. But, although there have been some valiant attempts to bring discussion back to earth and to direct attention to the problems of real life, notably by J. M. Clark and F. Machlup,[1] the general view seems still to regard the conception of competition currently employed by economists as the significant one and to treat that of the businessman as an abuse. It appears to be generally held that the so-called theory of "perfect competition" provides the appropriate model for judging the effectiveness of competition in real life and that, to the extent that real competition differs from that model, it is undesirable and even harmful.

For this attitude there seems to me to exist very little justification. I shall attempt to show that what the theory of perfect competition discusses has little claim to be called "competition" at all and that its conclusions are of little use as guides to policy. The reason for this seems to me to be that this theory throughout assumes that state of affairs already to exist which, according to the truer view of the older theory, the process of competition tends to bring about (or to approximate) and that, if the state of affairs assumed by the theory of perfect competition ever existed, it would not only deprive of their scope all the activities which the verb "to compete" describes but would make them virtually impossible.

* This essay reproduces the substance of the Stafford Little Lecture delivered at Princeton University on May 20, 1946.

1. J. M. Clark, "Toward a Concept of Workable Competition," *American Economic Review*, Vol. XXX (June, 1940); F. Machlup, "Competition, Pliopoly, and Profit," *Economica*, Vol. IX (new ser.; February and May, 1942).

The Meaning of Competition

If all this affected only the use of the word "competition," it would not matter a great deal. But it seems almost as if economists by this peculiar use of language were deceiving themselves into the belief that, in discussing "competition," they are saying something about the nature and significance of the process by which the state of affairs is brought about which they merely assume to exist. In fact, this moving force of economic life is left almost altogether undiscussed.

I do not wish to discuss here at any length the reasons which have led the theory of competition into this curious state. As I have suggested elsewhere in this volume,[2] the tautological method which is appropriate and indispensable for the analysis of individual action seems in this instance to have been illegitimately extended to problems in which we have to deal with a social process in which the decisions of many individuals influence one another and necessarily succeed one another in time. The economic calculus (or the Pure Logic of Choice) which deals with the first kind of problem consist of an apparatus of classification of possible human attitudes and provides us with a technique for describing the interrelations of the different parts of a single plan. Its conclusions are implicit in its assumptions: the desires and the knowledge of the facts, which are assumed to be simultaneously present to a single mind, determine a unique solution. The relations discussed in this type of analysis are logical relations, concerned solely with the conclusions which follow for the mind of the planning individual from the given premises.

When we deal, however, with a situation in which a number of persons are attempting to work out their separate plans, we can no longer assume that the data are the same for all the planning minds. The problem becomes one of how the "data" of the different individuals on which they base their plans are adjusted to the objective facts of their environment (which includes the actions of the other people). Although in the solution of this type of problem we still must make use of our technique for rapidly working out the implications of a given set of data, we have now to deal not only with several separate sets of

2. See the second and fourth chapters.

93

data of the different persons but also—and this is even more important —with a process which necessarily involves continuous changes in the data for the different individuals. As I have suggested before, the causal factor enters here in the form of the acquisition of new knowledge by the different individuals or of changes in their data brought about by the contacts between them.

The relevance of this for my present problem will appear when it is recalled that the modern theory of competition deals almost exclusively with a state of what is called "competitive equilibrium" in which it is assumed that the data for the different individuals are fully adjusted to each other, while the problem which requires explanation is the nature of the process by which the data are thus adjusted. In other words, the description of competitive equilibrium does not even attempt to say that, if we find such and such conditions, such and such consequences will follow, but confines itself to defining conditions in which its conclusions are already implicitly contained and which may conceivably exist but of which it does not tell us how they can ever be brought about. Or, to anticipate our main conclusion in a brief statement, competition is by its nature a dynamic process whose essential characteristics are assumed away by the assumptions underlying static analysis.

2

That the modern theory of competitive equilibrium *assumes* the situation to exist which a true explanation ought to account for as the effect of the competitive process is best shown by examining the familiar list of conditions found in any modern textbook. Most of these conditions, incidentally, not only underlie the analysis of "perfect" competition but are equally assumed in the discussion of the various "imperfect" or "monopolistic" markets, which throughout assume certain unrealistic "perfections."[3] For our immediate purpose, however, the theory of perfect competition will be the most instructive case to examine.

3. Particularly the assumptions that *at all times* a uniform price must rule for a given commodity throughout the market and that sellers know the shape of the demand curve.

The Meaning of Competition

While different authors may state the list of essential conditions of perfect competition differently, the following is probably more than sufficiently comprehensive for our purpose, because, as we shall see, those conditions are not really independent of each other. According to the generally accepted view, perfect competition presupposes:

1. A homogeneous commodity offered and demanded by a large number of relatively small sellers or buyers, none of whom expects to exercise by his action a perceptible influence on price.

2. Free entry into the market and absence of other restraints on the movement of prices and resources.

3. Complete knowledge of the relevant factors on the part of all participants in the market.

We shall not ask at this stage precisely for what these conditions are required or what is implied if they are assumed to be given. But we must inquire a little further about their meaning, and in this respect it is the third condition which is the critical and obscure one. The standard can evidently not be perfect knowledge of everything affecting the market on the part of every person taking part in it. I shall here not go into the familiar paradox of the paralyzing effect really perfect knowledge and foresight would have on all action.[4] It will be obvious also that nothing is solved when we assume everybody to know everything and that the real problem is rather how it can be brought about that as much of the available knowledge as possible is used. This raises for a competitive society the question, not how we can "find" the people who know best, but rather what institutional arrangements are necessary in order that the unknown persons who have knowledge specially suited to a particular task are most likely to be attracted to that task. But we must inquire a little further what sort of knowledge it is that is supposed to be in possession of the parties of the market.

If we consider the market for some kind of finished consumption goods and start with the position of its producers or sellers, we shall find, first, that they are assumed to know the lowest cost at which the commodity can be produced. Yet this knowledge which is assumed to

4. See O. Morgenstern, "Vollkommene Voraussicht und wirtschaftliches Gleichgewicht," *Zeitschrift für Nationalökonomie*, Vol. VI (1935).

be given to begin with is one of the main points where it is only through the process of competition that the facts will be discovered. This appears to me one of the most important of the points where the starting-point of the theory of competitive equilibrium assumes away the main task which only the process of competition can solve. The position is somewhat similar with respect to the second point on which the producers are assumed to be fully informed: the wishes and desires of the consumers, including the kinds of goods and services which they demand and the prices they are willing to pay. These cannot properly be regarded as given facts but ought rather to be regarded as problems to be solved by the process of competition.

The same situation exists on the side of the consumers or buyers. Again the knowledge they are supposed to possess in a state of competitive equilibrium cannot be legitimately assumed to be at their command before the process of competition starts. Their knowledge of the alternatives before them is the result of what happens on the market, of such activities as advertising, etc.; and the whole organization of the market serves mainly the need of spreading the information on which the buyer is to act.

The peculiar nature of the assumptions from which the theory of competitive equilibrium starts stands out very clearly if we ask which of the activities that are commonly designated by the verb "to compete" would still be possible if those conditions were all satisfied. Perhaps it is worth recalling that, according to Dr. Johnson, competition is "the action of endeavouring to gain what another endeavours to gain at the same time." Now, how many of the devices adopted in ordinary life to that end would still be open to a seller in a market in which so-called "perfect competition" prevails? I believe that the answer is exactly none. Advertising, undercutting, and improving ("differentiating") the goods or services produced are all excluded by definition—"perfect" competition means indeed the absence of all competitive activities.

Especially remarkable in this connection is the explicit and complete exclusion from the theory of perfect competition of all personal relationships existing between the parties.[5] In actual life the fact that our inadequate knowledge of the available commodities or services is made up for by our experience with the persons or firms supplying them—that competition is in a large measure competition for reputation or good will—is one of the most important facts which enables us to solve our daily problems. The function of competition is here precisely to teach us *who* will serve us well: which grocer or travel agency, which department store or hotel, which doctor or solicitor, we can expect to provide the most satisfactory solution for whatever particular personal problem we may have to face. Evidently in all these fields competition may be very intense, just because the services of the different persons or firms will never be exactly alike, and it will be owing to this competition that we are in a position to be served as well as we are. The reasons competition in this field is described as imperfect have indeed nothing to do with the competitive character of the activities of these people; it lies in the nature of the commodities or services themselves. If no two doctors are perfectly alike, this does not mean that the competition between them is less intense but merely that any degree of competition between them will not produce exactly those results which it would if their services were exactly alike. This is not a purely verbal point. The talk about the defects or competition when we are in fact talking about the necessary difference between commodities and services conceals a very real confusion and leads on occasion to absurd conclusions.

While on a first glance the assumption concerning the perfect knowledge possessed by the parties may seem the most startling and artificial of all those on which the theory of perfect competition is based, it may in fact be no more than a consequence of, and in part even justified by, another of the presuppositions on which it is founded. If, indeed, we start by assuming that a large number of people are producing the same commodity and command the same objective facili-

5. Cf. G. J. Stigler, *The Theory of Price* (1946), p. 24: "Economic relationships are never perfectly competitive if they involve any personal relationships between economic units" (see also *ibid.*, p. 226).

ties and opportunities for doing so, then indeed it might be made plausible (although this has, to my knowledge, never been attempted) that they will in time all be led to know most of the facts relevant for judging the market of that commodity. Not only will each producer by his experience learn the same facts as every other but also he will thus come to know what his fellows know and in consequence the elasticity of the demand for his own product. The condition where different manufacturers produce the identical product under identical conditions is in fact the most favorable for producing that state of knowledge among them which perfect competition requires. Perhaps this means no more than that the commodities can be identical in the sense in which it is alone relevant for our understanding human action only if people hold the same views about them, although it should also be possible to state a set of physical conditions which is favorable to all those who are concerned with a set of closely interrelated activities learning the facts relevant for their decisions.

However that be, it will be clear that the facts will not always be as favorable to this result as they are when many people are at least in a position to produce the same article. The conception of the economic system as divisible into distinct markets for separate commodities is after all very largely the product of the imagination of the economist and certainly is not the rule in the field of manufacture and of personal services, to which the discussion about competition so largely refers. In fact, it need hardly be said, no products of two producers are ever exactly alike, even if it were only because, as they leave his plant, they must be at different places. These differences are part of the facts which create our economic problem, and it is little help to answer it on the assumption that they are absent.

The belief in the advantages of perfect competition frequently leads enthusiasts even to argue that a more advantageous use of resources would be achieved if the existing variety of products were reduced by *compulsory* standardization. Now, there is undoubtedly much to be said in many fields for assisting standardization by agreed recommendations or standards which are to apply unless different requirements are explicitly stipulated in contracts. But this is something very different from the demands of those who believe that the variety of people's tastes should be disregarded and the constant experimentation with improvements should be suppressed in order to obtain the advantages of perfect competition. It would clearly not be an improvement to build all houses exactly alike in order to create a perfect market for houses, and the same is true of most other fields where differences between the individual products prevent competition from ever being perfect.

3

We shall probably learn more about the nature and significance of the competitive process if for a while we forget about the artificial assumptions underlying the theory of perfect competition and ask whether competition would be any less important if, for example, no two commodities were ever exactly alike. If it were not for the difficulty of the analysis of such a situation, it would be well worth while to consider in some detail the case where the different commodities could not be readily classed into distinct groups, but where we had to deal with a continuous range of close substitutes, every unit somewhat different from the other but without any marked break in the continuous range. The result of the analysis of competition in such a situation might in many respects be more relevant to the conditions of real life than those of the analysis of competition in a single industry producing a homogeneous commodity sharply differentiated from all others. Or, if the case where no two commodities are exactly alike be thought to be too extreme, we might at least turn to the case where no two producers produce exactly the same commodity, as is the rule not only with all personal services but also in the markets of many manufactured commodities, such as the markets for books or musical instruments.

For our present purpose I need not attempt anything like a complete analysis of such kinds of markets but shall merely ask what would be the role of competition in them. Although the result would, of course, within fairly wide margins be indeterminate, the market would still bring about a set of prices at which each commodity sold just cheap enough to outbid its potential close substitutes—and this in itself is no small thing when we consider the unsurmountable difficulties of discovering even such a system of prices by any other method except that of trial and error in the market, with the individual participants gradually learning the relevant circumstances. It is true, of course, that in such a market correspondence between prices and marginal costs is to be expected only to the degree that elasticities of demand for the individual commodities approach the conditions assumed by the theory of perfect competition or that elasticities of substitution between the different commodities approach infinity. But the point is that in this case this standard of perfection as something desirable or to be aimed at is wholly irrelevant. The basis of comparison, on the grounds of which the achievement of competition ought to be judged, cannot be a situation which is different from the objective facts and which cannot be brought about by any known means. It ought to be the situation as it would exist if competition were prevented from operating. Not the approach to an unachievable and meaningless ideal but the improvement upon the conditions that would exist without competition should be the test.

In such a situation how would conditions differ, if competition were "free" in the traditional sense, from those which would exist if, for example, only people licensed by authority were allowed to produce particular things, or prices were fixed by authority, or both? Clearly there would be not only no likelihood that the different things would be produced by those who knew best how to do it and therefore could do it at lowest cost but also no likelihood that all those things would be produced at all which, if the consumers had the choice, they would like best. There would be little relationship between actual prices and the lowest cost at which somebody would be able to produce these commodities; indeed, the alternatives between which both producers and consumers would be in a position to choose, their data, would be altogether different from what they would be under competition.

The real problem in all this is not whether we will get *given* commodities or services at *given* marginal costs but mainly by what commodities and services the needs of the people can be most cheaply satisfied. The solution of the economic problem of society is in this respect always a voyage of exploration into the unknown, an attempt to discover new ways of doing things better than they have been done before. This must always remain so as long as there are any economic problems to be solved at all, because all economic problems are created by unforeseen changes which require adaptation. Only what we have not foreseen and provided for requires new decisions. If no such adaptations were required, if at any moment we knew that all change had stopped and things would forever go on exactly as they are now, there would be no more questions of the use of resources to be solved.

A person who possesses the exclusive knowledge or skill which enables him to reduce the cost of production of a commodity by 50 per cent still renders an enormous service to society if he enters its production and reduces its price by only 25 per cent—not only through that price reduction but also through his additional saving of cost. But it is only through competition that we can assume that these possible savings of cost will be achieved. Even if in each instance prices were only just low enough to keep out producers which do not enjoy these or other equivalent advantages, so that each commodity were produced as cheaply as possible, though many may be sold at prices considerably above costs, this would probably be a result which could not be achieved by any other method than that of letting competition operate.

4

That in conditions of real life the position even of any two producers is hardly ever the same is due to facts which the theory of perfect competition eliminates by its concentration on a long-term equilibrium which in an ever changing world can never be reached. At any given moment the equipment of a particular firm is always largely determined by historical accident, and the problem is that it should make the best use of the given equipment (including the acquired capacities

101

of the members of its staff) and not what it should do if it were given unlimited time to adjust itself to constant conditions. For the problem of the best use of the given durable but exhaustible resources the long-term equilibrium price with which a theory discussing "perfect" competition must be concerned is not only not relevant; the conclusions concerning policy to which preoccupation with this model leads are highly misleading and even dangerous. The idea that under "perfect" competition prices should be equal to long-run costs often leads to the approval of such antisocial practices as the demand for an "orderly competition" which will secure a fair return on capital and for the destruction of excess capacity. Enthusiasm for perfect competition in theory and the support of monopoly in practice are indeed surprisingly often found to live together.

This is, however, only one of the many points on which the neglect of the time element makes the theoretical picture of perfect competition so entirely remote from all that is relevant to an understanding of the process of competition. If we think of it, as we ought to, as a succession of events, it becomes even more obvious that in real life there will at any moment be as a rule only one producer who can manufacture a given article at the lowest cost and who may in fact sell below the cost of his next successful competitor, but who, while still trying to extend his market, will often be overtaken by somebody else, who in turn will be prevented from capturing the whole market by yet another, and so on. Such a market would clearly never be in a state of perfect competition, yet competition in it might not only be as intense as possible but would also be the essential factor in bringing about the fact that the article in question is supplied at any moment to the consumer as cheaply as this can be done by any known method.

When we compare an "imperfect" market like this with a relatively "perfect" market as that of, say, grain, we shall now be in a better position to bring out the distinction which has been underlying this whole discussion—the distinction between the underlying objective facts of a situation which cannot be altered by human activity and the nature of the competitive activities by which men adjust themselves to the situation. Where, as in the latter case, we have a highly organized market of a fully standardized commodity produced by many producers, there is little need or scope for competitive activities because the situation is such that the conditions which these activities might bring about are already satisfied to begin with. The best ways of producing the commodity, its character and uses, are most of the time known to nearly the same degree to all members of the market. The knowledge of any important change spreads so rapidly and the adaptation to it is so soon effected that we usually simply disregard what happens during these short transition periods and confine ourselves to comparing the two states of near-equilibrium which exist before and after them. But it is during this short and neglected interval that the forces of competition operate and become visible, and it is the events during this interval which we must study if we are to "explain" the equilibrium which follows it.

It is only in a market where adaptation is slow compared with the rate of change that the process of competition is in continuous operation. And though the reason why adaptation is slow *may* be that competition is weak, e.g., because there are special obstacles to entry into the trade, or because of some other factors of the character of natural monopolies, slow adaptation does by no means necessarily mean weak competition. When the variety of near-substitutes is great and rapidly changing, where it takes a long time to find out about the relative merits of the available alternatives, or where the need for a whole class of goods or services occurs only discontinuously at irregular intervals, the adjustment must be slow even if competition is strong and active.

The confusion between the objective facts of the situation and the character of the human responses to it tends to conceal from us the important fact that competition is the more important the more complex or "imperfect" are the objective conditions in which it has to operate. Indeed, far from competition being beneficial only when it is "perfect," I am inclined to argue that the need for competition is nowhere greater than in fields in which the nature of the commodities or services makes it impossible that it ever should create a perfect market in the theoretical sense. The inevitable actual imperfections of competition are as little an argument against competition as the difficulties of achieving a perfect solution of any other task are an argument against attempting to solve it at all, or as little as imperfect health is an argument against health.

In conditions where we can never have many people offering the same homogeneous product or service, because of the ever changing character of our needs and our knowledge, or of the infinite variety of human skills and capacities, the ideal state cannot be one requiring an identical character of large numbers of such products and services. The economic problem is a problem of making the best use of what resources we have, and not one of what we should do if the situation were different from what it actually is. There is no sense in talking of a use of resources "as if" a perfect market existed, if this means that the resources would have to be different from what they are, or in discussing what somebody with perfect knowledge would do if our task must be to make the best use of the knowledge the existing people have.

5

The argument in favor of competition does not rest on the conditions that would exist if it were perfect. Although, where the objective facts would make it possible for competition to approach perfection, this would also secure the most effective use of resources, and, although there is therefore every case for removing human obstacles to competition, this does not mean that competition does not also bring about as effective a use of resources as can be brought about by any known means where in the nature of the case it must be imperfect. Even where free entry will secure no more than that at any one moment all the goods and services for which there would be an effective demand if they were available are in fact produced at the least current[6] expenditure of resources at which, in the given historical situation, they can be produced, even though the price the consumer is made to pay for them

6. "Current" cost in this connection excludes all true bygones but includes, of course, "user cost."

is considerably higher and only just below the cost of the next best way in which his need could be satisfied, this, I submit, is more than we can expect from any other known system. The decisive point is still the elementary one that it is most unlikely that, without artificial obstacles which government activity either creates or can remove, any commodity or service will for any length of time be available only at a price at which outsiders could expect a more than normal profit if they entered the field.

The practical lesson of all this, I think, is that we should worry much less about whether competition in a given case is perfect and worry much more whether there is competition at all. What our theoretical models of separate industries conceal is that in practice a much bigger gulf divides competition from no competition than perfect from imperfect competition. Yet the current tendency in discussion is to be intolerant about the imperfections and to be silent about the prevention of competition. We can probably still learn more about the real significance of competition by studying the results which regularly occur where competition is deliberately suppressed than by concentrating on the shortcomings of actual competition compared with an ideal which is irrelevant for the given facts. I say advisedly "where competition is deliberately suppressed" and not merely "where it is absent," because its main effects are usually operating, even if more slowly, so long as it is not outright suppressed with the assistance or the tolerance of the state. The evils which experience has shown to be the regular consequence of a suppression of competition are on a different plane from those which the imperfections of competition may cause. Much more serious than the fact that prices may not correspond to marginal cost is the fact that, with an intrenched monopoly, costs are likely to be much higher than is necessary. A monopoly based on superior efficiency, on the other hand, does comparatively little harm so long as it is assured that it will disappear as soon as anyone else becomes more efficient in providing satisfaction to the consumers.

In conclusion I want for a moment to go back to the point from which I started and restate the most important conclusion in a more general form. Competition is essentially a process of the formation of opinion: by spreading information, it creates that unity and coherence of the economic system which we presuppose when we think of it as one market. It creates the views people have about what is best and cheapest, and it is because of it that people know at least as much about possibilities and opportunities as they in fact do. It is thus a process which involves a continuous change in the data and whose significance must therefore be completely missed by any theory which treats these data as constant.

VI. "Free" Enterprise and Competitive Order*

1

IF DURING the next few years, that is, during the period with which practical politicians are alone concerned, a continued movement toward more government control in the greater part of the world is almost certain, this is due, more than to anything else, to the lack of a real program, or perhaps I had better say, to a consistent philosophy of the groups which wish to oppose it. The position is even worse than mere lack of program would imply; the fact is that almost everywhere the groups which pretend to oppose socialism at the same time support policies which, if the principles on which they are based were generalized, would no less lead to socialism than the avowedly socialist policies. There is some justification at least in the taunt that many of the pretending defenders of "free enterprise" are in fact defenders of privileges and advocates of government activity in their favor rather than opponents of all privilege. In principle the industrial protectionism and government-supported cartels and the agricultural policies of the conservative groups are not different from the proposals for a more far-reaching direction of economic life sponsored by the socialists. It is an illusion when the more conservative interventionists believe that they will be able to confine these government controls to the particular kinds of which they approve. In a democratic society, at any rate, once the principle is admitted that the government undertakes responsibility for the status and position of particular groups, it is inevitable that this control will be extended to satisfy the aspirations and prejudices of the great masses. There is no hope of a return to a freer system

* The substance of a paper which served to open a discussion on the subject indicated by its title held at a conference at Mont-Pélerin, Switzerland, in April, 1947.

107

until the leaders of the movement against state control are prepared first to impose upon themselves that discipline of a competitive market which they ask the masses to accept. The hopelessness of the prospect for the near future indeed is due mainly to the fact that no organized political group anywhere is in favor of a truly free system.

It is more than likely that from their point of view the practical politicians are right and that in the existing state of public opinion nothing else would be practicable. But what to the politicians are fixed limits of practicability imposed by public opinion must not be similar limits to us. Public opinion on these matters is the work of men like ourselves, the economists and political philosophers of the past few generations, who have created the political climate in which the politicians of our time must move. I do not find myself often agreeing with the late Lord Keynes, but he has never said a truer thing than when he wrote, on a subject on which his own experience has singularly qualified him to speak, that "the ideas of economists and political philosophers, both when they are right and when they are wrong, are more powerful than is commonly understood. Indeed the world is ruled by little else. Madmen in authority, who hear voices in the air, are distilling their frenzy from some academic scribbler of a few years back. I am sure that the power of vested interests is vastly exaggerated compared with the gradual encroachment of ideas. Not, indeed, immediately, but after a certain interval; for in the field of economic and political philosophy there are not many who are influenced by new theories after they are twenty-five or thirty years of age, so that the ideas which civil servants and politicians and even agitators apply are not likely to be the newest. But, soon or late, it is ideas, not vested interests, which are dangerous for good and evil."[1]

It is from this long-run point of view that we must look at our task. It is the beliefs which must spread, if a free society is to be preserved, or restored, not what is practicable at the moment, which must be our concern. But, while we must emancipate ourselves from that servitude

1. J. M. Keynes, *The General Theory of Employment, Interest, and Money* (London, 1936), pp. 383–84.

to current prejudices in which the politician is held, we must take a sane view of what persuasion and instruction are likely to achieve. While we may hope that, as regards the means to be employed and the methods to be adopted, the public may in some measure be accessible to reasonable argument, we must probably assume that many of its basic values, its ethical standards, are at least fixed for a much longer time and to some extent entirely beyond the scope of reasoning. To some extent it may be our task even here to show that the aims which our generation has set itself are incompatible or conflicting and that the pursuit of some of them will endanger even greater values. But we shall probably also find that in some respects during the last hundred years certain moral aims have firmly established themselves for the satisfaction of which in a free society suitable techniques can be found. Even if we should not altogether share the new importance attached to some of these newer values, we shall do well to assume that they will determine action for a long time to come and carefully to consider how far a place can be found for them in a free society. It is, of course, mainly the demands for greater security and greater equality I have here in mind. In both respects I believe very careful distinctions will have to be drawn between the sense in which "security" and "equality" can and cannot be provided in a free society.

Yet in another sense I think that we shall have to pay deliberate attention to the moral temper of contemporary man if we are to succeed in canalizing his energies from the harmful policies to which they are now devoted to a new effort on behalf of individual freedom. Unless we can set a definite task to the reformatory zeal of men, unless we can point out reforms which can be fought for by unselfish men, within a program for freedom, their moral fervor is certain to be used against freedom. It was probably the most fatal tactical mistake of many nineteenth-century liberals to have given the impression that the abandonment of all harmful or unnecessary state activity was the consummation of all political wisdom and that the question of *how* the state ought to use those powers which nobody denied to it offered no serious and important problems on which reasonable people could differ.

This is, of course, not true of all nineteenth-century liberals. About a hundred years ago John Stuart Mill, then still a true liberal, stated one of our present main problems in unmistakable terms. "The principle of private property has never yet had a fair trial in any country," he wrote in the first edition of his *Political Economy*. "The laws of property have never yet conformed to the principles on which the justification of private property rests. They have made property of things which never ought to be property, and absolute property where only a qualified property ought to exist ... if the tendency of legislators had been to favour the diffusion, instead of the concentration of wealth, to encourage the subdivision of the large units, instead of striving to keep them together; the principle of private property would have been found to have no real connection with the physical and social evils which have made so many minds turn eagerly to any prospect of relief, however desperate."[2] But little was in fact done to make the rules of property conform better to its rationale, and Mill himself, like so many others, soon turned his attention to schemes involving its restriction or abolition rather than its more effective use.

While it would be an exaggeration, it would not be altogether untrue to say that the interpretation of the fundamental principle of liberalism as absence of state activity rather than as a policy which deliberately adopts competition, the market, and prices as its ordering principle and uses the legal framework enforced by the state in order to make competition as effective and beneficial as possible—and to supplement it where, and only where, it cannot be made effective—is as much responsible for the decline of competition as the active support which governments have given directly and indirectly to the growth of monopoly. It is the first general thesis which we shall have to consider that competition can be made more effective and more beneficent by certain activities of government than it would be without them. With regard to some of these activities this has never been denied, although people speak sometimes as if they had forgotten about them. That a functioning market presupposes not only prevention of violence and fraud but the protection of certain rights, such as

2. *Principles of Political Economy* (1st ed.), Book II, chap. 1, §5 (Vol. I, p. 253).

property, and the enforcement of contracts, is always taken for granted. Where the traditional discussion becomes so unsatisfactory is where it is suggested that, with the recognition of the principles of private property and freedom of contract, which indeed every liberal must recognize, all the issues were settled, as if the law of property and contract were given once and for all in its final and most appropriate form, i.e., in the form which will make the market economy work at its best. It is only after we have agreed on these principles that the real problems begin.

It is this fact which I have wished to emphasize when I called the subject of this discussion " 'Free' Enterprise and Competitive Order." The two names do not necessarily designate the same system, and it is the system described by the second which we want. Perhaps I should at once add that what I mean by "competitive order" is almost the opposite of what is often called "ordered competition." The purpose of a competitive order is to make competition work; that of so-called "ordered competition," almost always to restrict the effectiveness of competition. Thus understood, this description of our subject at once distinguishes our approach as much from that of the conservative planners as from that of the socialists.

In this introductory survey I must confine myself to enumerating the main problems we shall have to discuss and must leave any detailed examination to later speakers. Perhaps I should begin by emphasizing more than I have yet done that, while our main concern must be to make the market work wherever it can work, we must, of course, not forget that there are in a modern community a considerable number of services which are needed, such as sanitary and health measures, and which could not possibly be provided by the market for the obvious reason that no price can be charged to the beneficiaries or, rather, that it is not possible to confine the benefits to those who are willing or able to pay for them. There are some obvious instances of the kind, like the one I have mentioned, but on closer examination we shall find that in some measure this kind of case shades somewhat gradually into those in which the whole of the services rendered can be sold to whoever wants to buy them. At some stage or other we shall certainly have to consider which services of this kind we must always expect the governments to provide *outside the market* and how far the fact that they must do so will also affect the conditions on which the market economy proceeds.

2

There are two other sets of problems which concern preconditions of a competitive order rather than what one might call market policy proper and which I must mention. The first is the question of the kind of monetary and financial policy required to secure adequate economic stability. We are probably all in agreement that any mitigation of cyclical unemployment depends at least in part on monetary policy. When we turn to these problems, one of our main concerns will have to be how far it is possible to make monetary management once more automatic or at least predictable because bound by fixed rule. The second major problem on which we shall have to assume some definite answer without going into detail at this stage is that in modern society we must take it for granted that some sort of provision will be made for the unemployed and the unemployable poor. All that we can usefully consider in this connection is not whether such provision is desirable or not but merely in what form it will least interfere with the functioning of the market.

I have mentioned these points mainly in order more sharply to delimit my main subject. Before I proceed to the bare enumeration with which I must content myself, I will add only that it seems to me highly desirable that liberals shall strongly disagree on these topics, the more the better. What is needed more than anything else is that these questions of a policy for a competitive order should once again become live issues which are being discussed publicly; and we shall have made an important contribution if we succeed in directing interest to them.

3

If I am not mistaken, the main headings under which the measures required to insure an effective competitive order ought to be considered are the law of property and contract, of corporations and associations, including, in particular, trade-unions, the problems of how to deal with those monopolies or quasi-monopolistic positions which would remain in an otherwise sensibly drawn-up framework, the problems of taxation, and the problems of international trade, particularly, in our time, of the relations between free and planned economies.

As far as the great field of the law of property and contract are concerned, we must, as I have already emphasized, above all beware of the error that the formulas "private property" and "freedom of contract" solve our problems. They are not adequate answers because their meaning is ambiguous. Our problems begin when we ask what ought to be the contents of property rights, what contracts should be enforceable, and how contracts should be interpreted or, rather, what standard forms of contract should be read into the informal agreements of everyday transactions.

Where the law of property is concerned, it is not difficult to see that the simple rules which are adequate to ordinary mobile "things" or "chattel" are not suitable for indefinite extension. We need only turn to the problems which arise in connection with land, particularly with regard to urban land in modern large towns, in order to realize that a conception of property which is based on the assumption that the use of a particular item of property affects only the interests of its owner breaks down. There can be no doubt that a good many, at least, of the problems with which the modern town planner is concerned are genuine problems with which governments or local authorities are bound to concern themselves. Unless we can provide some guidance in fields like this about what are legitimate or necessary government activities and what are its limits, we must not complain if our views are not taken seriously when we oppose other kinds of less justified "planning."

The problem of the prevention of monopoly and the preservation of competition is raised much more acutely in certain other fields to which the concept of property has been extended only in recent times. I am thinking here of the extension of the concept of property to such rights and privileges as patents for inventions, copyright, trade-marks, and the like. It seems to me beyond doubt that in these fields a slavish application of the concept of property as it has been developed for material things has done a great deal to foster the growth of monopoly and that here drastic reforms may be required if competition is to be made to work. In the field of industrial patents in particular we shall have seriously to examine whether the award of a monopoly privilege is really the most appropriate and effective form of reward for the kind of risk-bearing which investment in scientific research involves.

Patents, in particular, are specially interesting from our point of view because they provide so clear an illustration of how it is necessary in all such instances not to apply a ready-made formula but to go back to the rationale of the market system and to decide for each class what the precise rights are to be which the government ought to protect. This is a task at least as much for economists as for lawyers. Perhaps it is not a waste of your time if I illustrate what I have in mind by quoting a rather well-known decision in which an American judge argued that "as to the suggestion that competitors were excluded from the use of the patent we answer that such exclusion may be said to have been the very essence of the right conferred by the patent" and adds "as it is the privilege of any owner of property to use it or not to use it without any question of motive."[3] It is this last statement which seems to me to be significant for the way in which a mechanical extension of the property concept by lawyers has done so much to create undesirable and harmful privilege.

4

Another field in which a mechanical extension of the simplified conception of private property has produced undesirable results is in the field of trade-marks and proprietary names. I myself have no doubt that legislation has important tasks to perform in this field and that securing adequate and truthful information concerning the origin of any product is one, but only one, aspect of this. But the exclusive stress on the description of the producer and the neglect of similar provisions concerning the character and quality of the commodity has to some

3. *Continental Bag Co.* v. *Eastern Bag Co.*, 210 U.S. 405 (1909).

extent helped to create monopolistic conditions because trade-marks have come to be used as a description of the kind of commodity, which then of course only the owner of the trade-mark could produce ("Kodak," "Coca-Cola"). This difficulty might be solved, for example, if the use of trade-marks were protected only in connection with descriptive names which would be free for all to use.

The situation is rather similar in the field of contract. We cannot regard "freedom of contract" as a real answer to our problems if we know that not all contracts ought to be made enforceable and in fact are bound to argue that contracts "in restraint of trade" ought not to be enforced. Once we extend the power to make contracts from natural persons to corporations and the like, it no longer can be the contract but it must be the law which decides who is liable and how the property is to be determined and safeguarded which limits the liability of the corporation.

"Freedom of contract" is in fact no solution because in a complex society like ours no contract can explicitly provide against all contingencies and because jurisdiction and legislation evolve standard types of contracts for many purposes which not only tend to become exclusively practicable and intelligible but which determine the interpretation of, and are used to fill the lacunae in, all contracts which can actually be made. A legal system which leaves the kind of contractual obligations on which the order of society rests entirely to the ever new decision of the contracting parties has never existed and probably cannot exist. Here, as much as in the realm of property, the precise content of the permanent legal framework, the rules of civil law, are of the greatest importance for the way in which a competitive market will operate. The extent to which the development of civil law, as much where it is judge-made law as where it is amended by legislation, can determine the developments away from or toward a competitive system, and how much this change in civil law is determined by the dominant ideas of what would be a desirable social order is well illustrated by the development, during the last fifty years, of legislation and jurisdiction on cartels, monopoly, and the restraint of trade generally. It seems to me that no doubt is possible that this development, even where it fully maintained the principle of "freedom of contract," and partly because it did so, has greatly contributed to the decline of competition. But little intellectual effort has been directed to the question in what way this legal framework should be modified to make competition more effective.

The main field in which these problems arise and the one from which I can best illustrate my point it, of course, the law of corporations and particularly that concerning limited liability. I do not think that there can be much doubt that the particular form legislation has taken in this field has greatly assisted the growth of monopoly or that it was only because of special legislation conferring special rights—not so much to the corporations themselves as to those dealing with corporations—that size of enterprise has become an advantage beyond the point where it is justified by technological facts. It seems to me that, in general, the freedom of the individual by no means need be extended to give all these freedoms to organized groups of individuals, and even that it may on occasion be the duty of government to protect the individual against organized groups. It appears to me also as if historically in the field of the law of corporations we had a situation rather analogous to that in the field of the law of property to which I have already referred. As in the law of property the rules developed for ordinary mobile property were extended uncritically and without appropriate modifications to all sorts of new rights; thus the recognition of corporations as fictitious or legal persons has had the effect that all the rights of a natural person were automatically extended to corporations. There may be valid arguments for so designing corporation law as to impede the indefinite growth of individual corporations; and the ways in which this could be done without setting up any rigid limits or giving the government undesirable powers of direct interference is one of the more interesting problems which we might discuss.

5

I have so far deliberately spoken only of what is required to make competition effective on the side of employers, not because I regard this as of such exclusive importance, but because I am convinced that there is politically no chance to do anything about the other side of the problem—the labor side—until the employers have themselves shown their belief in competition and demonstrated that they are willing to put their own house in order. But we must not delude ourselves that in many ways the most crucial, the most difficult, and the most delicate part of our task consists in formulating an appropriate program of labor or trade-union policy. In no other respect, I believe, was the development of liberal opinion more inconsistent or more unfortunate or is there more uncertainty and vagueness even among the true liberals of today. Historically liberalism, first, far too long maintained an unjustified opposition against trade-unions as such, only to collapse completely at the beginning of this century and to grant to trade-unions in many respects exemption from the ordinary law and even, to all intents and purposes, to legalize violence, coercion, and intimidation. That, if there is to be any hope of a return to a free economy, the question of how the powers of trade-unions can be appropriately delimited in law as well as in fact is one of the most important of all the questions to which we must give our attention. I have many times already in the course of this outline felt tempted to refer you to the writings of the late Henry Simons, but I want now especially to draw your attention to his "Reflections on Syndicalism," which states this problem with rare courage and lucidity.[4]

The problem has recently, of course, become even bigger by the assumption on the part of most governments of the responsibility for what is called "full employment" and by all its implications, and I do not see how we can, when we reach these problems, any longer separate them from the more general problems of monetary policy which I have suggested we should, as far as possible, keep separate. The same is true of the next set of major problems, which I can now only briefly mention—those of international trade, tariffs and foreign exchange control, etc. While on all these our long-run point of view ought not

4. Henry C. Simons, "Some Reflections on Syndicalism," *Journal of Political Economy,* LII (March, 1944), 1–25; reprinted in his *Economic Policy for a Free Society* (Chicago: University of Chicago Press, 1948), pp. 121–58.

to be in doubt, they do, of course, raise real problems for the immediate future, which, however, we had probably better leave on one side as belonging to the questions of immediate policy rather than long-run principles. The same, I am afraid, we should probably not be entitled to do with regard to that other problem I have already mentioned—the problem of the relation between free and planned economies.

6

If I am to confine myself to the enunciation of the main problems, I must now hurry to a conclusion and just touch on one more major field—that of taxation. It is, of course, by itself very large. I want to pick out only two aspects of it. The one is the effect of progressive income taxation at the rate which has now been reached and used for extreme egalitarian ends. The two consequences of this which seem to me the most serious are, on the one hand, that it makes for social immobility by making it practically impossible for the successful man to rise by accumulating a fortune and that, on the other, it has come near eliminating that most important element in any free society—the man of independent means, a figure whose essential role in maintaining a free opinion and generally the atmosphere of independence from government control we only begin to realize as he is disappearing from the stage. Similar comments apply to modern inheritance taxation and particularly to estate duties as they exist in Great Britain. But, in mentioning this, I ought at once to add that inheritance taxes could, of course, be made an instrument toward greater social mobility and greater dispersion of property and, consequently, may have to be regarded as important tools of a truly liberal policy which ought not to stand condemned by the abuse which has been made of it.

There are many other important problems which I have not even mentioned. But I hope that what I have said will be sufficient to indicate the field which I had in mind when I suggested our present topic for discussion. It is too wide a field to treat the whole of it adequately even if we had much more time at our disposal. But, as I have said before, I hope that these discussions will be only a beginning and that it does not matter a great deal exactly where we start.

VII. Socialist Calculation I: *The Nature and History of the Problem**

1

THERE is reason to believe that we are at last entering an era of reasoned discussion of what has long uncritically been assumed to be a reconstruction of society on rational lines. For more than half a century the belief that deliberate regulation of all social affairs must necessarily be more successful than the apparent haphazard interplay of independent individuals has continuously gained ground until today there is hardly a political group anywhere in the world which does not want central direction of most human activities in the service of one aim or another. It seemed so easy to improve upon the institutions of a free society which had come more and more to be considered as the result of mere accident, the product of a peculiar historical growth which might as well have taken a different direction. To bring order to such a chaos, to apply reason to the organization of society, and to shape it deliberately in every detail according to human wishes and the common ideas of justice seemed the only course of action worthy of a rational being.

But at the present day it is clear—it would probably be admitted by all sides—that, during the greater part of the growth of this belief, some of the most serious problems of such a reconstruction have not even been recognized, much less successfully answered. For many years discussion of socialism—and for the greater part of the period it was only from socialism proper that the movement sprang—turned almost exclusively on ethical and psychological issues. On the one hand, there was the general question whether justice required a reorganization of society on socialist lines and what principles of the

* Reprinted from *Collectivist Economic Planning*, ed. F. A. Hayek (London: George Routledge & Sons, Ltd., 1935).

119

distribution of income were to be regarded as just. On the other hand, there was the question whether men in general could be trusted to have the moral and psychological qualities which were dimly seen to be essential if a socialist system was to work. But, although this latter question does raise some of the real difficulties, it does not really touch the heart of the problem. What was questioned was only whether the authorities in the new state would be in a position to make people carry out their plans properly. Only the practical possibility of the execution of the plans was called in question, not whether planning, even in the ideal case where these difficulties were absent, would achieve the desired end. The problem seemed therefore to be *only* one of psychology or education, the "only" meaning that after initial difficulties these obstacles would certainly be overcome.

If this were true, then the economist would have nothing to say on the feasibility of such proposals, and indeed it is improbable that any scientific discussion of their merits would be possible. It would be a problem of ethics, or rather of individual judgments of value, on which different people might agree or disagree, but on which no reasoned arguments would be possible. Some of the questions might be left to the psychologist to decide, if he has really any means of saying what men would be like under entirely different circumstances. Apart from this no scientist, and least of all the economist, would have anything to say about the problems of socialism. Many people, believing that the knowledge of the economist is only applicable to the problems of a capitalist society (i.e., to problems arising out of peculiar human institutions which would be absent in a world organized on different lines), still think this to be the case.

2

Whether this widespread belief is based on a clear conviction that there would be no economic problems in a socialist world, or whether it simply proves that the people who hold it do not know what economic problems are, is not always evident. Probably usually the latter.

This is not at all surprising. The big economic problems which the economist sees, and which he contends will also have to be solved in a collectivist society, are not problems which at present are solved deliberately by anybody in the sense in which the economic problems of a household reach solution. In a purely competitive society nobody bothers about any but his own economic problems. There is therefore no reason why the existence of economic problems, in the sense in which the economist uses the term, should be known to others. But the distribution of available resources between different uses, which is the economic problem, is no less a problem of society than for the individual, and, although the decision is not consciously made by anybody, the competitive mechanism does bring about some sort of solution.

No doubt, if it were put in this general way, everybody would be ready to admit that such a problem exists. But few realize that it is fundamentally different not only in difficulty but also in character from the problems of engineering. The increasing preoccupation of the modern world with problems of an engineering character tends to blind people to the totally different character of the economic problem and is probably the main cause why the nature of the latter was less and less understood. At the same time everyday terminology used in discussing either sort of problem has greatly enhanced the confusion. The familiar phrase of "trying to get the greatest results from the given means" covers both problems. The metallurgist who seeks for a method which will enable him to extract a maximum amount of metal from a given quantity of ore, the military engineer who tries to build a bridge with a given number of men in the shortest possible time, the optician who endeavors to construct a telescope which will enable the astronomer to penetrate to still more distant stars—all are concerned solely with technological problems. The common character of these problems is determined by the singleness of their purpose in every case, the absolutely determined nature of the ends to which the available means are to be devoted. Nor does it alter the fundamental character of the problem if the means available for a definite purpose is a fixed amount of money to be spent on factors of production with given prices. From this point of view the industrial engineer who decides on the best method of production of a given commodity on the basis of given prices is concerned only with technological problems, although he may speak of his trying to find the most economical method. But the only element which makes his decision *in its effects* an economic one is not any part of his calculations but the fact that he uses, as a basis for these calculations, prices as he finds them on the market.

The problems which the director of all economic activities of a community would have to face would be similar to those solved by an engineer only if the order of importance of the different needs of the community were fixed in such a definite and absolute way that provision for one could always be made irrespective of cost. If it were possible for him first to decide on the best way to produce the necessary supply of, say, food as the most important need, as if it were the only need, and would think about the supply, say of clothing, only if and when some means were left over after the demand for food had been fully satisfied, then there would be no economic problem, for in such a case nothing would be left over except what could not possibly be used for the first purpose, either because it could not be turned into food or because there was no further demand for food. The criterion would simply be whether the possible maximum of foodstuffs had been produced or whether the application of different methods might not lead to a greater output. But the task would cease to be merely technological in character and would assume an entirely different nature if it were further postulated that as many resources as possible should be left over for other purposes. Then the question arises what *is* a greater quantity of resources. If one engineer proposed a method which would leave a great deal of land but only little labor for other purposes, while another would leave much labor and little land, how in the absence of any standard of value could it be decided which was the greater quantity? If there were only one factor of production, this could be decided unequivocally on merely technical grounds, for then the main problem in every line of production would again be reduced to one of getting the maximum quantity of product out of any given amount of the same resources. The remaining economic problem of how much to produce in every line of production would in this case be of a very simple and almost negligible nature. As soon as there are two or more factors, however, this possibility is not present.

The economic problem arises, therefore, as soon as different purposes compete for the available resources. The criterion of its presence is that costs have to be taken into account. Cost here, as anywhere, means nothing but the advantages to be derived from the use of given resources in other directions. Whether this is simply the use of part of the possible working day for recreation, or the use of material resources in an alternative line of production, makes little difference. It is clear that decisions of this sort will have to be made in any conceivable kind of economic system, wherever one has to choose between alternative employments of given resources. But the decisions between two possible alternative uses cannot be made in the absolute way which was possible in our earlier example. Even if the director of the economic system were quite clear in his mind that the food of one person is always more important than the clothing of another, that would by no means necessarily imply that it is also more important than the clothing of two or ten others. How critical the question is becomes clearer if we look at the less elementary wants. It may well be that, although the need for one additional doctor is greater than the need for one additional schoolteacher, yet under conditions where it costs three times as much to train an additional doctor as it costs to train an additional schoolteacher, three additional schoolteachers may appear preferable to one doctor.

As has been said before, the fact that in the present order of things such economic problems are not solved by the conscious decision of anybody has the effect that most people are not conscious that such problems exist. Decisions whether and how much to produce of a thing are economic decisions in this sense. But the making of such a decision by a single individual is only part of the solution of the economic problem involved. The person making such a decision makes it on the basis of given prices. The fact that by this decision he influences these prices to a certain, probably very small, extent will not influence his choice. The other part of the problem is solved by the functioning of the price system. But it is solved in a way which only a systematic study of the working of this system reveals. It has already been suggested that it is not necessary, for the working of this system, that anybody should understand it. But people are not likely to let it work if they do not understand it.

The real situation in this respect is well reflected in the popular estimate of the relative merits of the economists and the engineer. It is probably no exaggeration to say that to most people the engineer is the person who actually does things and the economist the odious individual who sits back in his armchair and explains why the well-intentioned efforts of the former are frustrated. In a sense this is not untrue. But the implication that the forces which the economist studies and the engineer is likely to disregard are unimportant and ought to be disregarded is absurd. It needs the special training of the economist to see that the spontaneous forces which limit the ambitions of the engineer themselves provide a way of solving a problem which otherwise would have to be solved deliberately.

3

There are, however, other reasons besides the increasing conspicuousness of the elaborate modern technique of production which are responsible for our contemporary failure to see the existence of economic problems. It was not always so. For a comparatively short period in the middle of the last century, the degree to which the economic problems were seen and understood by the general public was undoubtedly much higher than it is at present. But the classical system of political economy whose extraordinary influence facilitated this understanding had been based on insecure and in part definitely faulty foundations, and its popularity had been achieved at the price of a degree of oversimplification which proved to be its undoing. It was only much later, after its teaching had lost influence, that the gradual reconstruction of economic theory showed that what defects there were in its basic concepts had invalidated its explanation of the working of the economic system to a much smaller degree than had at first seemed probable. But in the interval irreparable harm had been done. The downfall of the classical system tended to discredit the very idea of theoretical analysis, and it was attempted to substitute for an understanding of the why of economic phenomena a mere description of their occurrence. In consequence, the comprehension of the nature of the economic problem, the achievement of generations of teaching, was lost. The economists who were still interested in general analysis were far too much concerned with the reconstructing of the purely abstract foundations of economic science to exert a noticeable influence on opinion regarding policy.

It was largely owing to this temporary eclipse of analytical economics that the real problems connected with the suggestions of a planned economy have received so surprisingly little careful examination. But this eclipse itself was by no means due only to the inherent weaknesses and the consequent need for reconstruction of the old economics. Nor would it have had the same effect if it had not coincided with the rise of another movement definitely hostile to rational methods in economics. The common cause which at the same time undermined the position of economic theory and furthered the growth of a school of socialism, which positively discouraged any speculation of the actual working of the society of the future, was the rise of the so-called historical school in economics,[1] for it was the essence of the standpoint of this school that the laws of economics could be established only by the application to the material of history of the methods of the natural sciences. The nature of this material is such that any attempt of this kind is bound to degenerate into mere record and description and a total skepticism concerning the existence of any laws at all.

It is not difficult to see why this should happen. In all sciences except those which deal with social phenomena all that experience shows us

1. Some of the points on which I can only touch here I have developed at somewhat greater length in an address on the "Trend of Economic Thinking," *Economica*, May, 1933.

is the result of processes which we cannot directly observe and which it is our task to reconstruct. All our conclusions concerning the nature of these processes are of necessity hypothetical, and the only test of the validity of these hypotheses is that they prove equally applicable to the explanation of other phenomena. What enables us to arrive by this process of induction at the formulation of general laws or hypotheses regarding the process of causation is the fact that the possibility of experimenting, of observing the repetition of the same phenomena under identical conditions, shows the existence of definite regularities in the observed phenomena.

In the social sciences, however, the situation is the exact reverse. On the one hand, experiment is impossible, and we have therefore no knowledge of definite regularities in the complex phenomena in the same sense as we have in the natural sciences. But, on the other hand, the position of man, midway between natural and social phenomena —of the one of which he is an effect and of the other a cause—brings it about that the essential basic facts which we need for the explanation of social phenomena are part of common experience, part of the stuff of our thinking. In the social sciences it is the elements of the complex phenomena which are known beyond the possibility of dispute. In the natural sciences they can be at best only surmised. The existence of these elements is so much more certain than any regularities in the complex phenomena to which they give rise that it is they which constitute the truly empirical factor in the social sciences. There can be little doubt that it is this different position of the empirical element in the process of reasoning in the two groups of disciplines which is at the root of much of the confusion with regard to their logical character. There can be no doubt that the social as well as the natural sciences have to employ deductive reasoning. The essential difference is that in the natural sciences the process of deduction has to start from some hypothesis which is the result of inductive generalizations, while in the social sciences it starts directly from known empirical elements and uses them to find the regularities in the complex phenomena which direct observations cannot establish. They are, so to speak, empirically deductive sciences, proceeding from the known elements to the regularities in the complex phenomena which cannot be directly established. But this is not the place to discuss questions of methodology for their own sake. Our concern is only to show how it came that in the era of the great triumphs of empiricism in the natural sciences an attempt was made to force the same empirical methods on the social sciences which was bound to lead to disaster. To start here at the wrong end, to seek for regularities of complex phenomena which could never be observed twice under identical conditions, could not but lead to the conclusion that there were no general laws, no inherent necessities determined by the permanent nature of the constituting elements, and that the only task of economic science in particular was a description of historical change. It was only with this abandonment of the appropriate methods of procedure, well established in the classical period, that it began to be thought that there were no laws of social life other than those made by men and that all observed phenomena were all only the product of social or legal institutions, merely "historical categories," and did not in any way arise out of the basic economic problems which humanity has to face.

4

In many respects the most powerful school of socialism the world has so far seen is essentially a product of this kind of historicism. Although in some points Karl Marx adopted the tools of the classical economists, he made little use of their main permanent contribution —their analysis of competition. But he did wholeheartedly accept the central contention of the historical school that most of the phenomena of economic life were not the result of permanent causes but the product only of a special historical development. It is no accident that the country where the historical school had had the greatest vogue, Germany, was also the country where Marxism was most readily accepted.

Individualism and Economic Order

The fact that this most influential school of socialism was so closely related to the general antitheoretical tendencies in the social sciences of the time had a most profound effect on all further discussion of the real problems of socialism. Not only did the whole outlook create a peculiar inability to see any of the permanent economic problems which are independent of the historical framework, but Marx and the Marxians also proceeded, quite consistently, positively to discourage any inquiry into the actual organization and working of the socialist society of the future. If the change was to be brought about by the inexorable logic of history, if it was the inevitable result of evolution, there was little need for knowing in detail what exactly the new society would be like. If nearly all the factors which determined economic activity in the present society would be absent, if there would be no problems in the new society except those determined by the new institutions which the process of historical change would have created, then there was indeed little possibility of solving any of its problems beforehand. Marx himself had only scorn and ridicule for any such attempt deliberately to construct a working plan of such a utopia. Only occasionally, and then in this negative form, do we find in his works statements about what the new society would *not* be like. One may search his writings in vain for any definite statement of the general principles on which the economic activity in the socialist community would be directed.[2]

Marx's attitude on this point had a lasting effect on the socialists of his school. To speculate about the actual organization of the socialist society immediately stigmatized the unfortunate writer as being "unscientific," the most dreaded condemnation to which a member of the "scientific" school of socialism could expose himself. But even outside the Marxian camp the common descent of all modern branches of socialism from some essentially historical or "institutional" view of economic phenomena had the effect of successfully

2. A useful collection of the different allusions to this problem in Marx's works, particularly in the *Randglossen zum Gothaer Programm* (1875), will be found in K. Tisch, *Wirtschaftsrechnung und Verteilung im zentralistisch organisierten sozialistischen Gemeinwesen* (1932), pp. 110–15.

smothering all attempts to study the problems any constructive socialist policy would have to solve. As we shall see, it was only in reply to criticism from the outside that this task was ultimately undertaken.

5

We have now reached a point at which it becomes necessary clearly to separate several different aspects of the program which we have so far lumped together as socialistic. For the earlier part of the period in which the belief in central planning grew it is historically justified to identify, without much qualification, the idea of socialism and that of planning. In so far as the main economic problems are concerned, this is still the case today. Yet it must be admitted that in many other respects modern socialists and other modern planners are fully entitled to disclaim any responsibility for each other's program. What we must distinguish here are the ends aimed at and the means which have been proposed or are in fact necessary for the purpose. The ambiguities which exist in this connection arise out of the fact that the means necessary to achieve the ends of socialism in the narrower sense may be used for other ends and that the problems with which we are concerned arise out of the means and not the ends.

The common end of all socialism in the narrower sense, of "proletarian" socialism, is the improvement of the position of the propertyless classes of society by a redistribution of income derived from property. This implies collective ownership of the material means of production and collectivist direction and control of their use. The same collectivist methods may, however, be applied in the service of quite different ends. An aristocratic dictatorship, for example, may use the same methods to further the interest of some racial or other elite or in the service of some other decidedly anti-equalitarian purpose. The situation is further complicated by the fact that the method of collectivist ownership and control which is essential for any of these attempts to dissociate the distribution of income from the private ownership of the means of production admits of application in different degrees. For

129

the present it will be convenient to use the term "socialism" to describe the traditional socialist ends and to use the term "planning" to describe the method, although later we shall use "socialism" in the wider sense. In the narrower sense of the term it can be said, then, that it is possible to have much planning with little socialism or little planning and much socialism. The method of planning in any case can certainly be used for purposes which have nothing to do with the ethical aims of socialism. Whether it is equally possible to dissociate socialism completely from planning—and the criticisms directed against the method have led to attempts in this direction—is a question which we shall have to investigate later.

That it is possible, not only in theory but also in practice, to separate the problem of the method from that of the end is very fortunate for the purposes of scientific discussion. On the validity of the ultimate ends science has nothing to say. They may be accepted or rejected, but they cannot be proved or disproved. All that we can rationally argue about is whether and to what extent given measures will lead to the desired results. If, however, the method in question were only proposed as a means for one particular end, it might prove difficult, in practice, to keep the argument about the technical question and the judgments of value quite apart. But, since the same problem of means arises in connection with altogether different ethical ideals, one may hope that it will be possible to keep value judgments altogether out of the discussion.

The common condition necessary for the achievement of a distribution of income which is independent of individual ownership of resources—the common proximate end of socialism and other anticapitalistic movements—is that the authority which decides on the principles of this distribution should also have control over the resources. Now, whatever the substance of these principles of distribution, these ideas about the just or otherwise desirable division of income, they must be similar in one purely formal but highly important respect: They must be stated in the form of a scale of importance of a number of competing individual ends. It is this formal aspect, this fact that one

130

central authority has to solve the economic problem of distributing a limited amount of resources between a practically infinite number of competing purposes, that constitutes the problem of socialism as a method. The fundamental question is whether it is possible under the complex conditions of a large modern society for such a central authority to carry out the implications of any such scale of values with a reasonable degree of accuracy, with a degree of success equaling or approaching the results of competitive capitalism, not whether any particular set of values of this sort is in any way superior to another. It is the methods common to socialism in the narrower sense and all the other modern movements for a planned society, not the particular ends of socialism, with which we are here concerned.

6

Since in all that follows we shall be concerned only with the methods to be employed and not with the ends aimed at, from now onward it will be convenient to use the term "socialism" in this wider sense. In this sense it covers therefore any case of collectivist control of productive resources, no matter in whose interest this control is used. But while we need for our purpose no further definition of the concrete ends followed, there is still need for a further definition of the exact methods we want to consider. There are, of course, many kinds of socialism, but the traditional names of these different types, like "communism," "syndicalism," "guild socialism," have never quite corresponded to the classification of methods which we want, and most of them have in recent times become so closely connected with political parties rather than with definite programs that they are hardly useful for our purpose. What is relevant for us is essentially the degree to which the central control and direction of the resources is carried in each of the different types. To see to what extent variation on this point is possible, it is perhaps best to begin with the most familiar type of socialism and then to examine to what extent its arrangements can be altered in different directions.

Individualism and Economic Order

The program which is at once the most widely advocated and has the greatest prima facie plausibility provides not only for collective ownership but also for unified central direction of the use of all material resources of production. At the same time it envisages continued freedom of choice in consumption and continued freedom in the choice of occupation. At least it is essentially in this form that Marxism has been interpreted by the social-democratic parties on the Continent, and it is the form in which socialism is imagined by the greatest number of people. It is in this form, too, that socialism has been most widely discussed; most of the more recent criticism is focused on this variety. Indeed, so widely has it been treated as the only important socialist program that in most discussions on the economic problems of socialism the authors concerned have neglected to specify which kind of socialism they had in mind. This has had somewhat unfortunate effects, for it never became quite clear whether particular objections or criticisms applied only to this particular form or to all the forms of socialism.

For this reason it is necessary right from the outset to keep the alternative possibilities in mind and to consider carefully at every stage of the discussion whether any particular problem arises out of the assumptions which must underlie any socialist program or whether they are only due to assumptions made in some particular case. Freedom of the choice of the consumer or freedom of occupation, for example, are by no means necessary attributes of any socialist program, and although earlier socialists have generally repudiated the suggestion that socialism would abolish these freedoms, more recently criticisms of the socialist position have been met by the answer that the supposed difficulties would arise only if they were retained; and that it was by no means too high a price for the other advantages of socialism if their abolition should prove necessary. It is therefore necessary to consider this extreme form of socialism equally with the others. It corresponds in most respects to what in the past used to be called "communism," i.e., a system in which not only the means of production but all goods

were collectively owned and in which, in addition to this, the central
authority would also be in a position to order any person to do any task.

This kind of society where everything is centrally directed may be
regarded as the limiting case of a long series of other systems of a lesser
degree of centralization. The more familiar type discussed already
stands somewhat further in the direction of decentralization. But it
still involves planning on a most extensive scale—minute direction of
practically all productive activity by one central authority. The earlier
systems of more decentralized socialism like guild socialism or syndicalism need not concern us here, since it seems now to be fairly generally admitted that they provide no mechanism whatever for a rational
direction of economic activity. More recently, however, there has
arisen, again mainly in response to criticism, a tendency among socialist thinkers to reintroduce a certain degree of competition into their
schemes in order to overcome the difficulty which they admit would
arise in the case of completely centralized planning. There is no need
at this stage to consider in detail the forms in which competition between individual producers may be combined with socialism. This
will be done later on.[3] But it is necessary from the outset to be aware
of them. This for two reasons. In the first place, in order to remain
conscious throughout the further discussion that the completely centralized direction of all economic activity which is generally regarded
as typical of all socialism may conceivably be varied to some extent;
and, in the second—even more important—in order that we may see
clearly what degree of central control must be retained in order that
we may reasonably speak of socialism or what are the minimum
assumptions which will entitle us to regard a system as coming within
our field. Even if collective ownership of productive resources should
be found to be compatible with competitive determination of the purposes for which individual units of resources are to be used and the
method of their employment, we must still assume that the questions,
"Who is to exercise command over a given quantity of resources for the
community?" or "With what amount of resources are the different

3. See now chapter ix in this volume.

'entrepreneurs' to be intrusted?" will have to be decided by one central authority. This seems to be the minimum assumption consistent with the idea of collective ownership, the smallest degree of central control which would still enable the community to retain command over the income derived from the material means of production.

7

Without some such central control of the means of production, planning in the sense in which we have used the term ceases to be a problem. It becomes unthinkable. This would probably be agreed by the majority of economists of all camps, although most other people who believe in planning still think of it as something which could be rationally attempted inside the framework of a society based on private property. In fact, however, if by "planning" is meant the actual direction of productive activity by authoritative prescription, of either the quantities to be produced, the methods of production to be used, or the prices to be fixed, it can be easily shown, not that such a thing is impossible, but that any isolated measure of this sort will cause reactions which will defeat its own end, and that any attempt to act consistently will necessitate further and further measures of control until all economic activity is brought under one central authority.

It is impossible within the scope of this discussion of socialism to enter further into this separate problem of state intervention in a capitalistic society. It is mentioned here only to say explicitly that it is excluded from our considerations. In our opinion well-accepted analysis shows that it does not provide an alternative which can be rationally chosen or which can be expected to provide a stable or satisfactory solution of any of the problems to which it is applied.[4]

But here, again, it is necessary to guard against misunderstanding. To say that partial planning of the kind we are alluding to is irrational is, however, not equivalent to saying that the only form of capitalism which can be rationally advocated is that of complete laissez faire in the old sense. There is no reason to assume that the historically given

4. Cf. L. von Mises, *Interventionismus* (Jena, 1929).

134

legal institutions are necessarily the most "natural" in any sense. The recognition of the principle of private property does not by any means necessarily imply that the particular delimitation of the contents of this right as determined by the existing laws are the most appropriate. The question as to which is the most appropriate permanent framework which will secure the smoothest and most efficient working of competition is of the greatest importance and one which, it must be admitted, has been sadly neglected by economists.

But, on the other hand, to admit the possibility of changes in the legal framework is not to admit the possibility of a further type of planning in the sense in which we have used the word so far. There is an essential distinction here which must not be overlooked: the distinction between a permanent legal framework so devised as to provide all the necessary incentives to private initiative to bring about the adaptations required by any change and a system where such adaptations are brought about by central direction. It is this, and not the question of the maintenance of the existing order versus the introduction of new institutions, which is the real issue. In a sense both systems can be described as being the product of rational planning. But in the one case this planning is concerned only with the permanent framework of institutions and may be dispensed with if one is willing to accept the institutions which have grown in a slow historical process, while in the other it has to deal with day-to-day changes of every sort.

There can be no doubt that planning of this sort involves changes of a type and magnitude hitherto unknown in human history. It is sometimes urged that the changes now in progress are merely a return to the social forms of the preindustrial era. But this is a misapprehension. Even when the medieval guild system was at its height, and when restrictions to commerce were most extensive, they were not used as a means actually to direct individual activity. They were certainly not the most rational permanent framework for individual activity which could have been devised, but they were essentially only a permanent framework inside which current activity by individual initiative had free play. With our attempts to use the old apparatus of restrictionism as an instrument of almost day-to-day adjustment to change, we have already gone much further in the direction of central planning of current activity than has ever been attempted before. If we follow the path on which we have started, if we try to act consistently and to combat the self-frustrating tendencies of any isolated act of planning, we shall certainly embark upon an experiment which until recently had no parallel in history. But even at this stage we have gone very far. If we are to judge the potentialities aright, it is necessary to realize that the system under which we live, choked up with attempts at partial planning and restrictionism, is almost as far from any system of capitalism which could be rationally advocated as it is different from any consistent system of planning. It is important to realize in any investigation of the possibilities of planning that it is a fallacy to suppose capitalism as it exists today is the alternative. We are certainly as far from capitalism in its pure form as we are from any system of central planning. The world of today is just interventionist chaos.

8

Classical political economy broke down mainly because it failed to base its explanation of the fundamental phenomenon of value on the same analysis of the springs of economic activity which it had so successfully applied to the analysis of the more complex phenomena of competition. The labor theory of value was the product of a search after some illusory substance of value rather than an analysis of the behavior of the economic subject. The decisive step in the progress of economics was taken when economists began to ask what exactly were the circumstances which made individuals behave toward goods in a particular way. To ask the question in this form led immediately to the recognition that to attach a definite significance or value to the units of different goods was a necessary step in the solution of the general problem which arises everywhere when a multiplicity of ends compete for a limited quantity of means.

The omnipresence of this problem of value wherever there is rational action was the basic fact from which a systematic exploration of the forms, under which it would make its appearance under different organizations of economic life, could proceed. Up to a certain point from the very beginning the problems of a centrally directed economy found a prominent place in the expositions of modern economics. It was obviously so much simpler to discuss the fundamental problems on the assumption of the existence of a *single* scale of values consistently followed than on the assumption of a multiplicity of individuals following their personal scales that in the early chapters of the new systems the assumption of a Communist state was frequently used— and used with considerable advantage—as an expository device.[5] But it was used only to demonstrate that any solution would necessarily give rise to essentially the same value phenomena—rent, wages, and interest, etc.—which we actually observe in a competitive society, and the authors then generally proceeded to show how the interaction of independent activities of the individuals produced these phenomena spontaneously, without inquiring further whether they could be produced in a complex modern society by any other means. The mere absence of an agreed common scale of values seemed to deprive that problem of any practical importance. It is true that some of the earlier writers of the new school not only thought that they had actually solved the problem of socialism but also believed that their utility calculus provided a means which made it possible to combine individual utility scale into a scale of ends objectively valid for society as a whole. But it is now generally recognized that this latter belief was just an illusion and that there are no scientific criteria which would enable us to compare or assess the relative importance of needs of different persons, although conclusions implying such illegitimate interpersonal comparisons of utilities can still be found in discussions of special problems.

But it is evident that, as the progress of the analysis of the competitive system revealed the complexity of the problems which it solved spontaneously, economists became more and more skeptical about the possibility of solving the same problems by deliberate decision. It is

5. Cf. particularly F. von Wieser, *Natural Value* (London, 1893), *passim*.

137

perhaps worth noting that as early as 1854 the most famous among the predecessors of the modern "marginal utility" school, the German H. H. Gossen, had come to the conclusion that the central economic authority projected by the Communists would soon find that it had set itself a task which far exceeded the powers of individual men.[6] Among the later economists of the modern school the point in which Gossen had already based his objection, the difficulty of rational calculation when there is no private property, was frequently hinted at. It was particularly clearly put by Professor Cannan, who stressed the fact that the aims of socialists and Communists could only be achieved by "abolishing both the institution of private property and the practice of exchange, without which value, in any reasonable sense of the word, cannot exist."[7] But, beyond general statements of this sort, critical examination of the possibilities of a socialist economic policy made little headway, for the simple reason that no concrete socialist proposal of how these problems would be overcome existed to be examined.[8]

It was only early in the present century that at last a general statement of the kind we have just examined concerning the impracticability of socialism by the eminent Dutch economist, N. G. Pierson, provoked K. Kautsky, then the leading theoretician of Marxian social-

6. H. H. Gossen, *Entwicklung der Gesetze des menschlichen Verkehrs und der daraus fliessenden Regeln für menschliches Handeln* (Braunschweig, 1854), p. 231: "Dazu folgt aber ausserdem aus den im vorstehenden gefundenen Sätzen über das Geniessen, und infolgedessen über das Steigen und Sinken des Werthes jeder Sache mit Verminderung und Vermehrung der Masse und der Art, *dass nur durch Feststellung des Privateigenthums der Massstab gefunden wird zur Bestimmung der Quantität, welche den Verhältnissen angemessen am Zweckmässigsten von jedem Gegenstand zu produziren ist.* Darum würde denn die von Communisten projectierte Zentralbehörde zur Verteilung der verschiedenen Arbeiten sehr bald die Erfahrung machen, dass sie sich eine Aufgabe gestellt habe, deren Lösung die Kräfte einzelner Menschen weit übersteigt." (Italics in the original.)

7. E. Cannan, *A History of the Theories of Production and Distribution* (1893; 3d ed., 1917), p. 395. Professor Cannan has later also made an important contribution to the problem of the international relation between socialist states. Cf. his essay on "The Incompatibility of Socialism and Nationalism," in *The Economic Outlook* (London, 1912).

8. A completely neglected attempt to solve the problem from the socialist side, which shows at least some realization of the real difficulty, was made by G. Sulzer, *Die Zukunft des Sozialismus* (Dresden, 1899).

ism, to break the traditional silence about the actual working of the future socialist state and to give in a lecture, still somewhat hesitantly and with many apologies, a description of what would happen on the morrow of the Revolution.[9] But Kautsky only showed that he was not even really aware of the problem which the economists had seen. He thus gave Pierson the opportunity to demonstrate in detail, in an article which first appeared in the Dutch *Economist,* that a socialist state would have its problems of value just as any other economic system and that the task socialists had to solve was to show how in the absence of a pricing system the value of different goods was to be determined. This article is the first important contribution to the modern discussion of the economic aspects of socialism, and, although it remained practically unknown outside of Holland and was only made accessible in a German version after the discussion had been started independently by others, it remains of special interest as the only important discussion of these problems published before World War I. It is particularly valuable for its discussion of the problems arising out of the international trade between several socialist communities.[10]

All the further discussions of the economic problems of socialism which appeared before the first World War confined themselves more or less to the demonstration that the main categories of prices, as wages, rent, and interest, would have to figure at least in the calculations of the planning authority in the same way in which they appear today and would be determined by essentially the same factors. The modern development of the theory of interest played a particularly important role in this connection, and after Böhm-Bawerk[11] it was particularly Professor Cassel who showed convincingly that interest

9. An English translation of this lecture, originally given in Delft on April 24, 1902, and soon afterward published in German, together with that of another lecture given two days earlier at the same place, was published under the title, *The Social Revolution and On the Morrow of the Social Revolution* (London, 1907).

10. An English translation of Pierson's article is contained in the volume on *Collectivist Economic Planning* to which the present essay formed the Introduction.

11. In addition to his general work on interest, his essay on "Macht und ökonomisches Gesetz" (*Zeitschrift für Volkswirtschaft, Sozialpolitik und Verwaltung* [1914] should be specially mentioned, since in many ways it must be regarded as a direct predecessor of the later critical work.

would have to form an important element in the rational calculation of economic activity. But none of these authors even attempted to show how these essential magnitudes could be arrived at in practice. The one author who at least approached the problem was the Italian economist, Enrico Barone, who in 1908 in an article on the "Ministry of Production in the Collectivist State" developed certain suggestions of Pareto's.[12] This article is of considerable interest as an example of how it was thought that the tools of mathematical analysis of economic problems might be utilized to solve the tasks of the central planning authority.[13]

9

When, with the end of the war of 1914–18, socialist parties came into power in most of the states of central and eastern Europe, the discussion on all these problems necessarily entered a new and decisive phase. The victorious socialist parties had now to think of a definite program of action, and the socialist literature of the years immediately following World War I was for the first time largely concerned with the practical question of how to organize production on socialist lines. These discussions were very much under the influence of the experience of the war years when the states had set up food and raw material administrations to deal with the serious shortage of the most essential commodities. It was generally assumed that this had shown that not only was central direction of economic activity practicable and even superior to a system of competition but also that the special technique of planning developed to cope with the problems of war economics might be equally applied to the permanent administration of a socialist economy.

Apart from Russia, where the rapidity of change in the years immediately following the revolution left little time for quiet reflection, it was mainly in Germany and even more so in Austria that these

12. V. Pareto, *Cours d'économie politique*, II (Lausanne, 1897), 364 ff.
13. An English translation of Barone's essay forms the Appendix to the volume on *Collectivist Economic Planning*.

questions were most seriously debated. Particularly in the latter country whose socialists had long played a leading role in the intellectual development of socialism, and where a strong and undivided socialist party had probably exercised a greater influence on its economic policy than in any other country outside Russia, the problems of socialism had assumed enormous practical importance. It may perhaps be mentioned in passing that it is rather curious how little serious study has been devoted to the economic experiences of that country in the decade after the first World War, although they are probably more relevant to the problems of a socialist policy in the Western world than anything that has happened in Russia. But, whatever one may think about the importance of the actual experiments made in Austria, there can be little doubt that the theoretical contributions made there to the understanding of the problems will prove to be a considerable force in the intellectual history of our time.

Among these early socialist contributions to the discussions, in many ways the most interesting and in any case the most characteristic for the still very limited recognition of the nature of the economic problems involved, is a book by Otto Neurath which appeared in 1919, in which the author tried to show that war experiences had revealed that it was possible to dispense with any considerations of value in the administration of the supply of commodities and that all the calculations of the central planning authorities should and could be carried out *in natura*, i.e., that the calculations need not be carried through in terms of some common unit of value but that they could be made in kind.[14] Neurath was quite oblivious of the insuperable difficulties which the absence of value calculations would put in the way of any rational economic use of the resources and even seemed to consider it as an advantage. Similar strictures apply to the works published about the same time by one of the leading spirits of the Austrian social-democratic party, Bauer.[15] It is impossible here to give any detailed account

14. Otto Neurath, *Durch die Kriegswirtschaft zur Naturalwirtschaft* (München, 1919).

15. O. Bauer, *Der Weg zum Sozialismus* (Wien, 1919).

of the argument of these and a number of other related publications of that time. They have to be mentioned, however, because they are important as representative expression of socialist thought just before the impact of the new criticism and because much of this criticism is naturally directed or implicitly concerned with these works.

In Germany discussion centered round the proposals of the "socialization commission" set up to discuss the possibilities of the transfer of individual industries to the ownership and control of the state. It was this commission or in connection with its deliberations that economists like E. Lederer and E. Heimann and the ill-fated W. Rathenau developed plans for socialization which became the main topic of discussion among economists. For our purpose, however, these proposals are less interesting than their Austrian counterparts, because they did not contemplate a completely socialized system but were mainly concerned with the problem of the organization of individual socialized industries in an otherwise competitive system. For this reason their authors did not have to face the main problems of a really socialist system. They are important, nevertheless, as symptoms of the state of public opinion at the time when and in the nation in which the more scientific examination of these problems began. One of the projects of this period deserves perhaps special mention not only because its authors are the inventors of the now fashionable term "planned economy" but also because it so closely resembles the proposals for planning now [1935] so prevalent in Great Britain. This is the plan developed in 1919 by the Reichswirtschaftsminister, R. Wissel, and his undersecretary of state, W. von Moellendorf.[16] But interesting as their proposals of organization of individual industries are and relevant to many of the problems discussed in England at the present moment as is the discussion to which they gave rise, they cannot be regarded as socialist proposals of the kind discussed here but belong to the halfway house between capitalism and socialism, discussion of which for reasons mentioned above has been deliberately excluded from the present essay.

16. This plan was originally developed in a memorandum submitted to the cabinet of the Reich on May 7, 1919, and later developed by R. Wissel in two pamphlets, *Die Planwirtschaft* (Hamburg, 1920) and *Praktische Wirtschaftspolitik* (Berlin, 1919).

10

The distinction of having first formulated the central problem of socialist economics in such a form as to make it impossible that it should ever again disappear from the discussion belongs to the Austrian economist, Ludwig von Mises. In an article on "Economic Calculation in a Socialist Community," which appeared in the spring of 1920, he demonstrated that the possibility of rational calculation in our present economic system was based on the fact that prices expressed in money provided the essential condition which made such reckoning possible.[17] The essential point on which Professor Mises went far beyond anything done by his predecessors was the detailed demonstration that an economic use of the available resources was only possible if this pricing was applied not only to the final product but also to all the intermediate products and factors of production and that no other process was conceivable which would in the same way take account of all the relevant facts as did the pricing process of the competitive market. Together with the larger work in which this article was later incorporated Professor Mises' study represents the starting-point from which all the discussions of the economic problems of socialism, whether constructive or critical, which aspire to be taken seriously must necessarily proceed.

While Professor Mises' writings contain beyond doubt the most complete and successful exposition of what from then onward became the central problem, and while they had by far the greatest influence on all further discussions, it is an interesting coincidence that about the same time two other distinguished authors arrived independently at very similar conclusions. The first was the great German sociologist, Max Weber, who in his posthumous magnum opus, *Wirtschaft und Gesellschaft,* which appeared in 1921, dealt expressly with the condi-

17. "Die Wirtschaftsrechnung im sozialistischen Gemeinwesen," *Archiv für Sozialwissenschaften und Sozialpolitik,* Vol. XLVII, No. 1 (April, 1920), reproduced in an English translation in *Collectivist Economic Planning.* Most of this article has been embodied in the more elaborate discussion of the economic problems of a socalist community in Part II of Professor Mises' *Gemeinwirtschaft* (Jena, 1922; 2d ed., 1932); English trans. by J. Kahane under the title *Socialism* (London, 1936).

tions which in a complex economic system made rational decisions possible. Like Mises (whose article he quotes as having come to his notice only when his own discussion was already set up in print), he insisted that the *in natura* calculations proposed by the leading advocates of a planned economy could not provide a rational solution of the problems which the authorities in such a system would have to solve. He emphasized in particular that the rational use and the preservation of capital could be secured only in a system based on exchange and the use of money and that the wastes due to the impossibility of rational calculation in a completely socialized system might be serious enough to make it impossible to maintain alive the present populations of the more densely inhabited countries.

"The assumption that some system of accounting would in time be found or invented if one only tried seriously to tackle the problem of a moneyless economy does not help here: the problem is the fundamental problem of any complete socialization and it is certainly impossible to talk of a *rationally* 'planned economy' while in so far as the all-decisive point is concerned no means for the construction of a 'plan' is known."[18]

A practically simultaneous development of the same ideas is to be found in Russia. Here in the summer of 1920 in the short interval after the first military successes of the new system, when it had for once become possible to utter criticisms in public, Boris Brutzkus, a distinguished economist mainly known for his studies in the agricultural problems of Russia, subjected to a searching criticism in a series of lectures the doctrines governing the action of the Communist rulers. These lectures, which appeared under the title "The Problems of Social Economy under Socialism" in a Russian journal and were only many years later made accessible to a wider public in a German translation,[19]

18. Max Weber, *Wirtschaft und Gesellschaft* ("Grundriss der Sozialökonomik," Vol. III [Tübingen, 1921]), pp. 55–56.

19. The original title under which these lectures appeared in the winter of 1921–22 in the Russian journal *Ekonomist* was "Problems of Social Economy under Socialism." They were later reprinted in the original Russian as a pamphlet which appeared in Berlin in 1923, and a German translation under the title *Die Lehren des*

show in their main conclusion a remarkable resemblance to the doctrines of Mises and Max Weber, although they arose out of the study of the concrete problems which Russia had to face at that time and although they were written at a time when their author, cut off from all communication with the outside world, could not have known of the similar efforts of the Austrian and German scholars. Like Professor Mises and Max Weber, his criticism centers round the impossibility of a rational calculation in a centrally directed economy from which prices are necessarily absent.

11

Although to some extent Max Weber and Professor Brutzkus share the credit of having pointed out independently the central problem of the economics of socialism, it was the more complete and systematic exposition of Professor Mises, particularly in his larger work on *Die Gemeinwirtschaft,* which has mainly influenced the trend of further discussion on the Continent. In the years immediately succeeding its publication a number of attempts were made to meet his challenge directly and to show that he was wrong in his main thesis and that even in a strictly centrally directed economic system values could be exactly determined without any serious difficulties. But, although the discussion on this point dragged on for several years, in the course of which Mises twice replied to his critics,[20] it became more and more clear that, in so far as a strictly centrally directed planned system of the type originally proposed by most socialists was concerned, his central thesis could not be refuted. Much of the objections made at first were really more a quibbling about words caused by the fact that Mises had occasionally used the somewhat loose statement that socialism

---

Marxismus im Lichte der russischen Revolution was published in Berlin in 1928. This essay, together with a discussion of the development of economic planning in Russia, appeared in an English translation in B. Brutzkus, *Economic Planning in Soviet Russia* (London, 1935).

20. Mises, "Neue Beiträge zum Problem der sozialistischen Wirtschaftsrechnung," *Archiv für Sozialwissenschaften,* Vol. LI (1924), and "Neue Schriften zum Problem der sozialistischen Wirtschaftsrechnung," *Archiv für Sozialwissenschaften,* Vol. LX (1928).

was "impossible," while what he meant was that socialism made rational calculation impossible. Of course any proposed course of action, if the proposal has any meaning at all, is possible in the strict sense of the word, i.e., it may be tried. The question can only be whether it will lead to the expected results, that is, whether the proposed course of action is consistent with the aims which it is intended to serve. In so far as it had been hoped to achieve by means of central direction of all economic activity *at one and the same time* a distribution of income independent of private property in the means of production and a volume of output which was at least approximately the same or even greater than that procured under free competition, it was more and more generally admitted that this was not a practicable way to achieve these ends.

But it was only natural that, even where Professor Mises' main thesis was conceded, this did not mean an abandonment of the search for a way to realize the socialist ideals. Its main effect was to divert attention from what had so far been universally considered as the most practicable forms of socialist organization to the exploration of alternative schemes. It is possible to distinguish two main types of reaction among those who conceded his central argument. In the first place, there were those who thought that the loss of efficiency, the decline in general wealth which will be the effect of the absence of a means of rational calculation, would not be too high a price for the realization of a more just distribution of this wealth. Of course, if this attitude is based on a clear realization of what this choice implies, there is no more to be said about it, except that it seems doubtful whether those who maintain it would find many who would agree with their idea. The real difficulty here is, of course, that for most people the decision on this point will depend on the extent to which the impossibility of rational calculation would lead to a reduction of output in a centrally directed economy compared with that of a competitive system. Although in the opinion of the present writer it seems that careful study can leave no doubt about the enormous magnitude of that difference, it must be admitted that there is no simple way to prove how great that difference would be. The answer here cannot be derived from general considerations but will have to be based on a careful comparative study of the working of the two alternative systems and presupposes a much greater knowledge of the problems involved than can possibly be acquired in any other way but by a systematic study of economics.[21]

The second type of reaction to Professor Mises' criticism was to regard it as valid only as regards the particular form of socialism against which it was mainly directed and to try to construct other schemes that would be immune to that criticism. A very considerable and probably the more interesting part of the later discussions on the Continent tended to move in that direction. There are two main tendencies of such speculation. On the one hand, it was attempted to overcome the difficulties in question by extending the element of planning even further than had been contemplated before, so as to abolish completely the free choice of the consumer and the free choice of occupation. Or, on the other hand, it was attempted to introduce various elements of competition. To what extent these proposals really overcome any of the difficulties and to what extent they are practical is considered in various sections of *Collective Economic Planning*.

21. It is perhaps necessary in this connection to state explicitly that it would be wholly inconclusive if such a comparison were made between capitalism as it exists (or is supposed still to exist) and socialism as it might work under ideal assumptions—or between capitalism as it might be in its ideal form and socialism in some imperfect form. If the comparison is to be of any value for the question of principle, it has to be made on the assumption that either system is realized in the form which is most rational under the given condition of human nature and external circumstances which must of course be accepted.

VIII. Socialist Calculation II: *The State of the Debate* (1935)*

1

IN SPITE of a natural tendency on the part of socialists to belittle its importance, it is clear that the criticism of socialism has already had a very profound effect on the direction of socialist thought. The great majority of "planners" are, of course, still unaffected by it; the great mass of the hangers-on of any popular movement are always unconscious of the intellectual currents which produce a change of direction.[1] Moreover, the actual existence in Russia of a system which professes to be planned has led many of those who know nothing of·its development to suppose·that the main problems are solved; in fact, as we shall see, Russian experience provides abundant confirmation of the doubts already stated. But among the leaders of socialist thought not only is the nature of the central problem more and more recognized but the force of the objections raised against the types of socialism, which in the past used to be considered as most practicable, is also increasingly admitted. It is now rarely denied that, in a society which is to preserve freedom of choice of the consumer and free choice of occupation, central direction of all economic activity presents a task which cannot be rationally solved under the complex conditions of modern life. It is true, as we shall see, that even among those who see

* Reprinted from *Collectivist Economic Planning,* ed. F. A. Hayek (London: George Routledge & Sons, Ltd., 1935).

1. This also applies, unfortunately, to most of the organized collective efforts professedly devoted to the scientific study of the problem of planning. Anyone who studies such publications as the *Annales de l'économie collective,* or the material contributed to the World Social Economic Congress, Amsterdam, 1931, and published by the International Relations Institute under the title *World Social Economic Planning* (2 vols.; The Hague, 1931–32), will search in vain for any sign that the main problems are even recognized.

the problem, this position is not yet completely abandoned; but its defense is more or less of the nature of a rear-guard action where all that is attempted is to prove that "in principle" a solution is conceivable. Little or no claim is made that such a solution is practicable. We shall later have occasion to discuss some of these attempts. But the great majority of the more recent schemes try to get around the difficulties by the construction of alternative socialist systems which differ more or less fundamentally from the traditional types against which the criticism was directed in the first instance and which are supposed to be immune to the objections to which the latter are subject.

In this essay the recent English literature on the subject will be considered and an attempt will be made to evaluate the recent proposals that have been devised to overcome the difficulties which have now been recognized. Before we enter into this discussion, however, a few words on the relevance of the Russian experiment to the problems under discussion may be useful.

2

It is of course neither possible nor desirable to enter at this point into an examination of the concrete results of the Russian experiment. In this respect it is necessary to refer to detailed special investigations, particularly to those of Professor Brutzkus.[2] At this moment we are concerned only with the more general question of how the established results of such an examination of the concrete experiences fit in with the more theoretical argument and how far the conclusions reached by a priori reasoning are confirmed or contradicted by empirical evidence.

It is perhaps not unnecessary to remind the reader at this point that it was not the possibility of planning as such which has been questioned on the grounds of general considerations but the possibility of successful planning, of achieving the ends for which planning was undertaken. Therefore, we must first be clear as to the tests by which we are to judge success, or the forms in which we should expect failure to

2. B. Brutzkus, *Economic Planning in Russia* (London: George Routledge & Sons, Ltd., 1935).

manifest itself. There is no reason to expect that production would stop, or that the authorities would find difficulty in using all the available resources somehow, or even that output would be permanently lower than it had been before planning started. What we should anticipate is that output, where the use of the available resources was determined by some central authority, would be lower than if the price mechanism of a market operated freely under otherwise similar circumstances. This would be due to the excessive development of some lines of production at the expense of others and the use of methods which are inappropriate under the circumstances. We should expect to find overdevelopment of some industries at a cost which was not justified by the importance of their increased output and to see unchecked the ambition of the engineer to apply the latest developments made elsewhere, without considering whether they were economically suited in the situation. In many cases the use of the latest methods of production, which could not have been applied without central planning, would then be a symptom of a misuse of resources rather than a proof of success.

It follows, therefore, that the excellence, from a technological point of view, of some parts of the Russian industrial equipment, which often strikes the casual observer and which is commonly regarded as evidence of success, has little significance in so far as the answer to the central question is concerned. Whether the new plant will prove to be a useful link in the industrial structure for increasing output depends not only on technological considerations but even more on the general economic situation. The best tractor factory may not be an asset, and the capital invested in it is a sheer loss, if the labor which the tractor replaces is cheaper than the cost of the material and labor which goes to make a tractor, *plus* interest.

But, once we have freed ourselves from the misleading fascination by the existence of colossal instruments of production, which is likely to captivate the uncritical observer, only two legitimate tests of success remain: the goods which the system actually delivers to the consumer and the rationality or irrationality of the decisions of the central au-

150

thority. There can be no doubt that the first test would lead to a negative result, for the present, at any rate, or if applied to the whole population and not to a small privileged group. Practically all observers seem to agree that even compared with pre-war Russia the position of the great masses has deteriorated. Yet such a comparison still makes the results appear too favorable. It is admitted that czarist Russia did not offer conditions very favorable to capitalist industry and that, under a more modern regime, capitalism would have brought about rapid progress. It must also be taken into account that the suffering in the past fifteen years, that "starving to greatness" which was supposed to be in the interest of later progress, should by now have borne some fruits. It would provide a more appropriate basis of comparison if we assumed that the same restrictions of consumption, which has actually taken place, had been caused by taxation, the proceeds of which had been lent to competitive industry for investment purposes. It can hardly be denied that this would have brought about a rapid and enormous increase of the general standard of life beyond anything which is at present even remotely possible.

There remains, then, only the task of actually examining the principles on which the planning authority has acted. Although it is impossible to trace here, even shortly, the varied course of that experiment, all we know about it, particularly from Professor Brutzkus' study referred to above, fully entitles us to say that the anticipations based on general reasoning have been thoroughly confirmed. The breakdown of "war communism" occurred for exactly the same reasons, the impossibility of rational calculation in a moneyless economy, which Professors Mises and Brutzkus had foreseen. The development since, with its repeated reversals of policy, has only shown that the rulers of Russia had to learn by experience all the obstacles which a systematic analysis of the problem had revealed. But it has raised no important new problems, still less has it suggested any solutions. Officially the blame for nearly all the difficulties is still put on the unfortunate individuals who are persecuted for obstructing the plan by not obeying the orders of the central authority or by carrying them out too literally. But, although this means that the authorities only admit the obvious difficulty of making people follow out the plan loyally, there can be no doubt that the more serious disappointments are really due to the inherent difficulties of any central planning. In fact, from accounts such as that of Professor Brutzkus, we gather that, far from advancing toward more rational methods of planning, the present tendency is to cut the knot by abandoning the comparatively scientific methods employed in the past. Instead are substituted more and more arbitrary and uncorrelated decisions of particular problems as they are suggested by the contingencies of the day. In so far as political or psychological problems are concerned, Russian experience may be very instructive. But to the student of economic problems of socialism it does little more than furnish illustrations of well-established conclusions. It gives us no help toward an answer to the intellectual problem which the desire for a rational reconstruction of society raises. To this end we shall have to proceed with our systematic survey of the different conceivable systems which are no less important for existing so far only as theoretical suggestions.

3

As has been pointed out above in chapter vii, discussion of these questions in the English literature began relatively late and at a comparatively high level. Yet it can hardly be said that the first attempts really met any of the main points. Two Americans, F. M. Taylor and W. C. Roper, were first in the field. Their analyses, and to some extent also that of H. D. Dickinson in England, were directed to show that, on the assumption of a complete knowledge of all relevant data, the values and the quantities of the different commodities to be produced might be determined by the application of the apparatus by which theoretical economics explains the formation of prices and the direction of production in a competitive system.[3] Now, it must be admitted

3. F. M. Taylor, "The Guidance of Production in a Socialist State," *American Economic Review*, Vol. XIX (1929); W. C. Roper, *The Problem of Pricing in a Socialist State* (Cambridge, Mass., 1929); H. D. Dickinson, "Price Formation in a Socialist Community," *Economic Journal*, June, 1933.

that this is not an impossibility in the sense that it is logically contradictory. But the contention that a determination of prices by such a procedure being logically conceivable in any way invalidates the contention that it is not a possible solution only shows that the real nature of the problem has not been perceived. It is only necessary to attempt to visualize what the application of this method would imply in practice in order to rule it out as humanly impracticable and impossible. It is clear that any such solution would have to be based on the solution of some such system of equations as that developed in Barone's article.[4] But what is practically relevant here is not the formal structure of this system but the nature and amount of concrete information required if a numerical solution is to be attempted and the magnitude of the task which this numerical solution must involve in any modern community. The problem here is, of course, not how detailed this information and how exact the calculation would have to be in order to make the solution perfectly exact, but only how far one would have to go to make the result at least comparable with that which the competitive system provides. Let us look into this a little further.

In the first place it is clear that if central direction is really to take the place of the initiative of the manager of the individual enterprise and is not simply to be a most irrational limitation of his discretion in some particular respect, it will not be sufficient that it takes the form of mere general direction, but it will have to include and be intimately responsible for details of the most minute description. It is impossible to decide rationally how much material or new machinery should be assigned to any one enterprise and at what price (in an accounting sense) it will be rational to do so, without also deciding at the same time whether and in which way the machinery and tools already in use should continue to be used or be disposed of. It is matters of this sort, details of technique, the saving of one material rather than the other or any one of the small economies which cumulatively decide the success or failure of a firm; and in any central plan which is not to

4. "Ministry of Production in the Collectivist State," in *Collectivist Economic Planning* (London: George Routledge & Sons, Ltd., 1935), Appendix.

be hopelessly wasteful, they must be taken account of. In order to be able to do so, it will be necessary to treat every machine, tool, or building not just as one of a class of physically similar objects but as an individual whose usefulness is determined by its particular state of wear and tear, its location, etc. The same applies to every batch of commodities which is situated at a different place or which differs in any other respect from other batches. This means that, in order to achieve that degree of economy in this respect which is secured by the competitive system, the calculations of the central planning authority would have to treat the existing body of instrumental goods as being constituted of almost as many different types of goods as there are individual units. So far as ordinary commodities, i.e., nondurable semi-finished or finished goods, are concerned, it is clear that there would be many times more different types of such commodities to consider than we should imagine if they were classified only by their technical characteristics. Two technically similar goods in different places or in different packings or of a different age cannot possibly be treated as equal in usefulness for most purposes if even a minimum of efficient use is to be secured.

Now, since in a centrally directed economy the manager of the individual plan would be deprived of the discretion of substituting at will one kind of commodity for another, all this immense mass of different units would necessarily have to enter *separately* into the calculations of the planning authority. It is obvious that the mere statistical task of enumeration exceeds anything of this sort hitherto undertaken. But that is not all. The information which the central planning authority would need would also have to include a complete description of all the relevant technical properties of every one of these goods, including costs of movement to any other place where it might possibly be used with greater advantage, cost of eventual repair or changes, etc.

But this leads to another problem of even greater importance. The usual theoretical abstractions used in the explanation of equilibrium in a competitive system include the assumption that a certain range of technical knowledge is "given." This, of course, does not mean that all the best technical knowledge is concentrated anywhere in a single head but that people with all kinds of knowledge will be available and that among those competing in a particular job, speaking broadly, those that make the most appropriate use of the technical knowledge will succeed. In a centrally planned society the selection of the most appropriate among the known technical methods will be possible only if all that knowledge can be used in the calculations of the central authority. This means in practice that this knowledge will have to be concentrated in the heads of one or at best a very few people who actually formulate the equations to be worked out. It is hardly necessary to emphasize that this is an absurd idea even in so far as that knowledge is concerned which can properly be said to "exist" at any moment of time. But much of the knowledge that is actually utilized is by no means "in existence" in this ready-made form. Most of it consists in a technique of thought which enables the individual engineer to find new solutions rapidly as soon as he is confronted with new constellations of circumstances. To assume the practicability of these mathematical solutions, we should have to assume that the concentration of knowledge at the central authority would also include a capacity to discover any improvement of detail of this sort.[5]

There is a third set of data which would have to be available before the actual operation of working out the appropriate method of production and quantities to be produced could be undertaken—data relative to importance of the different kinds and quantities of consumers' goods. In a society in which the consumer was free to spend his income as he liked, these data would have to take the form of complete lists of the different quantities of all commodities which would be bought at any possible combination of prices of the different commodities which might be available. These figures would inevitably be of the nature of estimates for a future period based upon past experience. But past experience cannot provide the range of knowledge necessary, and, as tastes change from moment to moment, the lists would have to be in process of continuous revision.

5. On the more general problem of experimentation and the utilization of really new inventions, etc., see below, pp. 164 ff.

Individualism and Economic Order

It is probably evident that the mere assembly of these data is a task beyond human capacity. Yet, if the centrally run society were to work as efficiently as the competitive society, which, as it were, decentralizes the task of collecting them, they would have to be present. But let us assume for the moment that this difficulty, the "mere difficulty of statistical technique," as it is contemptuously referred to by most planners, is actually overcome. This would be only the first step in the solution of the main task. Once the material is collected, it would still be necessary to work out the concrete decisions which it implies. Now, the magnitude of this essential mathematical operation will depend on the number of unknowns to be determined. The number of these unknowns will be equal to the number of commodities which are to be produced. As we have seen already, we have to treat as different commodities all the final products to be completed at different times, whose production has to be started or to be continued at a given moment. At present we can hardly say what their number is, but it is scarcely an exaggeration to assume that, in a fairly advanced society, the order of magnitude would be at least in the hundreds of thousands. This means that, at each successive moment, every one of the decisions would have to be based on the solution of an equal number of simultaneous differential equations, a task which, with any of the means known at present [1935], could not be carried out in a lifetime. Yet these decisions would not only have to be made continuously but they would also have to be promptly conveyed to those who had to execute them.

It will probably be said that such a degree of exactitude would not be necessary, since the working of the present economic system itself does not come anywhere near it. But this is not quite true. It is clear that we never come near the state of equilibrium described by the solution of such a system of equations. But that is not the point. We should not expect equilibrium to be reached unless all external change had ceased. The essential thing about the present economic system is that it does react to some extent to all those small changes and differences which would have to be deliberately disregarded under the system we are discussing if the calculations were to be manageable. In this way ra-

156

tional decision would be impossible in all these questions of detail, which in the aggregate decide the success of productive effort.

It is improbable that anyone who has realized the magnitude of the task involved has seriously proposed a system of planning based on comprehensive systems of equations. What has actually been in the minds of those who have mooted this kind of analysis has been the belief that, starting from a given situation, which was presumably to be that of the pre-existing capitalistic society, the adaptation to the minor changes which occur from day to day could be gradually brought about by a method of trial and error. This suggestion suffers, however, from two fundamental mistakes. In the first instance, as has been pointed out many times, it is inadmissible to assume that the changes in relative values brought about by the transition from capitalism to socialism would be of a minor order, thus permitting prices of the pre-existing capitalistic system to be used as a starting-point, and making it possible to avoid a complete rearrangement of the price system. But, even if we neglect this very serious objection, there is not the slightest reason to assume that the task could be solved in this way. We need only to remember the difficulties experienced with the fixing of prices, even when applied to a few commodities only, and to contemplate further that, in such a system, price-fixing would have to be applied not to a few but to all commodities, finished or unfinished, and that it would have to bring about as frequent and as varied price changes as those which occur in a capitalistic society every day and every hour, in order to see that this is not a way in which the solution provided by competition can even be approximately achieved. Almost every change of any single price would make changes of hundreds of other prices necessary, and most of these other changes would by no means be proportional but would be affected by the different degrees of elasticity of demand, by the possibilities of substitution and other changes in the method of production. To imagine that all this adjustment could be brought about by successive orders by the central authority when the necessity is noticed, and that then every price is fixed and changed until some degree of equilibrium is obtained, is certainly

an absurd idea. That prices may be fixed on the basis of a total view of
the situation is at least conceivable, although utterly impracticable; but
to base authoritative price-fixing on the observation of a small section
of the economic system is a task which cannot be rationally performed
under any circumstances. An attempt in this direction will either have
to be made on the lines of the mathematical solution discussed before
or else entirely abandoned.

4

In view of these difficulties, it is not surprising that practically all
who have really tried to think through the problem of central planning
have despaired of the possibility of solving it in a world in which every
passing whim of the consumer is likely to upset completely the carefully worked-out plans. It is more or less agreed now that free choice
of the consumer (and presumably also free choice of occupation) and
planning from the center are incompatible aims. But this has given the
impression that the unpredictable nature of the tastes of the consumers
is the only or the main obstacle to successful planning. Maurice Dobb
has recently followed this to its logical conclusion by asserting that it
would be worth the price of abandoning the freedom of the consumer
if by the sacrifice socialism could be made possible.[6] This is undoubtedly a very courageous step. In the past, socialists have consistently protested against any suggestion that life under socialism would be like
life in a barracks, subject to regimentation of every detail. Dr. Dobb
considers these views as obsolete. Whether he would find many followers if he professed these views to the socialist masses is not a question
which need concern us here. The question is whether it would provide
a solution to our problem.

Dr. Dobb openly admits that he has abandoned the view, now held
by H. D. Dickinson and others, that the problem could or should be

6. See the article on "Economic Theory and the Problem of a Socialist Economy,"
Economic Journal, December, 1933. More recently (in his *Political Economy of Capitalism* [London, 1937], p. 310) Dr. Dobb has protested against this interpretation of his
earlier statement, but on re-reading it I still find it difficult to interpret it in any
other sense.

solved by a kind of pricing system under which the prices of the final products and the prices of the original agents would be determined in some kind of market, while the prices of all other products would be derived from these by some system of calculation. But he seems to suffer from the curious delusion that the necessity of any pricing is due only to the prejudice that consumers' preferences should be respected and that in consequence the categories of economic theory and apparently all problems of value would cease to have significance in a socialist society. "If equality of reward prevailed, market valuations would *ipso facto* lose their alleged significance, since money cost would have no meaning."

Now it is not to be denied that the abolition of free consumers' choice would simplify the problem in some respects. One of the unpredictable variables would be eliminated, and in this way the frequency of the necessary readjustments would be somewhat reduced. But to believe, as Dr. Dobb does, that in this way the necessity of some form of pricing, of an exact comparison between costs and results, would be eliminated surely indicates a complete unawareness of the real problem. Prices would cease to be necessary only if one could assume that in the socialist state production would have no definite aim whatever— that it would not be directed according to some well-defined order of preferences, however arbitrarily fixed, but that the state would simply proceed to produce something and consumers would then have to take what had been produced. Dr. Dobb asks what would be the loss. The answer is: almost everything. His attitude would be tenable only if costs determined value, so that, so long as the available resources were used somehow, the way in which they were used would not affect our well-being, since the very fact that they had been used would confer value on the product. But the question whether we have more or less to consume, whether we are to maintain or to raise our standard of life, or whether we are to sink back to the state of savages always on the edge of starvation depends mainly on how we use our resources. The difference between an economic and an uneconomic distribution and combination of resources among the different industries is the difference between scarcity and plenty. The dictator, who himself ranges in order the different needs of the members of the society according to his views about their merits, has saved himself the trouble of finding out what people really prefer and avoided the impossible task of combining the individual scales into an agreed common scale which expresses the general ideas of justice. But if he wants to follow this norm with any degree of rationality or consistency, if he wants to realize what he considers to be the ends of the community, he will have to solve all the problems which we have discussed already. He will not even find that his plans are not upset by unforeseen changes, since the changes in tastes are by no means the only, and perhaps not even the most important, changes that cannot be foreseen. Changes in the weather, changes in the numbers or the state of health of the population, a breakdown of machinery, the discovery or the sudden exhaustion of a mineral deposit, and hundreds of other constant changes will make it no less necessary for him to reconstruct his plans from moment to moment. The distance to the really practicable and the obstacles to rational action will have been only slightly reduced at the sacrifice of an ideal which few who realized what it meant would readily abandon.

5

In these circumstances it is easy to understand that Dr. Dobb's radical solution has not had many followers and that many of the younger socialists seek for a solution in quite the opposite direction. While Dr. Dobb wants to suppress the remnants of freedom or competition which are still assumed in the traditional socialist schemes, much of the more recent discussion aims at a complete reintroduction of competition. In Germany such proposals have actually been published and discussed. But in England thought on these lines is still in an embryonic stage. Mr. Dickinson's suggestions are a slight step in this direction. But it is known that some of the younger economists, who have given thought to these problems, have gone much further and are prepared to go the whole hog and to restore competition

160

completely, at least so far as in their view this is compatible with the state retaining the ownership of all the material means of production. Although it is not yet possible to refer to published work on these lines, what one has learned about them in conversations and discussions is probably sufficient to make worth while some examination of their content.[7]

In many respects these plans are very interesting. The common fundamental idea is that there should be markets and competition between independent entrepreneurs or managers of individual firms and that in consequence there should be money prices, as in the present society, for all goods, intermediate or finished, but that these entrepreneurs should not be owners of the means of production used by them but salaried officials of the state, acting under state instructions and producing, not for profit, but so as to be able to sell at prices which will just cover costs.

It is idle to ask whether such a scheme still falls under what is usually considered as socialism. On the whole, it seems it should be included under that heading. More serious is the question whether it still deserves the designation of planning. It appears not to involve much more planning than the construction of a rational legal framework for capitalism. If it could be realized in a pure form in which the direction of economic activity would be wholly left to competition, the planning would also be confined to the provision of a permanent framework within which concrete action would be left to individual initiative. And the kind of planning or central organization of production which is supposed to lead to an organization of human activity more rational than "chaotic" competition would be completely absent. But how far this would be really true would depend, of course, on the extent to which competition was reintroduced —that is to say, on the crucial question which is here crucial in every respect, namely, of what is to be the independent unit, the element which buys and sells on the markets.

At first sight two main types of such systems seem to be possible. We

7. For a discussion of two more recent publications on this subject see the next chapter.

may assume either that there will be competition between industries only, and that each industry is represented as it were by one enterprise, or that within each industry there are many independent firms which compete with one another. It is only in this latter form that this proposal really evades most of the objections to central planning as such and raises problems of its own. These problems are of an extremely interesting nature. In their pure form they raise the question of the rationale of private property in its most general and fundamental aspect. The question, then, is not whether all problems of production and distribution can be rationally decided by one central authority but whether decisions and responsibility can be successfully left to competing individuals who are not owners or are not otherwise directly interested in the means of production under their charge. Is there any decisive reason why the responsibility for the use made of any part of the existing productive equipment should always be coupled with a personal interest in the profits or losses realized on them, or would it really be only a question whether the individual managers, who deputize for the community in the exercise of its property rights under the scheme in question, served the common ends loyally and to the best of their capacity?

6

We may best discuss this question when we come to deal with the schemes in detail. Before we can do that, however, it is necessary to show why, if competition is to function satisfactorily, it will be necessary to go all the way and not to stop at a partial reintroduction of competition. The case which we have therefore to consider next is that of completely integrated industries standing under a central direction but competing wtih other industries for the custom of the consumer and for the factors of production. This case is of some importance beyond the problems of socialism which we are here chiefly concerned with, since it is by means of creating such monopolies for particular products that those who advocate planning within the

Socialist Calculation

framework of capitalism hope to "rationalize" the so-called "chaos" of free competition. This raises the general problem of whether it is ever in the general interest to plan or rationalize individual industries where this is only possible through the creation of a monopoly or whether, on the contrary, we must not assume that this will lead to an uneconomic use of resources and that the supposed economies are really diseconomies from the point of view of society.

The theoretical argument which shows that under conditions of widespread monopoly there is no determinate equilibrium position and that, in consequence, under such conditions there is no reason to assume that resources would be used to best advantage is now fairly well accepted. It is perhaps not inappropriate to open the discussion of what this would mean in practice by a quotation from the work of the great scholar who has been mainly responsible for establishing it.

"It has been proposed as an economic ideal that every branch of trade and industry should be formed into a separate union. The picture has some attractions. Nor is it at first sight morally repulsive; since, where all are monopolists, no one will be the victim of monopoly. But an attentive consideration will disclose an incident very prejudicial to industry—instability in the value of all those articles the demand for which is influenced by the prices of other articles, a class which is probably very extensive.

"Among those who would suffer by the new régime there would be one class which particularly interests readers of this Journal, namely abstract economists, who would be deprived of their occupation, the investigation of the conditions which determine value. There would survive only the empirical school, flourishing in the chaos congenial to their mentality."[8]

Now the mere fact that the abstract economists would be deprived of their occupation would probably be only a matter of gratification to most advocates of planning if it were not that at the same time the order which they study would also cease to exist. The instability of values, of which Edgeworth speaks, or the indeterminateness of

8. F. Y. Edgeworth, *Collected Papers*, I, 138.

equilibrium, as the same fact can be described in more general terms, is by no means a possibility only to disturb theoretical economists. It means in effect that in such a system there will be no tendency to use the available factors to the greatest advantage, to combine them in every industry in such a way that the contribution which every factor makes is not appreciably smaller than that which it might have made if used elsewhere. The actual tendency prevailing would be to adjust output in such a way, not that the greatest return is obtained from every kind of available resources, but so that the difference between the value of factors which can be used elsewhere and the value of the product is maximized. This concentration on maximum monopoly profits rather than on making the best use of the available factors is the necessary consequence of making the right to produce a good itself a "scarce factor of production." In a world of such monopolies this may not have the effect of reducing production all around in the sense that some of the factors of production will remain unemployed, but it will certainly have the effect of reducing output by bringing about an uneconomic distribution of factors between industries. This will remain true even if the instability feared by Edgeworth should prove to be of a minor order. The equilibrium that would be reached would be one in which the best use would have been made only of one scarce "factor": the possibility of exploiting consumers.

7

This is not the only disadvantage of a general reorganization of industry on monopolistic lines. The so-called "economies" which it is claimed would be made possible if industry were "reorganized" on monopolistic lines prove on closer examination to be sheer waste. In practically all the cases in which the planning of individual industries is advocated at present, the object is to deal with the effects of technical progress.[9] Sometimes it is claimed that the desirable introduction of a technical innovation is made impossible by competition. On

9. On these problems cf. A. C. Pigou, *Economics of Welfare* (4th ed., 1932), p. 188, and the present author's article, "The Trend of Economic Thinking," *Economica*, May, 1933, p. 132.

other occasions it is objected against competition that it causes waste by forcing the adoption of new machines, etc., when producers would prefer to continue using the old ones. But in both cases, as can be easily shown, planning which aims to prevent what would happen under competition would lead to social waste.

Once productive equipment of any kind is already in existence, it is desirable that it should be used so long as the costs of using it (the "prime costs") are lower than the total cost of providing the same service in an alternative way. If its existence prevents the introduction of more modern equipment, this means that the resources which are necessary to produce the same product with more modern methods can be used with greater advantage in some other connection. If older and more modern plants exist side by side, and the more modern firms are threatened by the "cutthroat competition" of the more obsolete works, this may mean one of two things. Either the newer method is not really better, i.e., its introduction has been based on a miscalculation and should never have taken place. In such a case, where operating costs under the new method are actually higher than under the old the remedy is, of course, to shut down the new plant, even if it is in some sense "technically" superior. Or—and this is the more probable case—the situation will be that, while operating costs under the new method are lower than under the old, they are not sufficiently lower to leave at a price which covers the operating costs of the old plant a margin sufficient to pay interest and amortization on the new plant. In this case, too, miscalculation has taken place. The new plant should never have been built. But, once it exists, the only way in which the public can derive at least some benefit from the capital which has been misdirected is for prices to be allowed to fall to the competitive level and part of the capital value of the new firms to be written off. Artificially to maintain capital values of the new plant by compulsory shutting-down of the old would simply mean to tax the consumer in the interest of the owner of the new plant without any compensating benefit in the form of increased or improved production.

All this is even clearer in the not infrequent case in which the new

165

plant is really superior in the sense that, if it had not already been built, it would be advantageous to build it now; but, where the firms using it are in financial difficulties because it has been erected at a time of inflated values, they are in consequence loaded with an excessive debt. Instances like this, in which the technically most efficient firms are at the same time the financially most unsound, are said to be not infrequent in some English industries. But here again any attempt to preserve capital values by suppressing competition from the less modern firms can only have the effect of enabling producers to keep prices higher than they otherwise would be, solely in the interests of the bondholders. The right course from the social point of view is to write down the inflated capital to a more appropriate level, and potential competition from the less modern concerns has therefore the beneficial effect of bringing prices down to a level appropriate to present costs of production. The capitalists who have invested at an unfortunate moment may not like this, but it is clearly in the social interest.

The effects of planning in order to preserve capital values are perhaps even more harmful when it takes the form of retarding the introduction of new inventions. If we abstract, as we are probably entitled to do, from the case where there is reason to assume that the planning authority possesses greater foresight and is better qualified to judge the probability of further technical progress than the individual entrepreneur, it should be clear that any attempt in this direction must have the effect that that which is supposed to eliminate waste is in fact the cause of waste. Given reasonable foresight on the part of the entrepreneur, a new invention will be introduced only if it makes it possible either to provide the same services as were available before at a smaller expenditure of current resources (i.e., at a smaller sacrifice of other possible uses of these resources) or to provide better services at an expenditure which is not proportionately greater. The fall in the capital values of existing instruments which will undoubtedly follow is in no way a social loss. If they can be used for other purposes, a fall of their value in their present use below that which they would attain elsewhere is a distinct indication that they should be transferred. If they have no other use but their present one, their former value is of interest only as an indication of how much cost of production must be lowered by the new invention before it becomes rational to abandon them entirely. The only persons who are interested in the maintenance of the value of already invested capital are its owners. But the only way this can be done in these circumstances is by withholding from the other members of society the advantages of the new invention.

8

It will probably be objected that these strictures may be true of capitalist monopolies aiming at maximum profits but that they would certainly not be true of the integrated industries in a socialist state whose managers would have instructions to charge prices which just covered costs. It is true that the preceding section has been essentially a digression into the problem of planning under capitalism. But it has enabled us not only to examine some of the supposed advantages which are commonly associated with any form of planning but also to indicate certain problems which will necessarily accompany planning under socialism. We shall meet some of these problems again at a later stage. For the moment, however, we must once more concentrate upon the case where the monopolized industries are conducted not so as to make the greatest profit but where it is attempted to make them act as if competition existed. Does the instruction that they should aim at prices which will just cover their (marginal) cost really provide a clear criterion of action?

It is in this connection that it almost seems as if excessive preoccupation with the conditions of a hypothetical state of stationary equilibrium has led modern economists in general, and especially those who propose this particular solution, to attribute to the notion of costs in general a much greater precision and definiteness than can be attached to any cost phenomenon in real life. Under conditions of widespread competition the term "cost of production" has indeed a very precise meaning. But as soon as we leave the realm of extensive competition and of a stationary state and consider a world where most of the existing means of production are the product of particular processes that will probably never be repeated; where, in consequence of incessant change, the value of most of the more durable instruments of production has little or no connection with the costs which have been incurred in their production but depends only on the services which they are expected to render in the future, the question of what exactly are the costs of production of a given product is a question of extreme difficulty which cannot be answered definitely on the basis of any processes which take place inside the individual firm or industry. It is a question which cannot be answered without first making some assumption as regards the prices of the products in the manufacture of which the same instruments will be used. Much of what is usually termed "cost of production" is not really a cost element that is given independently of the price of the product but a quasi-rent, or a depreciation quota which has to be allowed on the capitalized value of expected quasi-rents, and is therefore dependent on the prices which are expected to prevail in the future.

For every single firm in a competitive industry these quasi-rents, although dependent on price, are not a less reliable and indispensable guide for the determination of the appropriate volume of production than true cost. On the contrary, it is only in this way that some of the alternative ends which are affected by the decision can be taken into account. Take the case of some unique instrument of production which will never be replaced and which cannot be used outside the monopolized industry and which therefore has no market price. Its use does not involve any costs which can be determined independent from the price of its product. Yet, if it is at all durable and may be used up either more or less rapidly, its wear and tear must be counted as true cost if the appropriate volume of production at any one moment is to be rationally determined. This is true not only because its possible services in the future have to be compared with the results of a more intensive use at present but also because, while it exists, it saves the services of some other factor which would be needed to replace it and which can meanwhile be used for other purposes. The value of the services of this instrument is here determined by the sacrifices involved in the next best way of producing the same product; and these services have therefore to be economized because some alternative satisfactions depend on them in an indirect way. But their value can be determined only if the real or potential competition of the other possible methods of producing the same product is allowed to influence its price.

The problem which arises here is well known from the field of public utility regulation. The problem of how, in the absence of real competition, the effects of competition could be simulated and the monopolistic bodies be made to charge prices equivalent to competitive prices has been widely discussed in this connection. But all attempts at a solution have failed, and, as has recently been demonstrated by R. F. Fowler,[10] they were bound to fail because fixed plant is extensively used and one of the most important cost elements, interest and depreciation on such plant, can be determined only after the price which will be obtained for the product is known.

Again it may be objected that this is a consideration which may be relevant in a capitalistic society but that, since even in a capitalistic society fixed costs are disregarded in determining the short-run volume of production, they might also with much more reason be disregarded in a socialist society. But this is not so. If rational disposition of resources is to be attempted, and particularly if decisions of this sort are to be left to the managers of the individual industry, it is certainly necessary to provide for the replacement of the capital out of the gross proceeds of the industry, and it will also be necessary that the returns from this reinvested capital should be at least as high as they would be elsewhere. It would be as misleading under socialism as it is in a capitalistic society to determine the value of the capital which has thus to be recouped on some historic basis such as the past

10. *The Depreciation of Capital, Analytically Considered* (London, 1934), pp. 74 ff.

169

cost of production of the instruments concerned. The value of any particular instrument, and therefore the value of its services which have to be counted as cost, must be determined from a consideration of the returns expected, having regard to all the alternative ways in which the same result may be obtained and to all the alternative uses to which it may be put. All those questions of obsolescence due to technical progress or change of needs, which were discussed in the section 7, enter here into the problem. To make a monopolist charge the price that would rule under competition, or a price that is equal to the necessary cost, is impossible, because the competitive or necessary cost cannot be known unless there is competition. This does not mean that the manager of the monopolized industry under socialism will go on, against his instructions, to make monopoly profits. But it does mean that, since there is no way of testing the economic advantages of one method of production as compared with another, the place of monopoly profits will be taken by uneconomic waste.

There is also the further question of whether, under dynamic conditions, profits do not serve a necessary function, and whether they are not the main equilibrating force which brings about the adaptation to any change. Certainly, when there is competition within the industry, the question of whether it is advisable to start a new firm or not can be decided only on the basis of the profits made by the already existing industries. At least in the case of the more complete competition which we have yet to discuss, profits as an inducement to change cannot be dispensed with. But one might conceive that, where any one product is manufactured by only one single concern, it will adapt the volume of its output to the demand without varying the price of the product except in so far as cost changes. But how is it then to be decided who is to get the products before supply has caught up with an increased demand? Even more important, how is the concern to decide whether it is justified in incurring the initial cost of bringing additional factors to the place of production? Much of the cost of movement or transfer of labor and of other factors is of the nature of a nonrecurrent investment of capital which is only justified if interest at the market rate can permanently be earned on the sums involved. The interest on such nontangible investments connected with the establishment or expansion of a plant (the "good will," which is not only a question of popularity with the buyers but equally one of having all the required factors assembled in the proper place) is certainly a very essential factor in such calculations. But, once these investments have been made, it cannot in any sense be regarded as cost but will appear as profit which shows that the original investment was justified.

These are by no means all the difficulties which arise in connection with the idea of an organization of production on state monopolistic lines. We have said nothing about the problem of the delimitation of the individual industries, the problem of the status of a firm providing equipment needed in many different lines of production, or of the criteria on which the success or failure of any of the managers would be judged. Is an "industry" to include all processes that lead up to any single final product or is it to comprise all plants which turn out the same immediate product, in whatever further process it is used? In either case the decision will involve also a decision on the methods of production to be adopted. Whether every industry is to produce its own tools or whether it has to buy them from another industry which produces them at large scale will essentially affect the question of whether it will be advantageous to use a particular instrument at all. But these or very similar problems will have to be discussed in some detail in connection with proposals for readmitting competition in a much more complete form. What has been said here, however, seems sufficient to show that, if one wants to preserve competition in the socialist state in order to solve the economic problem, it would not really help to get a satisfactory solution to go only halfway. Only if competition exists not only *between* but also *within* the different industries can we expect it to serve its purpose. It is to the examination of such a more completely competitive system that we have now to turn.

At first sight it is not evident why such a socialist system with competition within industries as well as between them should not work as well or as badly as competitive capitalism. All the difficulties one might expect to arise seem likely to be only of that psychological or moral character about which so little that is definite can be said. It is true that the problems which arise in connection with such a system are of a somewhat different nature from those arising in a "planned" system, although on examination they prove to be not so very different as may appear at first.

The crucial questions in this case are: What is to be the independent business unit? Who is to be the manager? What resources are to be intrusted to him and how is his success or failure to be tested? As we shall see, these are by no means only minor administrative problems, questions of personnel such as those which have to be solved in any large organization today, but major problems whose solution will affect the structure of industry almost as much as the decisions of a real planning authority.

To begin with, it must be clear that the need for some central economic authority will not greatly diminish. It is clear, too, that this authority will have to be almost as powerful as in a planned system. If the community is the owner of all material resources of production, somebody will have to exercise this right for it, at least in so far as the distribution and the control of the use of these resources is concerned. It is not possible to conceive of this central authority simply as a kind of superbank which lends the available funds to the highest bidder. It would lend to persons who have no property of their own. It would therefore bear all the risk and would have no claim for a definite amount of money as a bank has. It would simply have rights of ownership of all real resources. Nor can its decisions be confined to the redistribution of free capital in the form of money and perhaps of land. It would also have to decide whether a particular plant or piece of machinery should be left further to the entrepreneur who has used it in the past, at his valuation, or whether it should be transferred to another who promises a higher return from it.

In imagining a system of this sort, it is most charitable to assume that the initial distribution of resources between individual firms will be made on the basis of the historically given structure of industry and that the selection of the managers is made on the basis of some efficiency test and of previous experience. If the existing organization of industry were not accepted, it could be improved or rationally changed only on the basis of very extensive central planning, and this would land us back with the systems which the competitive system is an attempt to replace. But acceptance of the existing organization would solve the difficulties only for the moment. Every change in circumstance will necessitate changes in this organization, and in the course of a comparatively short space of time the central authority will have to effect a complete reorganization.

On what principles will it act?

It is clear that in such a society change will be quite as frequent as under capitalism; it will also be quite as unpredictable. All action will have to be based on anticipation of future events, and the expectations on the part of different entrepreneurs will naturally differ. The decision to whom to intrust a given amount of resources will have to be made on the basis of individual promises of future return. Or, rather, it will have to be made on the statement that a certain return is to be expected with a certain degree of probability. There will, of course, be no objective test of the magnitude of the risk. But who is then to decide whether the risk is worth taking? The central authority will have no other grounds on which to decide but the past performance of the entrepreneur. But how are they to decide whether the risks he has run in the past were justified? And will its attitude toward risky undertakings be the same as if he risked his own property?

Consider first the question how his success or failure will be tested. The first question will be whether he has succeeded in preserving the value of the resources intrusted to him. But even the best entrepreneur will occasionally make losses and sometimes even very heavy losses. Is he to be blamed if his capital has become obsolete because of an invention or a change in demand? How is it to be decided whether he was entitled to take a certain risk? Is the man who never makes losses because he never takes a risk necessarily the man who acts most in the interest of the community? There will certainly be a tendency to prefer the safe to the risky enterprise.

But risky, and even the purely speculative, undertakings will be no less important here than under capitalism. Specialization in the function of risk-bearing by professional speculators in commodities will be as desirable a form of division of labor as it is today. But how is the magnitude of the capital of the speculator to be determined, and how is his remuneration to be fixed? How long is a formerly successful entrepreneur to be suffered to go on making losses? If the penalty for loss is the surrender of the position of "entrepreneur," will it not be almost inevitable that the possible chance of making a loss will operate as so strong a deterrent that it will outbalance the chance of the greatest profit? Under capitalism, too, loss of capital may mean loss of status as capitalist. But against this deterrent is always the attraction of the possible gain. Under socialism this cannot exist. It is even conceivable that general reluctance to undertake any risky business might drive the rate of interest down to nearly zero. But would this be an advantage to society? If it were due only to the satiation of all the absolutely safe channels of investment, it would be bought at a sacrifice of all experimentation with new and untried methods. Even if progress is inevitably connected with what is commonly called "waste," is it not worth having if on the whole gains exceed losses?

But, to turn back to the problem of the distribution and control of resources, there remains the very serious question of how to decide in the short run whether a going concern is making the best use of its resources. Even whether it is making profit or losses is a matter which will depend on one's estimate of the future returns to be expected from its equipment. Its results can be determined only if a definite value is to be given to its existing plant. What is to be the decision if another entrepreneur promises to get a higher return out of the plant (or even an individual machine) than that on which the present user bases his valuation? Is the plan or machine to be taken from him and to be given to the other man on his mere promise? This may be an extreme case, yet it only illustrates the constant shift of resources between firms which goes on under capitalism and which would be equally advantageous in a socialist society. In a capitalist society the transfers of capital from the less to the more efficient entrepreneur is brought about by the former making losses and the latter making profits. The question of who is to be entitled to risk resources and with how much he is to be trusted is here decided by the man who has succeeded in acquiring and maintaining them. Will the question in the socialist state be decided on the same principles? Will the manager of a firm be free to reinvest profits wherever and whenever he thinks it is worth while? At present he will compare the risk involved in further expansion of this present undertaking with the income which he will obtain if he invests elsewhere or if he consumes his capital. Will consideration of the alternative advantages which society might derive from that capital have the same weight in this computation of risk and gain as would his own alternative gain or sacrifice?

The decision about the amount of capital to be given to an individual entrepreneur and the decision thereby involved concerning the size of the individual firm under a single control are in effect decisions about the most appropriate combination of resources.[11] It will rest with the central authority to decide whether one plant located at one place should expand rather than another plant situated elsewhere. All this involves planning on the part of the central authority on much the same scale as if it were actually running the enterprise. While the individual entrepreneur would in all probability be given some definite contractual tenure for managing the plant intrusted to him, all new investment will necessarily be centrally directed. This division in the

11. For a more detailed discussion of how the size of the individual firm is determined under competition and of the way in which this affects the appropriateness of different methods of production and the costs of the product, cf. E. A. G. Robinson, *The Structure of Competitive Industry* (Cambridge Economic Handbooks, Vol. VII), London, 1931.

disposition over the resources would then simply have the effect that neither the entrepreneur nor the central authority would be really in a position to plan and that it would be impossible to assess responsibility for mistakes. To assume that it is possible to create conditions of full competition without making those who are responsible for the decisions pay for their mistakes seems to be pure illusion. It will at best be a system of quasi-competition where the person really responsible will not be the entrepreneur but the official who approves his decisions and where in consequence all the difficulties will arise in connection with freedom of initiative and the assessment of responsibility which are usually associated with bureaucracy.[12]

10

Without pretending any finality for this discussion of pseudo-competition, it may at least be claimed that it has been shown that its successful administration presents considerable obstacles and that it raises numerous difficulties which must be surmounted before we can believe that its results will even approach those of competition which is based on private property of the means of production. It must be said that in their present state, even considering their very provisional and tentative character, these proposals seem rather more than less impracticable than the older socialist proposals of a centrally planned economic system. It is true, even more true than in the case of planning proper, that all the difficulties which have been raised are due "only" to the imperfections of the human mind. But while this makes it illegitimate to say that these proposals are "impossible" in any absolute sense, it remains not the less true that these very serious obstacles to the achievement of the desired end exist and that there seems to be no way in which they can be overcome.

Instead of discussing any further the detailed difficulties which these proposals raise, it is perhaps more interesting to consider what it really

12. For further very illuminating discussion of these problems see R. G. Hawtrey, *The Economic Problem* (London, 1926), and J. Gerhardt, *Unternehmertum und Wirtschaftsführung* (Tübingen, 1930).

implies that so many of those of the younger socialists who have seriously studied the economic problems involved in socialism have
abandoned the belief in a centrally planned economic system and
pinned their faith on the hope that competition may be maintained
even if private property is abolished. Let us assume for the moment
that it is possible in this way to come very near the results which a
competitive system based on private property achieves. Is it fully
realized how much of the hopes commonly associated with a socialist
system are already abandoned when it is proposed to substitute for the
centrally planned system, which was regarded as highly superior to
any competitive system, a more or less successful imitation of competition? What are the advantages which will remain to compensate for
the loss of efficiency which, if we take account of our earlier objections,
it seems will be the inevitable effects of the fact that without private
property competition will necessarily be somewhat restricted and that
therefore some of the decisions will have to be left to the arbitrary decision of a central authority?

The illusions which have to be abandoned with the idea of a centrally planned system are indeed very considerable. The hope of a vastly
superior productivity of a planned system over that of "chaotic" competition has had to give place to the hope that the socialist system may
nearly equal the capitalist system in productivity. The hope that the
distribution of income may be made entirely independent of the price
of the services rendered and based exclusively on considerations of
justice, preferably in the sense of an egalitarian distribution, has to be
replaced by the hope that it will be possible to use part of the income
from the material factors of production to supplement income from
labor. The expectation that the "wage system" would be abolished,
that the managers of a socialized industry or firm would act on entirely different principles from the profit-seeking capitalist, has proved to
be equally wrong. Although there has been no occasion to discuss this
point in detail, the same must be said of the hope that such a socialist
system would avoid crises and unemployment. A centrally planned
system, although it could not avoid making even more serious mis-

takes of the sort which lead to crises under capitalism, would at least have the advantage that it would be possible to share the loss equally between all its members. It would be superior in this respect in that it would be possible to reduce wages by decree when it was found that this was necessary in order to correct the mistakes. But there is no reason why a competitive socialist system should be in a better position to avoid crises and unemployment than competitive capitalism. Perhaps an intelligent monetary policy may reduce their severity for both, but there are no possibilities in this respect under competitive socialism which would not equally exist under capitalism.

Against all this there is, of course, the advantage that it would be possible to improve the relative position of the working class by giving them a share in the returns from land and capital. This is, after all, the main aim of socialism. But that it will be possible to improve their position relative to that of those who were capitalists does not mean that their absolute incomes will be increased or that they will even remain as high as before. What will happen in this respect depends entirely on the extent to which general productivity is reduced. It must again be pointed out here that general considerations of the kind which can be advanced in a short essay can lead to no decisive conclusions. Only by intensive application of analysis on these lines to the phenomena of the real world is it possible to arrive at approximate estimates of the quantitive importance of the phenomena which have been discussed here. On this point opinions will naturally differ. But even if it could be agreed what exactly would be the effects of any of the proposed systems on the national income, there would still be the further question of whether any given reduction, either of its present absolute magnitude or of its future rate of progress, is not too high a price for the realization of the ethical ideal of greater equality of incomes. On this question, of course, scientific argument must give way to individual conviction.

But at least the decision cannot be made before the alternatives are known, before it is at least approximately realized what the price is that has to be paid. That there exists still so much confusion in this field

178

and that people still refuse to admit that it is impossible to have the best of both worlds is due mainly to the fact that most socialists have little idea of what the system they advocate is really to be like, whether it is to be a planned or a competitive system. It is at present effective tactics on the part of contemporary socialists to leave this point in the dark, and, while claiming all the benefits which used to be associated with central planning, refer to competition when they are asked how they are going to solve a particular difficulty. But nobody has yet demonstrated how planning and competition can be rationally combined; and, so long as this is not done, one is certainly entitled to insist that these two alternatives be kept clearly separate and that anybody who advocates socialism must decide for one or the other and then demonstrate how he proposes to overcome the difficulties inherent in the system he has chosen.

11

No pretense is made that the conclusions reached here in the examination of the alternative socialist constructions must necessarily be final. One thing, however, seems to emerge from the discussions of the last years with incontrovertible force: that today we are not yet intellectually equipped to improve the working of our economic system by "planning" or to solve the problem of socialist production in any other way without very considerably impairing productivity. What is lacking is not "experience" but intellectual mastery of a problem which so far we have learned only to formulate but not to answer. No one would want to exclude every possibility that a solution may yet be found. But in our present state of knowledge serious doubt must remain whether such a solution can be found. We must at least face the possibility that for the last fifty years thought has been on the wrong lines, attracted by a notion which on examination at close range proved not to be realizable. If this were so, it would be no proof that it would have been desirable to stay where we were before this tendency set in, but only that a development in another direction would have been more advantageous. There is indeed some reason to suppose that it might, for instance, have been more rational to seek for a smoother working of competition than to obstruct it so long with all kinds of attempts at planning that almost any alternative came to seem preferable to existing conditions.

But if our conclusions on the merits of the beliefs which are undoubtedly one of the main driving forces of our time are essentially negative, this is certainly no cause for satisfaction. In a world bent on planning, nothing could be more tragic than that the conclusion should prove inevitable that persistence on this course must lead to economic decay. Even if there is already some intellectual reaction under way, there can be little doubt that for many years the movement will continue in the direction of planning. Nothing, therefore, could do more to relieve the unmitigated gloom with which the economist today must look at the future of the world than if it could be shown that there is a possible and practicable way to overcome its difficulties. Even for those who are not in sympathy with all the ultimate aims of socialism there is strong reason to wish that, now that the world is moving in that direction, it should prove practicable and a catastrophe be averted. But it must be admitted that today it seems, to say the least, highly unlikely that such a solution can be found. It is of some significance that so far the smallest contributions to such a solution have come from those who have advocated planning. If a solution should ever be reached, this would be due more to the critics, who have at least made clear the nature of the problem—even if they have despaired of finding a solution.

IX. Socialist Calculation III: *The Competitive "Solution"**

* Reprinted from *Economica,* Vol. VII, No. 26 (new ser.; May, 1940). The two books with which this chapter is mainly concerned, Oskar Lange and Fred M. Taylor, *On the Economic Theory of Socialism,* ed. B. E. Lippincott (Minneapolis, 1938), and H. D. Dickinson, *Economics of Socialism* (Oxford, 1939), will be referred to throughout this chapter as "LT" (Lange-Taylor) and "D" (Dickinson), respectively.

1

TWO chapters in the discussion of the economics of socialism may now be regarded as closed. The first deals with the belief that socialism will dispense entirely with calculation in terms of value and will replace it with some sort of calculation *in natura* based on units of energy or of some other physical magnitude. Although this view is not yet extinct and is still held by some scientists and engineers, it has been definitely abandoned by economists. The second closed chapter deals with the proposal that values, instead of being left to be determined by competition, should be found by a process of calculations carried out by the planning authority, which would use the technique of mathematical economics. With regard to this suggestion, Pareto (who, curiously enough, is sometimes quoted as holding this view) has already said what probably will remain the final word. After showing how a system of simultaneous equations can be used to explain what determines prices on a market, he adds:

"It may be mentioned here that this determination has by no means the purpose to arrive at a numerical calculation of prices. Let us make the most favourable assumption for such a calculation, let us assume that we have triumphed over all the difficulties of finding the data of the problem and that we know the *ophélimités* of all the different commodities for each individual, and all the conditions of production of all the commodities, etc. This is already an absurd hypothesis to make. Yet it is not sufficient to make the solution of the problem possible. We have seen that in the case of 100 persons and 700 commodities there will be 70,699 conditions (actually a great number of circumstances which we have so far neglected will further increase that number); we shall therefore have to solve a system of 70,699 equations. This exceeds practically the power of algebraic analysis, and this is even more true if one contemplates the fabulous number of equations which one obtains for a population of forty millions and several thousand commodities. In this case the rôles would be changed: it would not be mathematics which would assist political economy, but political economy would assist mathematics. In other words, if one really could know all these equations, the only means to solve them which is available to human powers is to observe the practical solution given by the market."[1]

In the present article we shall be concerned mainly with a third stage in this discussion, for which the issue has now been clearly defined by the elaboration of proposals for a competitive socialism by Professor Lange and Dr. Dickinson. Since, however, the significance of the result of the past discussions is not infrequently represented in a way which comes very near to an inversion of the truth, and as at least one of the two books to be discussed is not quite free from this tendency, a few further remarks on the real significance of the past development seem not unnecessary.

The first point is connected with the nature of the original criticism directed against the more primitive conceptions of the working of a socialist economy which were current up to about 1920. The idea then current (and still advocated, e.g., by Otto Neurath) is well expressed by Engels in his *Anti-Dühring,* when he says that the social plan of production "will be settled very simply, without the intervention of the famous 'value.'" It was against this generally held belief that N. G. Pierson, Ludwig von Mises, and others pointed out that, if the socialist community wanted to act rationally, its calculation would have to be guided by the same *formal* laws which applied to a capitalist society. It seems necessary especially to underline the fact that this was a point

1. V. Pareto, *Manuel d'économie politique* (2d ed., 1927), pp. 233–34.

made by the critics of the socialist plans, since Professor Lange and particularly his editor[2] now seem inclined to suggest that the demonstration that the formal principles of economic theory apply to a socialist economy provides an answer to these critics. The fact is that it has never been denied by anybody, except socialists, that these formal principles *ought* to apply to a socialist society, and the question raised by Mises and others was not whether they ought to apply but whether they could in practice be applied in the absence of a market. It is therefore entirely beside the point when Lange and others quote Pareto and Barone as having shown that values in a socialist society would depend on essentially the same factors as in a competitive society. This, of course, had been shown long before, particularly by von Wieser. But none of these authors has made an attempt to show how these values, which a socialist society ought to use if it wants to act rationally, could be found, and Pareto, as we have seen, expressly denied that they could be determined by calculation.

It seems then that, on this point, the criticisms of the earlier socialist schemes have been so successful that the defenders, with few exceptions,[3] have felt compelled to appropriate the argument of their critics and have been forced to construct entirely new schemes of which nobody thought before. While against the older idea that it was possible to plan rationally without calculation in terms of value, it could be justly argued that they were logically impossible; the newer proposals designed to determine values by some process other than competition based on private property raise a problem of a different sort. But it is surely unfair to say, as Lange does, that the critics, because they deal in a new way with the new schemes evolved to meet the original criticism, "have given up the essential point" and "retreated to a second line of defense."[4] Is this not rather a case of covering up their own retreat by creating confusion about the issue?

There is a second point on which Lange's presentation of the present

2. See B. E. Lippincott in LT, p. 7.
3. The most notable exception is Dr. M. Dobb. See his *Political Economy and Capitalism* (1937), chap. viii, and his review of Professor Lange's book in the *Modern Quarterly*, 1939.
4. LT, p. 63.

state of the debate is seriously misleading. The reader of his study can hardly avoid the impression that the idea that values should and could be determined by using the technique of mathematical economics, i.e., by solving millions of equations, is a malicious invention of the critics, intended to throw ridicule on the efforts of modern socialist writers. The fact, which cannot be unknown to Lange, is, of course, that this procedure has more than once been seriously suggested by socialist writers as a solution of the difficulty—among others, by Dr. Dickinson, who now, however, expressly withdraws this earlier suggestion.[5]

2

The third stage in the debate has now been reached with the proposal to solve the problems of determining values by the reintroduction of competition. When five years ago the present author tried to appraise the significance of these attempts,[6] it was necessary to rely on what could be gathered from oral discussion among socialist economists, since no systematic exposition of the theoretical bases of competitive socialism was then available. This gap has now been filled by the two books here to be discussed. The first contains a reprint of an essay by Lange, originally published in 1936 and 1937, together with an older article by the late Professor Taylor (dating from 1928), an introduction by the editor, B. E. Lippincott, which, in addition to a quite unnecessary restatement of Lange's argument in cruder terms, does much, by the unmeasured praise he bestows on this argument and the extravagant claims he advances for it,[7] to prejudice the reader against the essentially scholarly piece of work that follows. Although written in a lively style and confining itself to the outlines of the subject, it does seriously grapple with some of the main difficulties in the field.

5. D, p. 104, and K. Tisch, *Wirtschaftsrechnung und Verteilung im zentralistisch organisierten sozialistischen Gemeinwesen* (1932).

6. In *Collectivist Economic Planning* (London, 1935), essay on "The Present State of the Debate," reprinted above, chap. ix.

7. Dr. Lange's essay is described as the "first writing to mark an advance on Barone's contribution" and to show by "irrefutable" argument the "evident feasibility and superiority" of a socialist system (LT, pp. 13, 24, 37).

Socialist Calculation

H. D. Dickinson's more recent book is a far more comprehensive survey of the field, proposing essentially the same solution.[8] It is unquestionably a book of great distinction, well organized, lucid, and concise, and should rapidly establish itself as the standard work on its subject. To the economist, the reading of the book provides indeed the rare pleasure of feeling that recent advances of economic theory have not been in vain and have even helped to reduce political differences to points which can be rationally discussed. Dr. Dickinson himself would probably agree that he shares all his economics with—and indeed has learned most of it from—nonsocialist economists and that in his essential conclusions on the desirable economic policy of a socialist community he differs much more from most of his socialist colleagues than from "orthodox" economists. This, together with the openmindedness with which the author takes up and considers the arguments advanced by his opponents, makes discussion of his views a real pleasure. If the socialists, like the economists, are ready to accept his book as the most up-to-date general treatment of the economics of socialism from the socialist point of view, it should provide the basis for much fruitful further discussion.

As has already been mentioned, the main outlines of the solution offered by the two authors are essentially the same. They both rely to some extent on the competitive mechanism for the determination of relative prices. But they both refuse to let prices be determined directly in the market and propose instead a system of price-fixing by a central authority, where the state of the market of a particular commodity, i.e., the relation of demand to supply, merely serves as an indication to the authority whether the prescribed prices ought to be raised or lowered. Neither of the two authors explains why he refuses to go the whole hog and to restore the price mechanism in full. But as I happen to agree (although probably for different reasons) that this would be impracticable in a socialist community, we can leave this question aside for the moment and shall take it for granted that in such a society com-

8. It is a curious fact that Dr. Dickinson nowhere in his book (except in the Bibliography) refers to Professor Lange's work.

petition cannot play quite the same role as it does in a society based on private property and that, in particular, the rates at which commodities will be exchanged by the parties in the market will have to be decreed by the authority.

We shall leave the details of the proposed organization for later consideration and first consider the general significance of this solution under three aspects. We shall ask, first, how far this kind of socialist system still conforms to the hopes that were placed on the substitution of a planned socialist system for the chaos of competition; second, how far the proposed procedure is an answer to the main difficulty, and, finally, how far it is applicable.

The first and most general point can be dealt with fairly briefly, although it is not unimportant if one wants to see these new proposals in their proper light. It is merely a reminder of how much of the original claim for the superiority of planning over competition is abandoned if the planned society is now to rely for the direction of its industries to a large extent on competition. Until quite recently, at least, planning and competition used to be regarded as opposites, and this is unquestionably still true of nearly all planners except a few economists among them. I fear that the schemes of Lange and Dickinson will bitterly disappoint all those scientific planners who, in the recent words of B. M. S. Blackett, believe that "the object of planning is largely to overcome the results of competition."[9] This would be even more true if it were really possible to reduce the arbitrary elements in a competitive socialist system as much as is believed by Dickinson, who hopes that his "libertarian socialism" "may establish, for the first time in human history, an effective individualism."[10] Unfortunately, as we shall see, this is not likely to be the case.

3

The second general question we must consider is how far the proposed method of central price-fixing, while leaving it to individual

9. See Sir Daniel Hall and others, *The Frustration of Science* (London, 1935), p. 142.
10. D, p. 26.

firms and consumers to adjust demand and supply to the given prices, is likely to solve the problem which admittedly cannot be solved by mathematical calculation. Here, I am afraid, I find it exceedingly difficult to understand the grounds on which such a claim is made. Lange as well as Dickinson asserts that even if the initial system of prices were chosen entirely at random, it would be possible by such a process of trial and error gradually to approach the appropriate system.[11] This seems to be much the same thing as if it were suggested that a system of equations, which was too complex to be solved by calculation within reasonable time and whose values were constantly changing, could be effectively tackled by arbitrarily inserting tentative values and then trying about until the proper solution was found. Or, to change the metaphor, the difference between such a system of regimented prices and a system of prices determined by the market seems to be about the same as that between an attacking army in which every unit and every man could move only by special command and by the exact distance ordered by headquarters and an army in which every unit and every man can take advantage of every opportunity offered to them. There is, of course, no *logical* impossibility of conceiving a directing organ of the collective economy which is not only "omnipresent and omniscient," as Dickinson conceives it,[12] but also omnipotent and which therefore would be in a position to change without delay every price by just the amount that is required. When, however, one proceeds to consider the actual apparatus by which this sort of adjustment is to be brought about, one begins to wonder whether anyone should really be prepared to suggest that, within the domain of practical possibility, such a system will ever even distantly approach the efficiency of a system where the required changes are brought about by the spontaneous action of the persons immediately concerned.

We shall later, when we consider the proposed institutional setting, come back to the question of how this sort of mechanism is likely to function in practice. In so far as the general question is concerned,

11. LT, pp. 70 and 86; D, pp. 103 and 113.
12. D, p. 191.

187

however, it is difficult to suppress the suspicion that this particular proposal has been born out of an excessive preoccupation with problems of the pure theory of stationary equilibrium. If in the real world we had to deal with approximately constant data, that is, if the problem were to find a price system which then could be left more or less unchanged for long periods, then the proposal under consideration would not be so entirely unreasonable. With given and constant data such a state of equilibrium could indeed be approached by the method of trial and error. But this is far from being the situation in the real world, where constant change is the rule. Whether and how far anything approaching the desirable equilibrium is ever reached depends entirely on the speed with which the adjustments can be made. The practical problem is not whether a particular method would eventually lead to a hypothetical equilibrium, but which method will secure the more rapid and complete adjustment to the daily changing conditions in different places and different industries. How great the difference in this respect would be between a method where prices are currently agreed upon by the parties of the market, and a method where these prices are decreed from above, is, of course, a matter of practical judgment. But I find it difficult to believe that anybody would doubt that in this respect the inferiority of the second method would be very great indeed.

The third general point is also one where I believe that preoccupation with concepts of pure economic theory has seriously misled both our authors. In this case it is the concept of perfect competition which apparently has made them overlook a very important field to which their method appears to be simply inapplicable. Wherever we have a market for a fairly standardized commodity, it is at least conceivable that all prices should be decreed in advance from above for a certain period. The situation is, however, very different with respect to commodities which cannot be standardized, and particularly for those which today are produced on individual orders, perhaps after invitation for tenders. A large part of the product of the "heavy industries," which, of course, would be the first to be socialized, belongs to this category. Much machinery, most buildings and ships, and many parts of other products are hardly ever produced for a market, but only on special contract. This does not mean that there may not be intense competition in the market for the products of these industries, although it may not be "perfect competition" in the sense of pure theory; the fact is simply that in those industries identical products are rarely produced twice in short intervals; and the circle of producers who will compete as alternative suppliers in each instance will be different in almost every individual case, just as the circle of potential customers who will compete for the services of a particular plant will differ from week to week. What basis is there in all these cases for fixing prices of the product so as "to equalize demand and supply"? If prices are here to be fixed by the central authority, they will have to be fixed in every individual case and on the basis of an examination by that authority of the calculations of all potential suppliers and all potential purchasers. It is hardly necessary to point out the various complications that will arise according as the prices are fixed before or after the prospective buyer has decided on the particular piece of machinery or building which he wants. Presumably it will be the estimates of the producer which, before they are submitted to the prospective customer, will have to be approved by the authority. Is it not clear that in all these cases, unless the authority in effect takes all the functions of the entrepreneur on itself (i.e., unless the proposed system is abandoned and one of complete central direction substituted), the process of price-fixing would become either exceedingly cumbersome and the cause of infinite delay or a pure formality?

4

All these considerations appear to be relevant whatever particular form of organization is chosen. Before we go further, however, it becomes necessary to consider somewhat more in detail the concrete apparatus of industrial control which the two authors propose. The sketches they provide of the organization are fairly similar, although in this respect Lange gives us somewhat more information than Dickinson, who, for most of the problems of economic organization, refers us to the works of the Webbs and G. D. H. Cole.[13]

Both authors contemplate a socialist system in which the choice of occupation would be free and regulated mainly by the price mechanism (i.e., by the wage system) and in which the consumers also would be free to spend their incomes as they chose. Apparently both authors also want prices of consumers' goods to be fixed by the ordinary market processes (although Dickinson does not seem to be quite decided on this point)[14] and also to leave the determination of wages to the bargaining between the parties concerned.[15] Both also agree that for various reasons not the whole of industry should be socialized but that besides the socialized there should also remain a private sector, consisting of small enterprises run on essentially capitalistic lines. I find it difficult to agree with their belief that the existence of such a private sector parallel with the socialized sector creates no special difficulties. But as it would be difficult within the space of this article to deal adequately with this problem, we shall, for the purposes of this discussion, disregard the existence of the private sector and assume that the whole of industry is socialized.

The determination of all prices, other than those of consumers' goods and of wages, is the main task of the central economic authority—Lange's Central Planning Board or Dickinson's Supreme Economic Council. (We shall, following Dickinson, henceforth refer to this body as the "S.E.C.") As regards the technique of how particular prices are announced and changed, we get more information, although by no means enough, from Lange, while Dickinson goes more fully into the question of the considerations by which the S.E.C. should be guided in the fixing of prices. Both questions have a special importance, and they must be considered separately.

According to Lange, the S.E.C. would, from time to time, issue what, following Professor Taylor, he calls "factor valuation tables,"

13. D, p. 30. 15. LT, p. 78; D, p. 126.
14. LT, p. 78; D, p. 60.

that is, comprehensive lists of prices of all means of production (except labor).[16] These prices would have to serve as the sole basis for all transactions between different enterprises and the whole calculation of all the industries and plants during the period of their validity, and the managers must treat these prices as constant.[17] What we are not told, however, either by Lange or by Dickinson, is for what period these prices are to be fixed. This is one of the more serious obscurities in the exposition of both authors, a gap in their exposition which makes one almost doubt whether they have made a real effort to visualize their system at work. Are prices to be fixed for a definite period in advance, or are they to be changed whenever it seems desirable? F. M. Taylor seemed to suggest the former alternative when he wrote that the appropriateness of particular prices would show itself at the end of the "productive period,"[18] and Lange, on at least one occasion, gives the same impression when he says that "any price different from the equilibrium price would show at the end of the accounting period a surplus or shortage of the commodity in question."[19] But on another occasion he says that "adjustments of those prices would be constantly made,"[20] while Dickinson confines himself to stating that after, "by a process of successive approximation," "a set of prices can ultimately be established in consonance with the principles of scarcity and substitution," "small adjustments will be sufficient to keep the system in equilibrium except in the case of major technical innovations or of big changes in consumers' tastes."[21] Could the failure to understand the true function of the price mechanism, caused by the modern preoccupation with stationary equilibrium, be better illustrated?

While Dickinson is very uninformative on the mechanism of bringing price changes into effect, he goes much more fully than Lange into the considerations on which the S.E.C. would have to base their decisions. Unlike Lange, Dickinson is not satisfied with the S.E.C. merely watching the market and adjusting prices when an excess of demand

16. LT, pp. 46 and 52.
17. LT, p. 81.
18. LT, p. 53.
19. LT, p. 82.
20. LT, p. 86.
21. D, pp. 100, 102, and 103.

or supply appears and then trying to find by experimentation a new equilibrium level. He rather wants the S.E.C. to use statistically established demand-and-supply schedules as a guide to determine the equilibrium prices. This is evidently a residue of his earlier belief in the possibility of solving the whole problem by the method of simultaneous equations. But, although he has now abandoned this idea (not because he regards it as impossible, since he still believes it could be done by solving merely "two or three thousand simultaneous equations,"[22] but because he realizes that "the data themselves, which would have to be fed into the equation-machine, are continually changing"), he still believes that the statistical determination of demand schedules would be useful as an aid to, if not as a substitute for, the method of trial and error and that it would be well worth while to try to establish the numerical values of the constants (*sic*) in the Walrasian system of equilibrium.

5

Whatever the method by which the S.E.C. fixes prices, and particularly whatever the periods at which and for which prices are announced, there are two points about which there can be little question: the changes will occur later than they would if prices were determined by the market parties, and there will be less differentiation between prices of commodities according to differences of quality and the circumstances of time and place. While with real competition price changes occur when the parties immediately concerned know that conditions have changed, the S.E.C. will be able to act only after the parties have reported, the reports have been verified, contradictions cleared up, etc.; and the new prices will become effective only after all the parties concerned have been notified, that is, either a date will have to be fixed in advance at which the new prices will become effective or the accounting will have to include an elaborate system by which every manager of production is constantly notified of the new prices

22. D, p. 104.

upon which he has to base his calculations. Since in fact every manager would have to be informed constantly on many more prices than those of the commodities which he is actually using (at least of those of all possible substitutes), some sort of periodic publication of complete lists of all prices would be necessary. It is clear that, while economic efficiency demands that prices should be changed as promptly as possible, practicability would confine actual changes to intervals of fair length.

That the price-fixing process will be confined to establishing uniform prices for classes of goods and that therefore distinctions based on the special circumstances of time, place, and quality will find no expression in prices is probably obvious. Without some such simplification, the number of different commodities for which separate prices would have to be fixed would be practically infinite. This means, however, that the managers of production will have no inducement, and even no real possibility, to make use of special opportunities, special bargains, and all the little advantages offered by their special local conditions, since all these things could not enter into their calculations. It would also mean, to give only one other illustration of the consequences, that it would never be practicable to incur extra costs to remedy a sudden scarcity quickly, since a local or temporary scarcity could not affect prices until the official machinery had acted.

For both these reasons, because prices would have to be fixed for definite periods and because they would have to be fixed generically for categories of goods, a great many prices would be at most times in such a system substantially different from what they would be in a free system. This is very important for the functioning of the system. Lange makes great play with the fact that prices act merely as "indices of terms on which alternatives are offered"[23] and that this "parametric function of prices,"[24] by which prices are guiding the action of individual managers without being directly determined by them, will be fully preserved under such a system of fixing prices. As he himself points out, "the determinateness of the accounting prices holds,

23. LT, p. 78.   24. LT, pp. 70 and 86.

193

Individualism and Economic Order

however, only if all discrepancies between demand and supply of a commodity are met by an appropriate change of price," and for this reason "rationing has to be excluded," and "the rule to produce at the minimum average cost has no significance unless prices represent the relative scarcity of the factors of production."[25] In other words, prices will provide a basis for rational accounting only if they are such that at the ruling prices anyone can always sell as much or buy as much as he wishes or that anyone should be free to buy as cheaply or to sell as dearly as is made possible by the existence of a willing partner. If I cannot buy more of a factor so long as it is worth more to me than the price, and if I cannot sell a thing as soon as it is worth less to me than the price which somebody else would be willing to pay for it, prices are no longer indices of alternative opportunities.

We shall see the significance of this more clearly when we consider the action of the managers of the socialist industries. But, before we can consider their action, we must see who these people are and with what functions they are invested.

6

The nature of the industrial unit under separate management and of the factors which determine its size and the selection of its management is another point on which both our authors are deplorably vague. Lange seems to contemplate the organization of the different industries in the form of national trusts, although this important point is merely touched upon once when the National Coal Trust is mentioned as an example.[26] The very important and relevant question of what is *one* industry is nowhere discussed, but he apparently assumes that the various "managers of production" will have monopolistic control of the particular commodities with which they are concerned. In general, Lange uses the term "managers of production" exceedingly vaguely,[27] leaving it obscure whether the directors of a whole "indus-

25. LT, pp. 93–94. 27. LT, pp. 75, 79, and 86.
26. LT, p. 78.

Individualism and Economic Order

however, only if all discrepancies between demand and supply of a commodity are met by an appropriate change of price," and for this reason "rationing has to be excluded," and "the rule to produce at the minimum average cost has no significance unless prices represent the relative scarcity of the factors of production."[25] In other words, prices will provide a basis for rational accounting only if they are such that at the ruling prices anyone can always sell as much or buy as much as he wishes or that anyone should be free to buy as cheaply or to sell as dearly as is made possible by the existence of a willing partner. If I cannot buy more of a factor so long as it is worth more to me than the price, and if I cannot sell a thing as soon as it is worth less to me than the price which somebody else would be willing to pay for it, prices are no longer indices of alternative opportunities.

try" or of a single unit are meant; but at critical points[28] a distinction between the managers of plant and the managers of a whole industry appears without any clear limitation of their functions. Dickinson is even more vague when he speaks of economic activities being "decentralized and carried on by a large number of separate organs of collective economy" which will have "their own nominal capital and their own profit and loss account and will be managed very much as separate enterprises under capitalism."[29]

Whoever these managers of production are, their main function would appear to be the decision how much and how to produce on the basis of the prices fixed by the S.E.C. (and the prices of consumers' goods and the wages determined by the market). They would be instructed by the S.E.C. to produce at the lowest possible average costs[30] and to expand production of the individual plants until marginal costs are equal to price.[31] According to Lange, the directors of the industries (as distinguished from the managers of individual plants) would have also the further task of seeing that the amount of equipment in the industry as a whole is so adjusted that "the marginal cost incurred by the industry" in producing an output which "can be sold or 'accounted for' at a price which equals marginal cost" is the lowest possible.[32]

In this connection a special problem arises which unfortunately cannot be discussed here, since it raises questions of such difficulty and complexity that a separate article would be required. It concerns the case of decreasing marginal costs where, according to both our authors, the socialist industries would act differently from capitalist industry by expanding production until prices are equal, not to average, but to marginal costs. Although the argument employed possesses a certain specious plausibility, it can hardly be said even that the problem is adequately stated in either of the two books, still less that the conclusions drawn are convincing. Within the space available on this occasion, however, we can do no more than seriously question Dr. Dickin-

28. LT, pp. 76 and 82 n.
29. D, p. 213.
30. LT, p. 75.

31. LT, p. 76; D, p. 107.
32. LT, p. 77.

son's assertion that "under modern technical conditions, diminishing costs are far commoner than increasing costs"—a statement which in the context in which it occurs clearly refers to marginal costs.[33]

Here we shall confine ourselves to considering one question arising out of this part of the proposal—the question of how the S.E.C. will insure the actual carrying-out of the principle that prices are equalized to the lowest marginal cost at which the quantity concerned can be produced. The question which arises here is not "merely" one of the loyalty or capacity of the socialist managers. For the purpose of this argument it may be granted that they will be as capable and as anxious to produce cheaply as the average capitalist entrepreneur. The problem arises because one of the most important forces which in a truly competitive economy brings about the reduction of costs to the minimum discoverable will be absent, namely, price competition. In the discussion of this sort of problem, as in the discussion of so much of economic theory at the present time, the question is frequently treated as if the cost curves were objectively given facts. What is forgotten is that the method which under given conditions is the cheapest is a thing which has to be discovered, and to be discovered anew, sometimes almost from day to day, by the entrepreneur, and that, in spite of the strong inducement, it is by no means regularly the established entrepreneur, the man in charge of the existing plant, who will discover what is the best method. The force which in a competitive society brings about the reduction of price to the lowest cost at which the quantity salable at that cost can be produced is the opportunity for anybody who knows a cheaper method to come in at his own risk and to attract customers by underbidding the other producers. But, if prices are fixed by the authority, this method is excluded. Any improvement, any adjustment, of the technique of production to changed conditions will be dependent on somebody's capacity of convincing the S.E.C. that the commodity in question can be produced cheaper and that therefore the price ought to be lowered. Since the man with the new idea will have no possibility of establishing himself by undercutting,

33. D, p. 108.

the new idea cannot be proved by experiment until he has convinced the S.E.C. that his way of producing the thing is cheaper. Or, in other words, every calculation by an outsider who believes that he can do better will have to be examined and approved by the authority, which in this connection will have to take over all the functions of the entrepreneur.

7

Let us briefly consider a few of the problems arising out of the relations between the "socialist managers of production" (whether of a plant or an industry) and the S.E.C. The manager's task is, as we have seen, to order production in such a way that his marginal costs are as low as possible and equal to price. How is he to do this and how is the fact of his success to be established? He has to take prices as given. This turns him into what has recently been called a pure "quantity adjuster," i.e., his decision is confined to the quantities of factors of production and the combination in which he uses them. But, as he has no means of inducing his suppliers to offer more (or to induce his purchasers to buy more) than they want to at the prescribed price, he will frequently be simply unable to carry out his instructions; or at least, if he cannot get more of a material required at the prescribed price, the only way for him, for example, to expand production so as to make his cost equal to price, would be to use inferior substitutes or to employ other uneconomic methods; and, when he cannot sell at the prescribed price and until the price is lowered by decree, he will have to stop production where under true competition he would have lowered his prices.

Another great difficulty arising out of the periodic price changes by decree is the problem of anticipations of future price movements. Lange, somewhat too bravely, cuts this Gordian knot by prescribing that "for purposes of accounting, prices must be treated as constant, as they are treated by entrepreneurs on a competitive market" (!). Does that mean that the managers, although they know for certain that a particular price will have to be raised or lowered, must act as if they did not know? Clearly this will not do. But if they are free to meet expected price movements by anticipatory action, are they to be allowed to take advantage of the administrative delays in making price changes effective? Who is to be responsible for losses caused by wrongly timed or wrongly directed price changes?

Closely connected with this problem is another question to which we also get no answer. Both our authors speak about "marginal costs" as if they were independent of the period for which the manager can plan. Clearly, actual costs depend in many instances, as much as on anything, on buying at the right time. In no sense can costs during any period be said to depend solely on prices during that period. They depend as much on whether these prices have been correctly foreseen as on the views that are held about future prices. Even in the very short run costs will depend on the effects which current decisions will have on future productivity. Whether it is economical to run a machine hard and to neglect maintenance, whether to make major adjustments to a given change in demand or to carry on as well as possible with the existing organization—in fact, almost every decision on how to produce—now depends at least in part on the views held about the future. But, while the manager clearly must hold some views on these questions, he can hardly be held responsible for anticipating future changes correctly if these changes depend entirely on the decision of the authority.

The success of the individual manager will, however, to a large extent not only depend on the action of the planning authority; he will also have to satisfy the same authority that he has done as well as was possible. Either beforehand, or more likely retrospectively, all his calculations will have to be examined and approved by the authority. This will not be a perfunctory auditing, directed to find out whether his costs have actually been what he says they have been. It will have to ascertain whether they have been the lowest possible ones. This means that the control will have to consider not only what he actually did but also what he might have done and ought to have done. From the point of view of the manager it will be much more important that he should always be able to prove that in the light of the knowledge

198

which he possessed the decision actually taken was the right one than that he should prove to be right in the end. If this will not lead to the worst forms of bureaucracy, I do not know what will.

This brings us to the general question of the responsibility of the managers. Dickinson clearly sees that "responsibility means in practice financial responsibility" and that unless the manager "bears responsibility for losses as well as for profits he will be tempted to embark upon all sorts of risky experiments on the bare chance that one of them will turn out successful."[34] This is a difficult problem with managers who have no property of their own. Dickinson hopes to solve it by a system of bonuses. This may indeed be sufficient to prevent managers from taking too great risks. But is not the real problem the opposite one—that managers will be afraid of taking risks if, when the venture does not come off, it will be somebody else who will afterward decide whether they have been justified in embarking on it? As Dickinson himself points out, the principle would be that, "although the making of profits is not necessarily a sign of success, the making of losses is a sign of failure."[35] Need one say more about the effects of such a system on all activities involving risk? It is difficult to conceive how under these circumstances any of the necessary speculative activities involving risk-bearing could be left to managerial initiative. But the alternative is to fall back for them on that system of strict central planning to avoid which the whole system has been evolved.

8

All this is even more true when we turn to the whole problem of new investments, that is, to all the questions which involve changes in the size (i.e., the capital) of the managerial units, whether they involve net changes in the total supply of capital or not. Up to a point it is possible to divide this problem into two parts—the decisions about the distribution of the available capital supply and the decisions about the rate at which capital is to be accumulated—although it is

34. D, p. 214.   35. D, p. 219.

dangerous to carry this division too far, since the decision about how much is to be saved is necessarily also a decision about which needs for capital are to be satisfied and which are not. Both our authors agree that, as regards the problem of the distribution of capital between industries and plants, the interest mechanism should as far as possible be retained but that the decision of how much to save and invest would necessarily have to be arbitrary.[36]

Now, however strong may be the desire to rely on the interest mechanism for the distribution of capital, it is fairly obvious that the market for capital can in no sense be a free market. While for Lange the rate of interest is also "simply determined by the condition that the demand for capital is equal to the amount available,"[37] Dr. Dickinson takes great pains to show how the S.E.C. will, on the basis of the alternative plans of activity drawn up by the different undertakings, construct an aggregate demand schedule for capital which will enable it to determine that rate of interest at which the demand for capital will equal supply. The ingenuity and the astounding trust in the practicability of even the most complicated constructions which Dickinson displays in this connection may be illustrated by his statement that in a certain case "it will be necessary to establish a provisional rate of interest, then to allow the different organs of collective economy to re-contract with each other on the basis of this provisional rate, and so to draw up their final demand schedule for capital."[38]

All this, however, does not meet the main difficulty. If, indeed, it were possible to accept at their face value the statements of all the individual managers and would-be managers about how much capital they could with advantage use at various rates of interest, some such scheme as this might appear feasible. It cannot be repeated too often, however, that the planning authority cannot be conceived "simply as a kind of superbank which lends the available funds to the highest bidder. It would lend to persons who have no property of their own. It would therefore bear all the risk and would have no

36. LT, p. 85; D, pp. 80 and 205.   38. D, p. 83 n.
37. LT, p. 84.

claim for a definite amount of money as a bank has. It would simply have rights of ownership over all real resources. Nor can its decisions be confined to the redistribution of free capital in the form of money and perhaps of land. It would have to decide whether a particular plant or piece of machinery should be left further to the entrepreneur who has used it in the past, at his valuation, or whether it should be transferred to another who promises a higher return for it."

These sentences are taken from the essay in which the present author discussed five years ago the "possibility of real competition under socialism."[39] At that time such systems had been only vaguely discussed, and one could hope to find an answer when systematic expositions of the new ideas became available. But it is most disappointing to find no answer whatever to these problems in the two books now under discussion. While throughout the two works claims are made about how beneficial the control of investment activity would be in many respects, no indication is given of how this control is to be exercised and of how the responsibilities are to be divided between the planning authorities and the managers of the "competing" industrial units. Such statements as we find, as, for instance, that "because the managers of socialist industry will be governed in some choices by the direction laid down by the planning authority, it does not follow that they will have no choice at all,"[40] are singularly unhelpful. All that seems to be fairly clear is that the planning authority will be able to exercise its function of controlling and directing investment only if it is in a position to check and repeat all the calculations of the entrepreneur.

It seems that here the two writers are unconsciously led to fall back on the earlier beliefs in the superiority of a centrally directed system over a competitive system and to console themselves with the hope that the "omnipresent, omniscient organ of the collective economy"[41] will possess at least as much knowledge as the individual entrepreneurs and will therefore be in a position to make the decisions at least

39. *Collectivist Economic Planning* (1935), pp. 232–37; see above, pp. 172–76.
40. D, p. 217. 41. D, p. 191.

as good if not better than that in which the entrepreneurs are now. As I have tried to show on another occasion, it is the main merit of real competition that through it use is made of knowledge divided between many persons which, if it were to be used in a centrally directed economy, would all have to enter the single plan.[42] To assume that all this knowledge would be automatically in the possession of the planning authority seems to me to miss the main point. It is not quite clear whether Lange means to assert that the planning authority will have all this information when he says that "the administrators of a socialist economy will have exactly the same knowledge, or lack of knowledge, of the production functions as the capitalist entrepreneurs have."[43] If the "administrators of a socialist economy" here means merely all the managers of the units as well as of the central organization taken together, the statement can, of course, be readily accepted but does in no way solve the problem. But, if it is intended to convey that all this knowledge can be effectively used by the planning authority in drawing up the plan, it is merely begging the whole question and seems to be based on the "fallacy of composition."[44]

On the whole of this all-important question of the direction of new investment and all that it involves, the two studies do not really give any new information. The problem remains where it was five years ago, and I can confine myself on this point to repeating what I said then: "The decision about the amount of capital to be given to an individual entrepreneur and the decisions thereby involved concerning the size of the individual firm under a single control are in effect decisions about the most appropriate combination of resources. It will rest with the central authority to decide whether one plant located

42. See the article on "Economics and Knowledge," reprinted above as chap. ii.
43. LT, p. 61.
44. Another and even worse instance of this fallacy occurs in Professor Lippincott's introduction to the essays of Professors Lange and Taylor, when he argues that "there can be no doubt that the Central Planning Board would exercise great power, but would it be any greater than that exercised collectively by private boards of directors? Because the decisions of private boards are made here and there, this does not mean that the consumer does not feel their collective impact, even though it may take a depression to make him aware of it."

at one place should expand rather than another plant situated elsewhere. All this involves planning on the part of the central authority on much the same scale as if it were actually running the enterprise. While the individual entrepreneur would in all probability be given some definite contractual tenure for managing the plant intrusted to him, all new investments will be necessarily centrally directed. This division in the disposition over the resources would then simply have the effect that neither the entrepreneur nor the central authority would be really in a position to plan and that it would be impossible to assess the responsibility for mistakes. To assume that it is possible to create conditions of full competition without making those who are responsible for the decisions pay for their mistakes seems to be pure illusion. It will be at best a system of quasi-competition where the persons really responsible will not be the entrepreneur but the official who approves his decisions and where in consequence all the difficulties will arise in connection with freedom of initiative and the assessment of responsibility which are usually associated with bureaucracy."[45]

9

The question of how far a socialist system can avoid extensive central direction of economic activity is of great importance quite apart from its relation to economic efficiency; it is crucial for the question of how much personal and political freedom can be preserved in such a system. Both authors show a reassuring awareness of the dangers to personal freedom which a centrally planned system would involve and seem to have evolved their competitive socialism partly in order to meet this danger. Dr. Dickinson even goes so far as to say that "capitalist planning can exist only on the basis of fascism" and that in the hands of an irresponsible controler even socialist planning "*could* be made the greatest tyranny the world has ever seen."[46] But

45. *Collectivist Economic Planning*, p. 237; see above, pp. 175–76.
46. D, pp. 22 and 227.

he and Lange believe that their competitive socialism will avoid this danger.

Now, if competitive socialism could really rely for the direction of production largely on the effects of consumers' choice as reflected in the price system, and if the cases where the authority will have to decide what is to be produced and how were made the exception rather than the rule, this claim would be to a large extent substantiated. How far is this really the case? We have already seen that, with the retention of the control over investment, the central authority wields most extensive powers over the direction of production—much more extensive, indeed, than is easily possible to show without making this discussion unduly long. To this have yet to be added, however, a further number of arbitrary elements of which Dickinson himself gives a quite substantial although by no means complete list.[47] There is, in the first instance, the "allocation of resources between present and future consumption," which, as we have already seen, always involves a decision about what particular needs will be satisfied and which needs will not be satisfied. There is, second, the need for arbitrary decision in respect to the "allocation of resources between communal and individual consumption," which, in view of the great extension of the "division of communal consumption" which he envisages, means that another very large part of the resources of the society is put outside the control of the price mechanism and made subject to purely authoritarian decision. Dickinson expressly adds to this only "the choice between work and leisure" and the "geographical planning and the pricing of land"; but at other points of his exposition further questions emerge on which he wants effective planning in order to correct the results of the market. But, although he (and still more so Lange) frequently hints at the possibilities of "correcting" the results of the price mechanism by judicious interference, this part of the program is nowhere clearly worked out.

What our authors here have in mind perhaps comes out clearest in Dickinson's attitude toward the problem of wage changes: "If wages

47. D, p. 205.

are too low in any one industry, it is the duty of the planning organ to adjust prices and quantities produced, so as to yield equal wages to work of equal skill, responsibility, and difficulty in every industry."[48] Apparently here the price mechanism and the free choice of occupation are not to be relied upon. Later we learn that, although "unemployment in any particular job affords a prima facie case for lowering the standard wage,"[49] a lowering of wages is objectionable "on social grounds, because a lowering in wages ... causes discontent; on economic grounds, because it perpetuates an uneconomic allocation of labor to different occupations." (How?) Therefore, "as invention and improved organization makes less labor necessary to satisfy human wants, society should set itself to discover new wants to satisfy."[50] "The powerful engine of propaganda and advertisement, employed by public organs of education and enlightenment instead of by the hucksters and panders of private profit-making industry, could divert demand into socially desirable directions while preserving the subjective impression [sic] of free choice."[51]

When we add to this, and many other similar points where Dickinson wants his S.E.C. to exercise a paternalistic control,[52] the fact that it will be necessary to co-ordinate national production "with a general plan of exports and imports,"[53] since free trade "is inconsistent with the principles of collectivism,"[54] it becomes fairly evident that there will be precious little economic activity which will not be more or less immediately guided by arbitrary decisions. In fact, Dickinson expressly contemplates a situation where "the state, through a definite planning organ, makes itself responsible for the consideration of economic activity as a whole" and even adds that this destroys the "illusion" maintained in a capitalist society that "the division of the product is governed by forces as impersonal and inevitable as those

48. D, p. 21. 50. D, p. 131.
49. D, p. 127. 51. D, p. 32.
52. Cf., e.g., the passage (D, p. 52) where Dickinson speaks about the "people who will not pay voluntarily beforehand for what they are only too glad to have once they have it."
53. D, p. 169. 54. D, p. 176.

which govern the weather."[55] This can mean only that, with most other planners, he himself thinks of production in his system as one which is largely directed by conscious and arbitrary decisions. Yet, in spite of this extensive role which arbitrary decisions are to play in his system, he is confident (and the same applies to Lange) that his system will not degenerate into an authoritarian despotism.

Dickinson merely mentions the argument that "even if a socialist planner wished to realize freedom he could not do so and remain a planner," yet the answer he gives makes one doubt whether he has quite seen on what considerations this argument is based. His answer is merely that "a plan can always be changed."[56] But this is not the point. The difficulty is that, in order to plan at all on an extensive scale, a much more extensive agreement among the members of the society about the relative importance of the various needs is required than will normally exist and that, in consequence, this agreement will have to be brought about and a common scale of values will have to be imposed by force and propaganda. I have developed this argument at length elsewhere, and I have not space here to restate it.[57] The thesis I have developed there—that socialism is bound to become totalitarian—now seems to receive support from the most unexpected quarters. This at least appears to be the meaning when Max Eastman, in a recent book on Russia, states that "Stalinism *is* socialism, in the sense of being an inevitable, although unforeseen, political and cultural accompaniment."[58]

In fact, although he does not seem to see it, Dickinson himself, in the concluding passages of his book, makes a statement which comes very much to the same thing. "In a socialist society," he says, "the distinction, always artificial, between economics and politics will break down; the economic and the political machinery of society will

55. D, p. 21.
56. D, pp. 227–28.
57. See *Freedom and the Economic System* ("Public Policy Pamphlet" No. 29 [Chicago: University of Chicago Press, 1939]) and, since this article first appeared, in *The Road to Serfdom* (Chicago, 1944).
58. *Stalin's Russia and the Crisis in Socialism* (New York, 1940).

fuse into one."[59] This is, of course, precisely the authoritarian doctrine preached by Nazis and Fascists. The distinction breaks down because in a planned system all economic questions become political questions, because it is no longer a question of reconciling as far as possible individual views and desires but one of imposing a single scale of values, the "social goal" of which socialists ever since the time of Saint-Simon have been dreaming. In this respect it seems that the schemes of an authoritarian socialist, from those of Professor Hogben and Lewis Mumford, whom Dickinson mentions as an example,[60] to those of Stalin and Hitler, are much more realistic and consistent than the beautiful and idyllic picture of the "libertarian socialism" in which Dickinson believes.

10

There can be no better testimony of the intellectual quality of the two books under discussion than that, after having written about them at such length, one is conscious of having merely scratched the surface of the problems raised by them. But an examination in greater detail would clearly exceed the scope of an article; and, since many of the doubts which are left with the reader concern points which are not answered in the two books, an adequate treatment of the subject would require another book even longer than those discussed. There are, however, also important problems which are discussed at some length, particularly in Dickinson's book, which we have scarcely been able to mention. This applies not only to the difficult problem of the combination of a private sector with the socialized sector, which both authors propose, but also to such important problems as the international relations of a socialist community and to the problems of monetary policy, to which Dickinson devotes a very brief, and on the whole least satisfactory, section.

A fuller discussion would also have to point out various passages in the argument of both authors where apparently residues of earlier

59. D, p. 235.   60. D, p. 25.

beliefs or views which are purely matters of political creed creep in and which strike one as curiously inconsistent with the plane of the rest of the discussion. This applies, for instance, to Dickinson's repeated references to class conflict and exploitation or to his gibes at the wastes of competition,[61] and to much of Lange's interesting section on the "economist's case for socialism," where he employs arguments that seem to be of somewhat questionable validity.

These, however, are minor points. On the whole, the books are so thoroughly unorthodox from a socialist point of view that one rather wonders whether their authors have not retained too little of the traditional trappings of socialist argument to make their proposals acceptable to socialists who are not economists. As courageous attempts to face some of the real difficulties and completely to remold socialist doctrine in order to meet them they deserve our gratitude and respect. Whether the solution offered will appear particularly practicable, even to socialists, may perhaps be doubted. To those who, with Dickinson, wish to create "for the first time in human history, an effective individualism,"[62] a different path will probably appear more promising.

61. D, pp. 22 and 94.   62. D, p. 26.

X. A Commodity Reserve Currency[*]

1

THE gold standard as we knew it undoubtedly had some grave defects. But there is some danger that the sweeping condemnation of it which is now the fashion may obscure the fact that it also had some important virtues which most of the alternatives lack. A wisely and impartially controlled system of managed currency for the whole world might, indeed, be superior to it in all respects. But this is not a practical proposition for a long while yet. Compared, however, with the various schemes for monetary management on a national scale, the gold standard had three very important advantages: it created in effect an international currency without submitting national monetary policy to the decisions of an international authority; it made monetary policy in a great measure automatic and thereby predictable; and the changes in the supply of basic money which its mechanism secured were on the whole in the right direction.

2

The importance of these advantages should not be lightly underestimated. The difficulties of a deliberate co-ordination of national policies are enormous, because our present knowledge gives us unambiguous guidance in only a few situations, and decisions in which nearly always some interests must be sacrificed to others will have to rest on subjective judgments. Unco-ordinated national policies, however, directed solely by the immediate interests of the individual countries, may in their aggregate effect on every country well be worse than the most imperfect international standard. Similarly, though the auto-

* Reprinted from the *Economic Journal*, LIII, No. 210 (June–September, 1943), 176–84.

matic operation of the gold standard is far from perfect, the mere fact that under the gold standard policy is guided by known rules, and that, in consequence, the action of the authorities can be foreseen, may well make the imperfect gold standard less disturbing than a more rational but less comprehensible policy. The general principle that the production of gold is stimulated when its value begins to rise and discouraged when its value falls is right at least in the direction, if not in the way in which it operates in practice.

It will be noticed that none of these points claimed in favor of the gold standard is directly connected with any property inherent to gold. Any internationally accepted standard based on a commodity whose value is regulated by its cost of production would possess essentially the same advantages. What in the past made gold the only substance on which in practice an international standard could be based was mainly the irrational, but no less real, factor of its prestige—or, if you will, of the ruling superstitious prejudice in favor of gold, which made it universally more acceptable than anything else. So long as this belief prevailed, it was possible to maintain an international currency based on gold without much design or deliberate organization to support it. But if it was prejudice which made the international gold standard possible, the existence of such a prejudice at least made an international money possible at a time when any international system based on explicit agreement and systematic co-operation was out of the question.

3

The decisive change which has occurred in recent times, and which has fundamentally altered our prospects and opportunities in this field, is the psychological one that the unreasoning prejudice in favor of gold, which gave gold what special advantage it possessed, has been gravely shaken—though perhaps not so much as many people imagine; that in many quarters it has even been replaced by an equally strong and unreasoned prejudice against gold; and that people generally are much more ready to consider rational alternatives. It is therefore important that we should seriously reconsider alternative systems which preserve the advantages of an automatic international standard with freedom from the special defects of gold. One such alternative in particular, which has recently been worked out in its practical detail by competent students of monetary problems, is of a kind which makes it appeal to many who in the past have defended the gold standard—not because they regarded it as ideal, but because it seemed to them superior to anything else which was practical politics.

Before describing this new proposal, it is necessary briefly to consider the real faults of the gold standard which we want to avoid. They are not mainly those which are most generally recognized. The much-discussed "vagaries" in the production of gold can easiy be exaggerated. The great increases in the supply of gold in the past have in fact occurred when a prolonged scarcity had created a real need for them. The really serious objection against gold is rather the slowness with which its supply adjusts itself to genuine changes in demand. A temporary increase in the general demand for highly liquid assets, or the adoption of the gold standard by a new country, was bound to cause great changes in the value of gold while the supply adjusted itself only slowly. By a sort of delay action the increased supplies often became available only when they were no longer needed. Not only did these new supplies thus tend to become an embarrassment rather than a relief, but the increase of the stock of gold in response to a temporary increase in demand remained permanent and provided the basis for an excessive expansion of credit as soon as the demand again fell.

This last point is closely connected with the one really paradoxical feature of the gold standard: namely, the fact that the striving of all individuals to become more liquid did not put society into a more liquid position at all. Yet there are times when the desire of the individuals to put themselves in a more liquid position expresses a real social need. There will always be periods in which increased uncertainty about the future will make it desirable that a larger portion of our assets should be given forms in which they can be readily converted to the needs of what are still unpredictable circumstances. A rational arrangement of our affairs would require that at such times production is in some measure switched from things of more restricted usefulness to the kind of things which will be needed in all conditions, such as the most widely used raw materials. The true irony of the gold standard is that under its rule a general increase in the desire for liquidity leads to the increase in the production of the one thing which can be used for practically no other purpose than to provide a liquidity reserve to individuals; and of a thing, moreover, which not only has few other uses but which can be supplied in increased quantity only so slowly that an increase in the demand for it will act much more on its value than on its quantity or, in other words, will cause a general fall in prices; while once the supply has increased and the demand again falls, the excess supply can be worked off only by a fall in its value or by a general rise of prices.

4

More rational schemes relying on the use of commodities other than gold have often been proposed, but so long as the universal prejudice was in favor of gold they were scarcely of practical interest. In the present situation, however, at least one of these proposals, recently elaborated in detail by two American scholars, deserves close attention for its successful combination of great theoretical and practical merits. Benjamin Graham, of New York, and Frank D. Graham, of Princeton, who had, unknown to each other, arrived at very similar ideas, have in recent years fully elaborated their proposal in a series of important publications.[1] Though at first their plan may appear strange and complicated, it is in fact very simple and eminently practical.

The basic idea is that currency should be issued solely in exchange

1. See particularly Benjamin Graham, *Storage and Stability* (New York: McGraw-Hill Book Co., 1937), and Frank D. Graham, *Social Goals and Economic Institutions* (Princeton: Princeton University Press, 1942). An almost identical proposal had been made earlier by the Dutch economist, Professor J. Goudrian, in a pamphlet, *How To Stop Deflation* (London, 1932), which I had not seen at the time of writing the above article. Benjamin Graham has since further elaborated his proposals in a book, *World Commodities and World Currency* (New York: McGraw-Hill Book Co., 1945).

212

A Commodity Reserve Currency

against a fixed combination of warehouse warrants for a number of storable raw commodities and be redeemable in the same "commodity unit." For example, £100, instead of being defined as so-and-so many ounces of gold, would be defined as so much wheat, *plus* so much sugar, *plus* so much copper, *plus* so much rubber, etc. Since money would be issued only against the complete collection of all the raw commodities in their proper physical quantities (twenty-four different commodities in Benjamin Graham's plan), and since money would also be redeemable in the same manner, the aggregate price of this collection of commodities would be fixed, but only the aggregate price and not the price of any one of them. In this respect the different commodities would be connected with money not in the way in which gold and silver were connected with it under bimetallism, so that a unit of money was obtainable *either* for a fixed quantity of gold *or* for a fixed quantity of silver; but rather as if (according to the plan suggested by Alfred Marshall under the name of "symmetallism") only the price of a certain weight of gold and a certain weight of silver together were fixed, but the price of each metal by itself was allowed to fluctuate.

With this system in operation an increase in the demand for liquid assets would lead to the accumulation of stocks of raw commodities of the most general usefulness. The hoarding of money, instead of causing resources to run to waste, would act as if it were an order to keep raw commodities for the hoarder's account. As the hoarded money was again returned to circulation, and demand for commodities increased, these stocks would be released to satisfy the new demand. Since the collection of commodities could always be exchanged against a fixed sum of money, its aggregate price could never fall below that figure; and, since money would be redeemable at the same (or an only slightly different) rate, their aggregate price could never rise above that figure. In this respect the aim of the proposal is similar to that of the "tabular standard" or the "index currencies," which were at one time much discussed. But it differs from them in its direct and automatic operation. It is at least doubtful whether the price level of any selection of commodities could be effectively kept constant by deliberate adjustments of the quantity of money. But there can be no doubt that the aggregate price of the selected raw commodities could not vary so long as the monetary authority stood ready to sell and buy the commodity unit at a fixed price.

As proposed by its American protagonists, the plan is designed primarily for adoption on a national scale by the United States. The arguments in its favor apply, however, no less to other countries. As the adoption of the plan by several countries, who based it, however, on different collections of commodities, would produce a new cause of serious instability, it would appear that the plan not only could but, to achieve its ends, ought to be adopted internationally—or, what comes in practice to the same thing, that it ought to be operated on the same principle by all the major countries. The particular collection of raw commodities on which Benjamin Graham's scheme is based (five grains, four fats and oilseeds, three other foodstuffs, four metals, three textile fibers, tobacco, hides, rubber, and petroleum) and certain other details would have to be modified; but the principle raises no serious difficulties to international application. In the following outline of the way in which the scheme would operate it will be assumed that commodity units of the same composition are adopted as the basis of currency at least in the British Empire and the United States.

5

For reasons which will presently appear, the plan is most easily put into operation when a fall of demand threatens. It can be made automatically to come into effect at such a time by fixing beforehand a buying price for the commodity unit slightly below the ruling market value. Once the demand for raw commodities then begins to slacken and their prices to fall, the monetary authorities of the participating countries will be offered any commodity units which cannot be disposed in the market at the fixed price. Their purchases will make up for the fall of the industrial demand—and for every amount of money that is being accumulated in private hands a corresponding amount of raw commodities is accumulated in the warehouses. The demand for raw commodities in general is thus maintained—but only the demand for the group as a whole and not that for any particular commodity, the output of which may well be excessive and in need of curtailment.

It will be readily seen how the operation of the scheme would tend to stabilize the demand for raw commodities. As in the past gold-mining used to be the only industry that regularly prospered during periods of depression, so the producers of raw commodities might under this plan enjoy in the same circumstances even a moderate increase in prosperity through being able to exchange their products at more favorable terms against manufactures. But while gold-mining is far too small an industry for its prosperity to have significant effects outside it, the secure income of the producers of raw commodities would also go far to stabilize the demand for manufactures and to prevent the depression from becoming serious. The benefit would indeed not be confined to the producers of the commodities included in the commodity unit. Even a country in which none of these commodities was produced would gain from its operation hardly less than the others. So long as it stood ready to buy commodity units at a fixed price in its national currency, any money thus issued to the producers of raw commodities would be of no use to them except for buying the products of the country to which they had sold their raw produce.

6

At first it may appear as if the operation of the plan might create the danger of serious inflationary expansion. But on examination it proves that its effect could not be really inflationary in any significant sense of that word; whatever monetary expansion it would permit could hardly lead either to a general rise of prices or to that shortage of consumers' goods through which the most harmful effects of inflation operate. It is, in fact, one of the great merits of the scheme that it provides an automatic check to any expansion before it can become dangerous. We have considered its operation during a depression first, because its effectiveness during a boom depends on the previous accumulation of commodity stocks such as would take place during a period of slackening activity. The manner in which the scheme would operate while an improvement in the general outlook leads to a mobilization of the idle cash reserves is, however, no less important.

The aggregate price of the raw commodities making up the commodity unit could not rise so long as the monetary authorities are able to sell from their stocks at the fixed figure. Instead of a rise in prices and a consequent increase in output as demand increased, and *pari passu* with the return into circulation of the accumulated money hoards, raw commodities would be released from the stocks and the money received for them impounded. The savings made by individuals in the form of cash during the slack period would not have run to waste but would be waiting in the form of raw commodities ready to be used. In consequence, the revival of activity will not lead to an extra stimulus to the production of raw commodities which would continue on an even keel. There is reason to regard the temporary stimulus to an excessive expansion of the production to raw commodities, which used to be given by the sharp rise of their prices in boom periods, as one of the most serious causes of general instability. This would be entirely avoided under the proposed scheme—at least so long as the monetary authority had any stocks from which to sell. But since it would necessarily possess sufficient reserves to redeem all the extra cash accumulated during the period of slackness (and considerably more if the commodity stocks held by governments at the initiation of the scheme were brought in), the boom would almost certainly be damped down by the contraction of the circulation before the reserves are exhausted.

7

As has been remarked before, the scheme *sounds* complicated, but is, in fact, exceedingly simple to operate. There would, in particular, be no need for the monetary authorities or the government in any way directly to handle the many commodities of which the commodity unit is composed. Both the bringing-together of the required assortment of warrants and the actual storing of the commodities could be safely left to private initiative. Specialist brokers would soon take care of the collecting and tendering of warrants as soon as their aggregate market price fell ever so little below the standard figure and of withdrawing and redistributing the warrants to their various markets if their aggregate price rose above that figure. In this respect the business of the monetary authority would be as mechanical as the buying and selling of gold under the gold standard.

This is not to say that the proposal does not raise numerous problems, which cannot be fully discussed in this short outline. At least the more important of these problems have been considered and practicable solutions suggested in the publications already referred to. To mention only a few of these points: the cost of the physical storage of the commodities could be defrayed out of the difference between the prices at which the monetary authority buys and sells commodity units. (It should be noticed that the cost of storage would not include any interest charge, because the loss of interest would be voluntarily borne by the holders of the money issued against the commodities.) The problems raised by the composition of the commodity unit and the periodical changes in it which will become necessary can also be solved by the adoption of an objective principle which would lift it out of the sphere of political wrangle. Similarly the problems of the differences of quality and distinctions according to the place of storage and the like do not raise insuperable difficulties. It should be remembered in this connection that for the purposes of the plan the inclusion of the most important variety of any commodity would have nearly the same effect on the prices of its close substitutes as if they were themselves included.

Two special points must, however, be mentioned even in so brief a survey. The first is the important feature of the plan that the monetary authority shall be empowered in precisely defined circumstances to accept in place of (or substitute for) warrants for stored commodi-

217

ties contracts for future delivery of any commodity. This meets the difficulties which would otherwise be caused by a temporary shortage of any one commodity included in the unit and makes it possible to use the reserves for some measure of stabilization even of individual commodity prices. This would be achieved, for example, by substituting "futures" for present commodities whenever the current price rose by more than a fixed percentage over the "future" price.

The second point is that, if it were wished to preserve the value of gold or to prevent a too rapid decline of it, it would not be difficult to link up the value of gold in such a way with the commodity scheme that, though gold would have no significant effect on the value of money, the value of gold would be stabilized at the same time with the value of money. Whether this is desirable in view of the interest whole nations have in the preservation of the value of gold, and whether it ought to be used to maintain the production of gold indefinitely near its present level or rather to bring about a gradual but predictable decline of the resources devoted to it, is a political problem we need not consider here. The important point is merely that there are many ways in which gold could be linked with the new scheme if desired without thereby impairing the advantages of the scheme.

It is probably true to·say that all the rational arguments which can be advanced in favor of the gold standard apply even more strongly to this proposal, which is at the same time free from most of the defects of the former. In judging the feasibility of the plan, it must, however, not be regarded solely as a scheme for currency reform. It must be borne in mind that the accumulation of commodity reserves is certain to remain part of national policy and that political considerations render it unlikely that the markets for raw commodities will in any future for which we can now plan be left entirely to themselves. All plans aiming at the direct control of the prices of particular commodities are, however, open to the most serious objections and certain to cause grave economic and political difficulties. Even apart from monetary consideration, the great need is for a system under which these controls are taken from the separate bodies which can but act in what is essentially an arbitrary and unpredictable manner and to make the controls instead subject to a mechanical and predictable rule. If this can be combined with the reconstruction of an international monetary system which would once more secure to the world stable international currency relations and a greater freedom in the movement of raw commodities, a great step would have been taken in the direction toward a more prosperous and stable world economy.

XI. The Ricardo Effect *

Machinery and labour are in constant competition, and the former can frequently not be employed until labour rises.—DAVID RICARDO.

1

WHEN in a recent essay on industrial fluctuations the author introduced "the familiar Ricardian proposition that a rise in wages will encourage capitalists to substitute machinery for labour,"[1] this was done under the illusion that thus an argument he had long employed could be stated in a more familiar and readily acceptable form. That illusion has been dispelled by the various comments on that essay;[2] and a re-examination of the earlier literature on the subject has revealed a rather peculiar situation: while the proposition has been supported and used by numerous writers ever since it was first enounced by Ricardo,[3] it seems never to have been adequately expounded. In particular, although it is fundamental to the discussions of interest in the works of Böhm-Bawerk, Wicksell, and Mises, none of these authors develops it at any length. The frequent brief references to it in other general theoretical works in modern times,[4] which seemed to confirm the impression that it was widely accepted, prove

* Reprinted from *Economica*, IX, No. 34 (new ser.; May, 1942), 127–52.

1. *Profits, Interest, and Investment* (1939); cf. also *The Pure Theory of Capital* (1941), chap. xxvii.
2. Cf. particularly the review of *Profits, Interest, and Investment*, by H. Townsend in the *Economic Journal*, March, 1940, and T. Wilson, "Capital Theory and the Trade Cycle," *Review of Economic Studies*, June, 1940. I have not been able to see C. Welinder, "Hayek och 'Ricardoeffekten,' " *Ekonomisk Tidskrift*, March, 1940.
3. The relevant passages of Ricardo's *Principles* will be found mainly in *Works*, ed. McCulloch, pp. 26 and 241.
4. E.g., N. G. Pierson, *Principles of Economics*, I (1902), 219, 308; G. Cassel, *The Nature and Necessity of Interest* (1903), p. 116: "Supposing the rate of interest to be constant, the more expensive labor becomes, the greater will be the substitution of waiting for it"; F. A. Fetter, *Economic Principles* (1915), p. 340; H. R. Seager, *Principles of Economics* (2d ed., 1917), pp. 278, 289; R. G. Hawtrey, *The Economic Problem* (1926), pp. 324 ff.; see also H. G. Hayes, "The Rate of Wages and the Use of

on examination not only to be inadequate but often to be based on faulty reasoning. Although it used to be treated as a commonplace in realistic studies of the influence of high wages on the use of machinery, there, too, we search in vain for a reasoned argument.[5] The relatively fullest discussion in recent times is to be found in some German publications.[6] But when in England a few years ago Professor Hicks made use of the proposition in a chapter of his *Theory of Wages*, Mr. Shove in his review of that work produced what has become the standard reply—that, as long as the rate of interest is unchanged, a general change in wages will affect the cost of production of the different methods of production in the same proportion (which is undeniable) and that, therefore, it cannot alter their relative advantages (which does not follow);[7] and Professor Hicks's later withdrawal of the whole chapter in which occurred the passage criticized seemed to imply that he abandoned the contention.[8] Still more recently Mr. Kaldor, in an article to which we shall have to refer later, while admitting the principle, seemed to restrict its significance to rather special conditions.[9]

Machinery," and C. O. Fisher, "An Issue in Economic Theory: The Rate of Wages and the Use of Machinery," in *American Economic Review*, 1923, a particularly characteristic discussion in which a faulty presentation of the argument by the first author was easily demolished by the second.

5. E.g., G. von Schulze-Gaevernitz, *Der Grossbetrieb* (1892); J. Schœnhof, *The Economy of High Wages* (1893), pp. 33, 279; L. Brentano, *Hours and Wages in Their Relation to Production* (1894); and J. A. Hobson, *The Evolution of Modern Capitalism* (1894), p. 81.

6. See particularly H. Neisser, "Lohnhöhe und Beschäftigungsgrad im Marktgleichgewicht," *Weltwirtschaftliches Archiv*, Vol. XXXVI (October, 1932); and A. Kähler, *Die Theorie der Arbeiterfreisetzung durch die Maschine* (Leipzig, 1933), pp. 75 ff. I should perhaps add that it is partly due to Professor Neisser that I was confirmed in the belief that the proposition was generally accepted; since when, about the same time as his article appeared, I got (in an article in the same journal) badly mixed up on the point, it was he who promptly caught me out and orally pointed out to me the confusion.

7. J. R. Hicks, *The Theory of Wages* (1932), chap. ix, and G. F. Shove's review in *Economic Journal*, XLIII (September, 1933), 471.

8. J. R. Hicks, "Wages and Interest: The Dynamic Problem," *Economic Journal*, Vol. XLV (September, 1935).

9. N. Kaldor, "Capital Intensity and the Trade Cycle, *Economica*, Vol. VI, No. 21 (new ser.; February, 1939); cf. also his "Annual Survey of Economic Theory: The Recent Controversy on the Theory of Capital," *Econometrica*, Vol. V, No. 3 (July, 1937).

Individualism and Economic Order

The proposition in question is of importance far beyond the special context in which it has been used in recent discussions. It is not surprising that those who completely reject it seem at the same time to be unable to attach any meaning to the conception of a given and limited supply of real capital[10] because it is through this effect that the scarcity of real capital will make itself ultimately felt, however much the rate of interest may be affected by purely monetary factors, and that the volume of investment must ultimately be adjusted to a level compatible with the demand for consumers' goods. The proposition thus is an essential part of the elementary theory of production. If this is true, the lack of agreement on it would go far to explain the sharp and apparently irreconcilable conflict of economists on the more complex problems of industrial fluctuations, and an attempt at a fuller statement of the argument on which the proposition is based seems to be urgently needed.

Such a statement will be attempted here in terms which should make it as far as possible independent of disputed points of the theory of capital, and without direct application to the problems of industrial

10. As I have attempted to show elsewhere (*Pure Theory of Capital*, esp. p. 147), the only adequate description of this "supply of capital" is a complete enumeration of the range of possible output streams of different time shapes that can be produced from the existing resources. Which of these different output streams will be produced depends in the first instance on what may be called the "rate of employment" (i.e., the rate at which people will be employed at successive moments of time during the period in question) and on the form that employment will take, factors which in turn depend on final demand, the level of money wages, and the result of these, the relation of money wages to the prices of the products. There will, as a rule, be only one output stream which in its production will generate an income stream of such size and time shape that the part of that income which at any time will be spent on consumers' goods will just equal the cost of the current output of consumers' goods, inclusive of that rate of return on capital in the expectation of which the method of production actually employed has been decided upon.

It was the fatal mistake of Böhm-Bawerk (and to much less an extent of Wicksell) that, although he was quite aware that the existing stock of capital goods was capable of producing more than one single output stream, he attempted to simplify his exposition by identifying the stock of capital goods with a definite quantity of consumers' goods and to represent this in his illustrations by a fixed amount of available money capital. The analysis of the famous final chapter on "The Market for Capital in Its Full Development" of the *Positive Theory* makes perfect sense if we remember this simplification but must seem to have no relevance to anything in the real world to anyone who takes literally the representation of the supply of capital by a sum of money.

fluctuations beyond (1) a general stress on short-run rather than long-run effects, and (2) concentration on the effect of a fall rather than a rise of wages relative to product prices, because it is in this form that the principle seems to be particularly relevant for the exploration of industrial crises. In order to separate the various parts of the argument, the problem will be approached in stages. The next section will be devoted to an explanation of the concepts used and an exposition of the general principle on assumptions which will enable us to disregard the money rate of interest. After the general principle has thus been established, the concrete ways in which it is likely to affect investment demand will be discussed in Section 3. The interplay between the Ricardo effect and the rate of interest on money loans will be taken up in Section 4 and will be discussed first on assumptions concerning the supply of credit which are approximately true of the real world. In Sections 5 and 6 the same problem will be considered on the assumption of a "perfectly elastic supply of credit," which, though highly unrealistic, raises theoretical problems of considerable interest. In a final section will be added a few considerations which have to be taken into account in any attempt at statistical verification of the theorem.

2

The proposition here described as the Ricardo effect asserts that a general change in wages relative to the prices of the products will alter the relative profitability of different industries or methods of production which employ labor and capital ("indirect labor") in different proportions. In its original form it asserts that a general rise in wages relative to the prices of the products will not reduce the profitability of the industries or methods employing relatively more capital to the same extent as those employing relatively less capital. We are here more particularly concerned with the inverse of this, namely, with the proposition that a general fall in wages relative to product prices will have the opposite effect.[11]

11. As a result of a criticism of this article in the proof stage by G. F. Shove, I am no longer so sure that the establishment of the truth of the proposition in the inverse form also proves the correctness of the original proposition.

A general change in the relationships between wages and product prices may be caused by a general change in product prices, by a general change in wages, or by a change in technical knowledge or the physical quantities of other factors available which change the productivity of labor. While any of these changes may serve for our purpose as the independent variable, we must, of course, not treat in the same way changes in the productivity of labor which are the consequence of variations in the proportion between capital and labor employed, since this is the dependent variable of our problem.

The particular kind of change on which we shall here illustrate the proposition will be a general rise in the prices of final products (or consumers' goods, henceforth briefly referred to as "commodities") while money wages are assumed to remain constant (and thus to fall *relatively* to commodity prices). We shall assume this rise of prices to be due to an increase of demand, caused by a growth of incomes earned from producing investment goods, and exceeding the amount beyond which the output of commodities can be readily increased. We shall further assume that entrepreneurs expect commodity prices to remain at least for some considerable time at the new higher level. No assumption will be made concerning any change in the price of capital goods, this being part of our problem.

The assumption of a general rise in the prices of commodities while wages remain unchanged means, of course, that *all* wages fall relative to commodity prices. It is important to emphasize this because the theorem has often been misunderstood to refer to a situation where only the wages of labor co-operating with machinery change relative to prices, while the wages used in the production of machinery remain unaffected.[12] It should be at once admitted that, with such a general change in the wage level relative to final prices, the costs of producing final goods by different methods must, if we assume a uniform rate of interest, be changed in the same proportion. Our con-

12. While many later authors were confused on this point, Ricardo clearly assumed a general change in wages; the starting-point of his brief discussion of the whole problem is the question whether, if wages rose by 10 per cent, "will not machinery rise in price" to the same extent? See *Works*, ed. McCulloch, p. 26.

The Ricardo Effect

tention is that nevertheless the attractiveness of investing in different industries or methods of production will be affected differently.

In order to exclude, for the purpose of the present section, any influence exercised by the money rate of interest, we shall assume for the time being that there is no lending of money of any kind during the period with which we are concerned: entrepreneurs either owning all the capital they employ and being effectively prevented from lending any of it, or being limited by a strict rationing of credit. We shall assume, however, that before the rise in commodity prices occurred, the rates of return on capital had been the same in all the firms. By excluding any consideration of the rate of interest in discussing the effects of the changes in commodity prices, we are, for the moment, deliberately avoiding what will later become our main problem. This temporary shelving of the central issue will, however, help us to isolate the more elementary parts of the argument which seem still to need explicit statement.

Our present problem thus is how, with unchanged wages, the rise in commodity prices will affect the current distribution of the funds at the command of the entrepreneurs between expenditure on wages (or investment in "circulating capital") and expenditure on machinery (investment in "fixed capital"). To avoid complications arising from changes in the prices of raw materials, etc., which I have discussed elsewhere,[13] we can assume that the firms with which we are concerned are all of the type represented by a brickyard on marginal land in which the labor employed produces not only all the raw material but also the fuel.

It remains to introduce an unambiguous and, so far as possible, uncontroversial measure of the proportions in which capital and labor are combined in the various firms and possible methods of production. For the purpose in hand, the most convenient measure which has also the advantage of being familiar to businessmen, is the concept of the "rate of turnover," applied either to the whole or to any part of the capital of a firm. That some firms can expect to "turn over" their

13. *Profits, Interest, and Investment*, pp. 29 ff.

capital (i.e., to reinvest out of current receipts an amount equal to their capital) once in two months, while others can expect to do so only once in five or even ten years, and that this rate of turnover depends, at least in part,[14] on the nature of the business and the character of the methods adopted is a familiar fact. Similarly, it will also be true that within any given firm some parts of its assets will be "turned over," or wholly turned into cash and reinvested, twelve times a year, while others may be thus completely amortized and replaced only once in twenty years. The "rate of turnover" expresses (as an integer or fraction) the number of times the capital is turned over in the course of one year. As it will be convenient to have an adjective describing firms or methods with a relatively high or relatively low rate of turnover, we shall, for reasons which will be obvious, occasionally employ the technical term "more capitalistic" for firms or methods with a relatively low rate of turnover, and "less capitalistic" for firms or methods with a relatively high method of turnover.

The concept of the rate of turnover of capital provides a specially useful starting-point for our discussion, because changes in the wage-price relationship will evidently in the first instance affect the gain made each time the product of a given expenditure can be sold. As long as the prices of commodities remain high relative to costs, the difference will be a source of a given proportional profit on the capital every time the capital is turned over, and any given rise in product prices relative to costs will enable entrepreneurs to make higher profits *per unit of time* from their given capital according as they are able to turn over their capital more frequently.

14. The rate of turnover depends, of course, not only on the nature of the business and on the technical methods adopted but also (apart from the "state of trade") on the skill and success of the entrepreneur. The entrepreneur who in the same trade and with the same technical methods can make a given amount of capital go further than his marginal colleague will unquestionably derive from this skill a differential profit; but this does not alter the fact, to be discussed presently, that entrepreneurs of the same skill, in different trades and with different technical methods, will have to earn different profit margins on each turnover in order to earn the same rate of return on their capital. It is well known, e.g., that a secondhand bookseller, because his rate of turnover is very much smaller than that of a dealer in new books, will have to earn a much larger percentage on each book sold than the latter.

The Ricardo Effect

In the situation of long-period equilibrium which we assume to have existed before prices rose, a situation in which the rate of return on capital will be the same for all firms, the relation between the rate of turnover and the proportional gain on each turnover is very simple. In order to avoid the ambiguous term "profit," we shall henceforth employ the following terms: (1) The per annum net percentage return on the whole capital of a firm (or on any part of it for which we find it necessary to compute it separately), net of "wages of management" and of risk premium, we shall designate as the "internal rate of return."[15] In the position of long-term equilibrium to which we have just referred, these internal rates of return will be the same for all firms and each part of the capital of any firm. (2) The proportional gain on each sale, and therefore on the capital at each turnover, expressed in percentage, we shall designate as the "profit margin." When it is remembered that the rate of turnover expresses the number of times total sales (or rather the costs of the products sold in a year) exceed the value of the capital of the firm, it is clear that, if the internal rate of return is to be uniform for all firms, profit margins will have to vary inversely with the rates of turnover. Thus, if we call the internal rate of return I, the rate of turnover T, and the profit margin M, the relationship will be represented by

$$I = TM \qquad \text{or} \qquad M = \frac{I}{T}.$$

If, for example, the internal rate is 6 per cent, the profit margin of a firm turning over its capital six times a year will have to be 1 per cent, while a firm turning over its capital only once in two years will have to earn 12 per cent on all sales, and a firm turning over its capital only once in every ten years will have to earn a profit margin of 60 per cent.[16]

15. The term "internal rate of return" is borrowed from K. E. Boulding, "The Theory of a Single Investment," *Quarterly Journal of Economics*, XLIX (May, 1935), 478 ff. Its German equivalent (more precisely the term "innerer Zinssatz") has been used earlier, I believe in discussions of the effects of credit rationing, but I cannot now recollect when or by whom.

16. To simplify calculations, compound interest is disregarded throughout.

How will these internal rates of return of the different firms be affected by a general rise of prices of, say, 5 per cent? As such a rise means a proportional increase of the receipts from the sale of any quantity of commodities, the cost of production of which is unchanged, it will mean a clear addition to the profit margins earned on each turnover equal to the amount of the rise. For the three firms which we have just considered by way of illustration, the first (with an annual rate of turnover $T = 6$) will find its profit margin increased from 1 to 6 per cent; the second (with $T = 1$) from 6 to 11 per cent; and the third (with $T = 1/10$) from 60 to 65 per cent. Multiplying these profit margins by the corresponding rates of turnover, we obtain the new internal rates of return of $6 \times 6 = 36$ per cent for the first, $1 \times 11 = 11$ per cent for the second, and $1/10 \times 65 = 6.5$ per cent for the third firm.[17]

In the circumstances assumed these differences of the internal rates of return of the different firms cannot, in the short run, bring about any change in the capital at their disposal (beyond any reinvestment of profits)—although the effect these differences would have in the real world on the distribution of capital between the firms will be readily seen. Let us therefore turn from the differences between the effects on the return of the different firms to the differences between the effects of the same change on the rate of return on the different parts of the capital of any one firm. The concept of separate and ascertainable rates of turnover of, and rates of return on, different parts of the capital of any firm (certainly known, although probably never precisely determined in practice) depends on the possibility of ascertaining the marginal contribution to the product of the different parts of the capital; and this, in turn, depends in the familiar manner on the possibility of varying the proportions in which the different forms of capital are combined. We shall in the next section explain why we think that in the relevant sense this variability is fairly high,

17. These figures show, of course, the impact effect of the rise of prices on the profits of the different firms and will be changed by the adjustments in the composition of their capital, which we are going to discuss.

even in the short run. For the present we shall proceed on the assumption that this is so and that we are consequently in a position to determine the rate of turnover as well as the marginal product of, and therefore the profit margin earned on, any part of the capital of the firms.[18]

We can use for the purpose of this analysis the same numerical illustration which we have just used in connection with different firms; that is, we can assume that, for the major component parts of the capital of the particular firm which we now consider, the rates of turnover are 6 for the sums invested in current wages, 1 for the operating parts of the machine tools, etc., and 1/10 for the heavier machinery, buildings, etc. We shall again assume that after a uniform internal rate of return of 6 per cent had been established, product prices rise by 5 per cent and that in consequence the internal rates of return earned on the different kinds of capital rise as before to 36 per cent, 11 per cent, and 6.5 per cent, respectively. This can clearly be only a temporary position if the proportions between the forms of capital with different rates of turnover can be varied. It will now pay to redistribute current outlay so as to increase investment in capital with a high rate of turnover and to reduce investment in capital with a low rate of turnover. This change will be continued until the expected rates of return are once more the same on all forms of investment, and current investment will continue in this new form so long as the same conditions prevail, until ultimately all the capital of the firm has been

18. Dr. Hawtrey, in his review of my *Pure Theory of Capital* (*Economic Journal*, June–September, 1941, p. 286) attempts to draw a distinction between the measurement of the yield of any investment in terms of "net cost saving capacity" and in terms of its marginal contribution to final output and asserts that, while the former will be regularly possible, the latter will be possible only in exceptional cases. But these two approaches are surely merey different aspects of the same thing, and neither seems to be more likely to be useful than the other: the difference between them is merely that in the first instance we assume the proportions between the different factors to be so adjusted as to leave output constant, while in the second we assume the quantity of all the resources except one to be constant and observe the effects of the change in the one on the quantity of output. Or, in other words, the first approach is in terms of movements along an equiproduct curve and changes in the marginal rates of substitution between the factors, while the second is in terms of movements parallel to the axes of the same diagram and of the consequent changes in the marginal product.

adapted to the new conditions. As a result, a new and once more uniform internal rate of return for the firm will be established somewhere between the extremes of 6.5 and 36 per cent, and at this new rate of return the total yield that can be earned from the limited resources of the firm (augmented only by any reinvested extra profits) will have reached its maximum.

Although once more uniform for any one firm, the internal rates of return will, however, remain different for different industries and (to a lesser extent) different firms in the same industry. Where the internal rate will be fixed for any one firm will depend on the original composition of the capital of the firm and on the degree to which costs will be raised by any transition to less capitalistic methods. But, generally speaking, the rates of return will remain higher in the industries which, because of the nature of their product, need relatively less capital, and lower in the industries which need relatively more capital, although both kinds of industries will tend to change so far as possible to less capitalistic methods of production.[19]

19. It has been argued (by Wilson in the article quoted before) that the numerical illustrations I have again employed in the preceding argument are misleading because under modern conditions the practical choice is not between capital lasting a few months and other capital lasting one or two years, but between various kinds of machinery all lasting many years, and that as between them the difference in the rates of return caused by changes in product prices is so small as to be negligible. It is perfectly true that, e.g., in our illustration, where the return on capital with a rate of turnover of 1/10 is raised from 6 to 6.5 per cent, the rate of return on capital with a rate of turnover of 1/12 would be raised from 6 to 6.417 per cent—a difference which is indeed insignificant. But this objection entirely misses the point of the argument. It is based on a confusion, owing, presumably, to the verbal similarity of two different statements. It is true that the new, more durable (or more laborsaving) machine will replace a less durable or less laborsaving machine. But it does so in a sense different from that in which it can be said that the additional capital displaces other factors. The extra capital, the extra amount that is invested in the new, more expensive (because more durable or more laborsaving) machine, above what would be necessary to replace the old machine by an identical one, is not destined to replace the old machine. There would be no point in this. It is destined to save further costs, to reduce the amount of other factors required, and it is with the return on capital invested in these other factors for which the extra capital is substituted with which its return must be compared. Slightly simplifying, we can say that the extra capital invested in the machine is used to displace more *labor* by making the machine more durable, with the result that the additional investment in the machine will displace more labor than would have been true of the amounts invested in less durable machinery (because, at any positive rate of

The Ricardo Effect

3

Before going further, it will be advisable to consider briefly the probable quantitative significance in the short run of the phenomenon considered. The belief has been expressed, and appears to be widely held, that although the argument may be correct, the practical importance of the effect in question could only be small. Although it would be convenient to postpone these considerations of a more concrete kind until the theoretical argument is complete, it is probably as well to forestall a feeling of impatience on the part of the reader who may feel that all this lengthy argument is wasted on a point the practical significance of which, even if proved, would be negligible.

This widely held belief seems, however, to be based on a misconception. Of course, the proportion in which fixed capital and circulating capital (or more and less durable or laborsaving machinery) are used in production can be changed only gradually and slowly over a long period of time. But this is not the point. We are interested not in the proportions between the existing *stocks* of fixed capital and circulating capital but in the relative rates at which firms will spend their current outlay on renewing (or adding to) the two kinds of capital assets. Here both common experience and general considerations suggest that this proportion is highly variable in the short run.

The mistaken impression is probably caused by the kind of illustrations of the transition from less to more capitalistic methods common-

---

interest, it will be profitable to make machines more durable only if their life is increased more than in proportion to the extra expenditure); or that it is used to make the machine more laborsaving, in which case it is even more evident that the additional capital is substituted not for other machines but for current labor. By comparing (in the illustration to which Wilson objected) the effects of a price rise on a two years' investment with that on investments for a few months, I was understating my case, and what appeared to be true on these assumptions must be a fortiori true of the more realistic situations where machinery that will last ten or even twenty years is introduced to save current labor.

It remains true, of course, that if we compute the rate of turnover (or the "average period of investment") and the rate of return for the whole of the capital of a firm, the changes in either will be small. But the point is precisely that at any moment the decision has *not* to be made for the whole of the capital and that the alternative gains to be made on the sums currently to be reinvested will differ very considerably, absolutely, as well as expressed as percentages of these amounts currently to be reinvested.

ly used in textbooks and describing alternative positions of long-term equilibrium. The familiar instances of "changes in the method of production" through replacement of all machines by those of another kind, of less durable by more durable, of less laborsaving by more laborsaving machinery, or of processes which are altogether shorter by processes which are altogether longer, stress an aspect which would indeed seem to be relatively unimportant in the short run. To realize how the same tendency operates no less strongly in the short run, we must overcome our prepossession with the "comparative statics" of the textbook and try to think more realistically of the concrete decision which entrepreneurs will continuously have to make.

Within limited space we can illustrate this only by selected examples. But they will, I hope, show the width of the range of variations possible in the very short run.

We have to think of entrepreneurs equipped at any given moment with a given stock of durable machinery of which only a small part needs replacement during any short period of time. If conditions had remained what they had been, they would have continued period after period to invest their earned depreciation allowances in machinery of the same kind. But they will do so merely because this would be the most profitable method of using their funds, and we must not assume that they will continue to do so after conditions have changed. Particularly when demand increases there will be any number of possible ways of increasing output other than by multiplying machinery of the kind they have been using before. If they cannot borrow so as to bring their internal rate down to the former level, some of these will appear more profitable than those used before.

There will be mainly two kinds of changes which will now appear advantageous: an entrepreneur may use his existing machinery more intensively (i.e., with more labor)—employing for this purpose part of the funds which would have otherwise been invested to replace the machinery by new machines of the same kind—or he may replace those machines that wear out by a larger number of cheaper ones. Both of these methods will probably be resorted to, although the first is probably the more important one.

The Ricardo Effect

The obvious methods of quickly increasing output as commodity prices rise is to work overtime, to introduce double or treble shifts, to provide extra assistance to relieve the workers on the existing machines from ancillary operations, etc. This will normally raise labor costs per unit of output, and this fact will have prevented these devices from being used before prices had risen. But if the adoption of any of these methods increases marginal labor cost per unit of output by, say, 4 per cent,[20] this would, with a 5 per cent rise in prices, still leave an extra profit of 1 per cent, which, with a rate of turnover of 6, would make the internal rate of return on this form of investment still 12 per cent compared with the 6.5 per cent on the machine with a rate of turnover of 1/10. This more expensive method of production will therefore now become the one through which, with the limited resources at the disposal of the entrepreneur, the largest profits can be realized; and the labor co-operating with the machinery will be increased until the fall of the return on funds invested in more labor and the rise of returns on funds invested in machines make the two rates of return once more equal at an intermediate figure.

The kinds of changes in the machinery used which have to be taken into account even in the short run will be equally numerous and will also all have the effect of raising marginal costs. There will, in the first instance, be the possibility of less perfect maintenance and attention, makeshift instead of thorough repairs, shorter or fewer periods of laying off for inspection and overhaul, which will reduce the efficiency and shorten the life of the existing machinery but may well be worth while if current output can thus be increased. There will be, second, the possibility of outright nonrenewal, not, of course, of essential parts of the equipment, but of the many auxiliary laborsaving devices such as automatic feeders and other gadgets performing operations which can also be done by hand. Third, there will be the possibility of using obolete or secondhand machines instead of new ones. Many older fac-

20. If it be objected that the increase of costs which we assumed to be caused by the adoption of overtime or similar devices is improbably small, this would mean merely that the very small rise of prices of 5 per cent, which we have assumed, would not have this particular effect and that it would require a rise of, say, 20 or 25 per cent to bring it about.

tories have a certain amount of such old machinery for temporary use to meet peak-time demands or in an emergency, for which it would not pay to keep a new machine in reserve. There exists in many branches a supply of secondhand machinery which can be used in the same way. Fourth, and last, there will be the possibility of replacing those machines that wear out by new but cheaper and less efficient ones. So long as the internal rate of return of any firm remains above what it has been before, it may well be profitable to buy two less efficient machines at the price of one more efficient one, if the two less efficient machines enable the firm, though with the co-operation of much more labor, to increase output more than with the more efficient one.

If we consider the effect of all these possible changes, *not* on the proportion in which the stock of capital of any firm is composed of different parts, but on the *rates* at which its current outlay is *spent* on different kinds of resources, or on the *proportion* in which total outlay is *distributed* between fixed and circulating capital, it seems to be clear that, in consequence of a general change in commodity prices, large changes in the latter magnitudes may be brought about in a comparatively short time. In extreme cases it may even be profitable for entrepreneurs temporarily to discontinue all demand for machinery and yet for a considerable period greatly to increase output. But while this extreme result may not be probable, it does not seem unlikely that the demand for certain kinds of new equipment will be absolutely reduced. This would seem to be likely particularly where, as is true in the case of buildings and most heavy machinery, the equipment has to be made to order and large sums will have to be locked up in it by the buyer during the period of production without bringing any current yield; the same would seem to be true wherever a gradual transition to some new (e.g., more laborsaving) but more expensive kind of machinery has been under way, which will now be stopped; and generally wherever the change in the methods of production adopted will involve a change from equipment made by one group of people to that made by another group of people.[21] In so far as any labor is specific to the production of the kind of equipment, the demand for which now decreases or ceases entirely, the consequence of the rise in final demand will thus be unemployment in the capital goods industries.

4

We have now to introduce the possibility of borrowing money at rates of interest determined by the market and not necessarily changed in response to an increase in the demand for funds. In the present section we shall consider how far this modifies the conclusions thus far reached if we make assumptions which in the most important respects approximately correspond to conditions in the real world and which will therefore enable us to judge what the practical significance of our conclusions is likely to be. The theoretically very interesting but practically irrelevant case of a "perfectly elastic supply of credit" will be deferred until the next section.

The sharp distinction between the two cases and the order of treatment is indicated by the frequent but misleading application to this problem of the category of "perfect competition"; this concept is quite inappropriate to it, simply because successive (additional) loans to the same borrower will never represent the "same commodity" in the sense in which the term is used in the theory of competition. While in a commodity market "perfect competition" means that any single buyer can buy at the given market price any quantity he likes, it would, of course, be absurd to assume that even in the most perfectly competitive

21. It seems that the term "structure of production," which I introduced in *Prices and Production* to describe the distribution of *current* labor between the different "stages of production" has sometimes been interpreted in a materialistic sense which supported the misunderstanding that the "changes in the methods of production" I was discussing implied an instantaneous change in the machines actually used. But the "structure of production" in the sense in which I used the term, can, of course, change fundamentally without any change in the equipment actually used; this latter change will come about only gradually as a consequence of the change in the former; and the most radical change of this sort would indeed be the entire cessation of the production of machines, although the people might yet go on for a long time using the same machines in the production of consumers' goods.

money market every borrower (or, for that matter, any borrower) can at the given rate of interest borrow any amount he likes. This is precluded by the fact that in given circumstances the security a borrower has to offer is not so good for a large amount as for a small one. In consequence, every prospective borrower will have to face an upward sloping supply curve of credit—or, rather, not a continuous supply curve, but an upward stepped "curve," showing that the rate of interest, while constant within certain limits, will go up by distinct steps whenever one of the limits is reached up to which he can borrow at a given rate.

The most important, though not the sole, factor limiting the borrowing capacity of a firm at any given rate of interest will be the size of the capital owned by it. Bankers, as a rule, will not be willing to lend to any one firm more than a given proportion of its own capital and take very good care that no firm borrows at the same time from more than one bank; and beyond this limit the firm will be able to obtain funds only at a higher rate of interest, or, what comes to the same thing, on more onerous conditions of some other kind. This limitation of the amount of funds any firm can raise to increase its output will be further strengthened where banks provide loans only for investment in circulating capital and effectively refuse to provide funds for the investment in fixed capital. The general fact we have to remember in this connection is that, in the existing institutional framework, lending (in the strict sense of the word), and particularly short-term lending, will secure mobility of capital only to a limited extent and that, in a world where risk is ever present, it will by itself not be sufficient to bring about an equalization of the rates of return on capital invested in different firms or completely to adjust these rates to a given market rate of interest. For this, in addition to lending, transfers of capital by way of full participation in the risk of the business, i.e., changes in the share capital or what we may quite generally describe as the "own capital" (as distinguished from the borrowed capital) of the firms will be necessary. But this latter process is necessarily much slower than the provision of additional bank loans, and it will therefore frequently be

The Ricardo Effect

true that in the short run most firms will not be able to raise as much capital as they could profitably use or that they will be able to do so only at rates much higher than the "market rate."

This is not to say that the maximum a firm will be able to borrow at a given rate of interest will be rigidly fixed in proportion to its own capital. The director of a firm who can convince his bank manager that he has an exceptional opportunity of making large profits on additional capital and thus can provide a large margin of safety in case his optimism should prove not to be quite justified will be able to borrow proportionally more than another. In general, when prospects are good all firms may be able to borrow more in proportion to their own capital than when prospects are poor.[22] The stepped supply "curves" of credit which all firms face will be shifted to the right as general prospects get better (and to the left when prospects get worse), and such sideways shifts of the supply curves will frequently act, and often be deliberately used, in exactly the same way as an outright change in the rate of interest (i.e., as a raising or lowering of the whole curve).

But, although any general increase in expected profits is likely to increase the amounts firms can borrow, it will in many instances increase the amounts they would like to borrow at the current rates of interest still more and thus bring firms up to the limit beyond which they can raise capital only at higher costs. Though there will be, at the ruling rate of interest, an unsatisfied demand, this demand will not be "effective" demand, because it will not fall within the categories to which the ruling rates apply, and these rates will therefore remain unchanged. The situation is similar to that caused by credit rationing, although it will arise, without the intervention of authority or a monopolist, merely as a result of the views the banks hold about the "credit-worthiness" of the borrowers.

22. It should be noted that the limit thus imposed on the borrowing capacity of the firms will be a sliding limit, fixed only in the short run, but rising gradually as, in consequence of each addition to the volume of credits already granted, incomes and final demand and thereby the prospects of profits rise. In other words, it will limit merely the rate of expansion of credit but may not prevent a continuous, progressive, and (if for the purpose of estimating the security of the borrower the value of his assets is written up with rising prices) even limitless expansion of credit.

There is no need to explain at any length that, whenever the amounts people would like to borrow at the current rate of interest are larger than the amounts they can obtain at that rate, it will be these *amounts* and not the ruling market rate which will determine the internal rates of return of the different firms. As in the situation discussed in the last section these internal rates will be different for different firms according to the circumstances then enumerated (to which we must now add the limitations on the borrowing facilities of any particular firm), and the investment of each firm will be governed by its own internal rate, which may be very much higher than the market rate, which may not have changed at all. The rise in internal rates would lead to a general change to less capitalistic methods of production, different in extent according as the internal rate has changed in the different firms.

There remains, however, the question whether, to the extent that the firms are able to procure additional credits, this will reduce the degree to which their internal rates will rise, and therefore the degree to which they will change to less capitalistic methods of production, compared with the case where no additional credit at all was available. The problem which arises here is the same as that which we intend to consider in its more general form in the next section, since, if our proposition holds true even when the supply of credit is completely elastic, it must apply still more in the present case. We can, therefore, immediately proceed to this "stronger" case.

5

The assumption that the supply of credit at a given rate of interest is perfectly elastic is not only unrealistic but, when we contemplate its implications, perfectly fantastic; and it makes the analysis rather complicated. But, as it brings us face to face with a fundamental theoretical problem, it is well worth undertaking. It raises in its purest form the question of the relationship between the monetary and the real factors affecting the relative profitability of different methods of production.

The Ricardo Effect

The contention that if the supply of credit is perfectly elastic it must be the money rate of interest which will determine which forms of investment are most profitable may be based on either of two assertions which ought to be clearly distinguished: it may be asserted that in this case the cost-price relations (or the relation between wages and commodity prices) must necessarily be so adjusted by either a change in wages or a change in commodity prices as to make the difference correspond to the money rate of interest; or it may be asserted that even when this does not happen and wages remain, for example, too low relative to commodity prices, it will still be the money rate of interest and not the cost-price relationship that will govern the form of investment.

With regard to both these arguments, but particularly with regard to the first, it is important to remember that the situation which we consider is eminently *not* one of equilibrium but one in which the causes of continuous and cumulative change are inherent. It is indeed the classical instance of a cumulative process with which we are dealing; the perfectly elastic supply of credit at a rate of interest lower than the internal rate of all or most of the firms will be the cause of continuous changes of prices and money incomes where each change makes further changes necessary. There is no point in saying with respect to such a situation that "in equilibrium there must" exist such and such a relationship, because it necessarily follows from the assumptions that the relationship between at least some prices must be out of equilibrium. This is important particularly with reference to the two propositions: first, that prices must be equal to marginal costs, and, second, that the prices of the factors must be equal to the expected price of their marginal product discounted at the rate of interest at which credit can be freely obtained. All we need to say with respect to the first proposition is that, except in a very special and for our purpose irrelevant sense,[23] it is just not true in the very short run, although a

23. The proposition can be made true in the shortest of short runs if we include in marginal costs all costs (including the personal effort of the entrepreneur) of increasing output during the short period in question—that is, if we include in marginal costs the costs of increasing output at a certain rate. But, if we do so, marginal costs are no longer

dogmatic belief that prices must always be equal to marginal costs in the relevant sense is probably responsible for a great many confusions in this field. The second proposition is the one with which we are here more directly concerned.

The belief that, if the supply of money at a given rate of interest is perfectly elastic while investment demand is inelastic, the former will uniquely determine the rate of return at which supply and demand will be equal, is derived by analogy from the general rule that, if either the quantity demanded or the quantity supplied of anything is completely elastic at a given price, it follows necessarily that this will be the price. But, while this statement is true enough when we discuss demand and supply in "real" terms, it neglects an essential difference of the present case where the "price" in question is the relationship between the prices of two groups of goods (labor and commodities), while the supply which is infinitely elastic is not that of one of the two goods but merely of the money that is in the first instance to be spent on one of the two goods; it neglects the fact that any increase of money expenditure on the one kind of good is bound to cause an increase of money expenditure on the other kind of good.

When it was said before that we are dealing with a position of disequilibrium, this meant precisely that we had to deal with two sets of forces tending to fix the same price (or rather the same relationship between two groups of prices) at different figures. On the one hand, we have a given output of consumers' goods (only slowly variable) and a given propensity of the people to spend a certain proportion of their income on consumers' goods, which together would for each volume of employment (and therefore of total income) determine a definite ratio between the prices of commodities and the prices of all factors; and, on the other hand, we have an infinitely elastic supply of money which tends to determine the prices of factors in a certain fixed

uniquely correlated with the volume of output, and we have to consider separate marginal cost curves for each rate at which output is increased, becoming steeper as we assume a faster rate of increase until, for a strictly instantaneous increase of output, the marginal cost curve becomes perpendicular.

relation to the prices of the products which is different from that determined by the first set of factors.

It is not to be denied, of course, that through changes in the money stream the relation between the prices of goods as determined by the real factors can be very considerably modified. The problem is merely whether there is no limit to the extent to which, and the period of time for which, the price structure as determined by the "real" factors can be thus distorted, or whether the fact that the extra money which has first raised one group of prices will soon work round to affect the other group of prices in the same direction does not set a limit to the possible degree of distortion. The question is rather similar to that whether, by pouring a liquid fast enough into one side of a vessel, we can raise the level at that side above that of the rest to any extent we desire. How far we shall be able to raise the level of one part above that of the rest will clearly depend on how fluid or viscid the liquid is; we shall be able to raise it more if the liquid is syrup or glue than if it is water. But in no case shall we be at liberty to raise the surface in one part of the vessel above the rest to any extent we like.

Just as the viscosity of the liquid determines the extent to which any part of its surface can be raised above the rest, so the speed at which an increase of incomes leads to an increase in the demand for consumers' goods limits the extent to which, by spending more money on the factors of production, we can raise their prices relative to those of the products.[24] The problem arises most sharply when we assume that the money rate is arbitrarily lowered to a very low figure in a new country with little capital and a very high "marginal efficiency of capital." If the proposition we are considering were true at all, it would have to hold in this case also, i.e., the availability of an unlimited quantity of

24. The economic equilibrium differs, of course, from our hydrostatic simile by the fact that the equilibrium position between the prices is not constant but will be affected by changes in the real quantities of goods available. These real changes, however, will only strengthen the tendency, because they will necessarily work in a direction opposite from the monetary factors: in our case their effect will be to increase the proportion of people engaged in producing things other than consumers' goods to the available output of consumers' goods and thus to increase the difference between wages and commodity prices which will establish itself as soon as the flow of new money ceases.

money at the low rate of interest would bring it about that wages would be driven up to the discounted value—not merely of the present marginal product of labor but of the marginal product which labor could be expected to produce after the machinery had been installed which it would be profitable to instal at the low rate of interest. The aggregate value of the services of labor at that real wage might be very considerably larger than the total current output of consumers' goods and certainly very much larger than the whole current output of labor. The effect of this must be that the demand for consumers' goods and their prices would rise accordingly. If this rise of prices stimulated entrepreneurs to borrow and invest still more, this would only make prices rise still further, and the faster entrepreneurs expected prices to rise, the more they would necessarily speed up this price rise beyond their expectations. Although they might succeed at times in driving wages up to the discounted value of the *expected* price of the marginal product of labor, they could not possibly, whatever their effort, actually raise real wages to the figure corresponding to the low rate of interest, because the stuff to provide this real income just would not be there.

In the situation to which we have to apply these considerations, such as will exist in a modern society in the late stages of a boom, the position will be different only in degree. It still remains true that entrepreneurs, by offering higher money wages, cannot effectively raise real wages to the level which would correspond to the low money rate of interest, because the more they raise money wages, the more the prices of commodities will rise.[25] In this case, too, the limiting factor is simply

25. This if, of course, not to say that the share of labor as a whole in the real income of society is rigidly fixed. An increase in the sum of money wages will enable labor to encroach on the real income of the *rentier* class. But the rise in money wages necessary to give an increased number of people the same real income per head at the expense of the people with fixed money incomes would have to be very large indeed—so large that it is not likely to be offered by entrepreneurs until they have come to expect a galloping inflation. In other words, we do, of course, not wish to deny that there will be some forced saving largely at the expense of the *rentier* class; what we deny is merely that it is likely that by forced saving it will be possible to give an ever increasing number of men employed in producing investment goods a constant wage in terms of consumers' goods. Perhaps it should also be added that the argument of the text does *not* imply that *all* the additional money income paid out in wages is promptly spent on consumers' goods, but only that this is true of a substantial part of it (see, on this, *Profits, Interest, and Investment*, pp. 52 ff.).

that the consumers' goods are not there and that, so long as all investment takes highly capitalistic forms, every increase in employment adds only a fraction of its value to the output of consumers' goods. This brings us to the second hard fact which dominates the situation we are considering: that in this situation there will not be enough labor available to increase at the same time the current output of consumers' goods and to push investment to the limit indicated by the rate of interest. So long as unused reserves of labor are available, there is indeed, as we shall presently see, no reason why the entrepreneurs should not use the unlimited funds to do both: to increase the output of consumption goods for the near future by the expensive but quick methods and to provide for cheaper production by investing on a large scale. This is the reason why in the early stage of a boom the money rate of interest will control the situation. But, although this would mean that in these circumstances the low rate of interest was effective so far as the volume of investment was concerned, it would still not mean that, once consumers' goods prices began to rise, real wages could be maintained by proportional adjustments in the money wages.

6

That in the circumstances considered it will sooner or later become inevitable that real wages should fall, and investment expenditure be reduced, will be evident if we consider for a moment the paradoxical results that would follow if things worked as appears to be assumed by the contrary view. The increase in the prices of commodities, with unlimited amounts of money available at a fixed rate of interest, would lead to an increase of investment expenditure and of real investment, which, since no reserves of labor are available, could take place only at the expense of the output of consumers' goods in the near future. The consequent increase of money incomes and of final demand, coupled with the decrease in the output of consumers' goods, would cause a further rise in their prices relative to wages. This further rise in the prices of consumers' goods would, according to that view, bring about a further increase of investment at the expense of the output of consumers' goods, and so on, presumably until there are no people left producing consumers' goods and everybody is engaged in providing machinery destined to produce consumers' goods in some distant future when the men will all have died of starvation in the interval. While some tendency in this direction probably exists during the earlier part of a boom, it hardly needs any superstitious belief in the self-righting forces of the economic system to suspect that, some time before that extreme result is produced, counterforces will operate to check such a development. This brings us to the second version of the argument according to which it must be the money rate of interest which rules the roost.

This version, which admits that wages may remain relatively too low compared with the rate of interest but insists that in spite of this, if the supply of money is perfectly elastic, it will be the rate of interest and not the level of wages which will govern the form of investment, is represented mainly by Kaldor and Wilson.[26] These two writers, however, as we shall try to show, so much simplify their task that they do not prove what they mean to demonstrate. All they do prove, in a quite unnecessarily elaborate manner, is that, so long as an unlimited amount of money can be obtained at the given rate of interest, it will depend solely on the rate of interest which method will bring the highest *current* profit above *current* costs *after* the equipment appropriate to that method has been procured. This is no more than another version of the truism which we have emphasized from the beginning that, so long as the rate of interest remains constant, a change in real wages cannot alter the relative costs of the different methods of production. What Kaldor and Wilson completely disregard is that, in comparing the profits obtained from producing with different methods, they are comparing methods employing different amounts of capital without counting in any way the cost of creating the extra real capital required for one of the two methods. They do this by omit-

26. N. Kaldor, "Capital Intensity and the Trade Cycle," *Economica*, February, 1939, and T. Wilson, "Capital Theory and the Trade Cycle," *Review of Economic Studies*, June, 1940.

ting to give any attention to what will happen during the period of transition before the new equipment is available. Whether this equipment will ever be available will depend, however, precisely on what happens during this interval. The problem is not answered by the statement that, if we adopt a certain course, the excess of current receipts over current outlay will be largest from a certain future date onward, if we are not also told what happens between now and that future date. In choosing between the two alternative methods, we cannot decide merely on the basis of what the position would be after *some* new long-term equilibrium has been established, but we must also consider what will happen between now and then, because *which* long-term equilibrium will be established will depend on this. What the procedure of Kaldor and Wilson amounts to is to leave out from their data the real factors which determine the supply of capital and to assume that the quantity of capital will in the long run necessarily adjust itself so as to bring its "marginal efficiency" to the level of a rate of interest determined solely by monetary factors.

To speak more concretely, Kaldor and Wilson assume that, if only the funds were available, it will, in the circumstances assumed, necessarily be most profitable to meet an increased demand for the product by increasing equipment in proportion to the increase in the amount of the product that can be sold at a given price, although in this way it will as a rule be possible to catch up with increased demand only after some considerable interval. Only if (and to the extent that) we can assume the extra equipment needed to be waiting in the shops ready to be bought and instantaneously to be installed would no such interval occur. This assumption (which amounts to presupposing that all the real capital required for an expansion is already in existence) is evidently one which might be true for any one firm, but which will not be true when all firms are simultaneously in the same position. In the situation with which we are concerned the additional equipment and still more the output produced by it will be available only after considerable delay. In the interval until this output is available profits which might have been made by quicker methods will be lost and ought to be counted as part of the cost of the production for the more distant future.

To this it will no doubt be answered that there is no reason why the entrepreneurs should not do both: provide for the output in the near future by the quick but expensive methods *and* provide for the more distant future by ordering more machinery. But this brings us up to the fundamental issue whether the amount of real resources, and particularly of labor, will be sufficient to make both possible at the same time. Or, in other words, the question arises, which it is now fashionable to disregard in discussion of these problems, whether an unlimited supply of funds secures an equally unlimited supply of real resources. We have already seen that, in the kind of situation with which we are concerned, this is not likely to be the case.

It is instructive, however, to examine a little more closely how some economists manage to gloss over this difficulty and thereby apparently succeed in eliminating the given supply of capital from the relevant data of the problem. Kaldor's treatment of the question in the article referred to is in this respect most illuminating. He explicitly claims to deal with all the cases where the output of individual firms is limited by "falling demand curves for the products *and/or rising supply curves for its factors*"[27] as the only possible alternative to a limitation by an inelastic supply of credit. But, when he comes to discuss the case, he assumes, and, finally, even introduces in a footnote, the explicit assumption that *"the elasticity of supply of factors, to the individual firm, is infinite."*[28] But, although he has thus in fact confined his proof to only part of the group of cases for which he has originally undertaken to provide it, he proceeds as if he had proved it for all and continues to treat his original alternative (inelastic supply or credit *or* falling demand curves for the product and/or rising supply curves for the factors) as corresponding to the distinction between situations where

27. *Op. cit.*, p. 46. (Our italics.)
28. *Ibid.*, p. 50, n. 4. The assumption is implied in the whole discussion on this and the preceding page, since only if unlimited amounts of labor are available at the given price is the "supply curve of capital horizontal" in the real sense in which the term "capital" is there used.

either only the rate of wages or only the rate of interest determines the methods of production that will be profitable.

Kaldor's omission to face the effects of limitation in the supply of labor is so significant because it is through the rise in the supply price of labor that the shortage of real resources available for investment (caused by the competing demand of the producers of consumers' goods) makes itself felt. His conclusion follows solely from the assumption that, and is true only if, the elasticity of the supply of labor (and other factors) is infinite. When this is true, there is indeed no reason why entrepreneurs should not succeed in using the unlimited money funds to increase output quickly by costly methods and at the same time making arrangements for a more economical production of a larger output at a later date. So long as unused reserves of labor are available at an unchanged price, unlimited funds mean unlimited control over resources. But this is not the condition which is relevant for the position of full employment that will prevail near the top of a boom.

We shall see the problem involved more clearly if for a moment we assume that each firm represents a completely integrated process of production, that is, not only that the production of the final commodity and of all the various raw materials, etc., used but also that of all machinery required for the production of that output is produced within the firm. In the circumstances we are considering, each of these integrated firms would be able to attract additional labor only by offering higher wages; and, although the relatively less capitalistic industries might find it profitable to increase their labor in this way at the expense of the more capitalistic industries, this will, if there are no unemployed available, not be possible for all firms or for industries or firms of average "capital intensity."

For each of these firms, which for our purpose may serve as representatives of a general trend, the problem will therefore be how to distribute its given labor force between the production of commodities and the production of machinery. The way to maximize the excess of current receipts over current outlay for all periods after the change had been completed would be temporarily to transfer labor from the production of commodities to the production of machinery. This would involve a reduction of the current output of commodities, and therefore of current profits, not only below what they would be if the past volume of output had been maintained, but still more below the level which could be achieved if current output were increased, by adopting quick and more costly methods until marginal cost just equaled price. These profits, which will have to be foregone if the additional machinery is to be provided, would have to be regarded as costs of, and would therefore have to be offset against, the larger profits which in consequence could be continuously earned from some future date onward. It is this item which represents the costs of the extra waiting which the more capitalistic methods involve and which nowhere enters into the calculations of Kaldor or Wilson. Since these profits which will be earned during this interval are, as we have seen, likely to be very considerable, it is more than likely that they will turn the scales against the more capitalistic process. In other words, profits will be higher on the method with the higher rate of turnover, *not* because they would accrue at a higher rate *after* the new equilibrium envisaged by Kaldor had been established (which they would not do), but because the profits on the less capitalistic method will *begin to accrue* earlier than those on the more capitalistic method. It is the profits from now onward, not merely profits after the additional equipment has been created, which must be considered in deciding whether that additional equipment is to be created at all. It is for this reason that our integrated firms, if their internal rates of return only rise high enough, will certainly not transfer labor from the production of commodities to the production of machinery, but, on the contrary, will transfer labor from the production of machinery to the production of commodities. This change will not be merely temporary but will evidently have to be maintained so long as the conditions continue which made it appear profitable in the first instance, that is, so long as the prices of consumers' goods remain high relative to wages.

Before leaving the integrated firms, it is worth while to consider a little more closely exactly what will happen in their machine shops. These machine shops will have to give up some of their labor that can also be used indirectly to produce consumers' goods, and they will have to turn to the production of less elaborate, less costly machinery. Both of these changes will have the effect of making superfluous other kinds of labor which are specific to the production of the more elaborate kind of machinery or to jobs (such as the extraction of certain raw materials used in the production of machinery) which are wanted in a rigid quantitative proportion to the total output of machinery. In other words, the result of the shortage of the more generally employable labor will be unemployment of certain particular kinds of labor—that which is highly specific to the production of some kinds of machinery.

While it seems fairly evident that the results must be the same if we abandon the assumption of complete integration of the different industries, I must admit that I find it difficult to visualize precisely how it will be brought about. The physical conditions of the problem are, of course, the same: it will still be true that there will not be enough labor available at the same time to increase the output of consumers' goods quickly and to provide more machinery to produce a still larger output by more efficient methods at a later date. And it will also still be true that, if entrepreneurs decide for the costlier but speedier methods, this will bring them the larger profits. The problem is what will enable them to foresee this result; because, so long as they believe that at the ruling price they will be able both to get the labor to increase the output immediately and to get the manufacturers of machines to produce machines for them, it will appear profitable to try to do both; the individual entrepreneur will no longer be directly faced with the problem of using the same labor either to produce more commodities or to produce more machinery; and it will be only when he and all the other entrepreneurs who are in the same position try to do so that they will find out that it cannot be done.

The answer, I think, is to be sought, first, in the fact that the provision for the near future will necessarily have the first attention of the entrepreneur, because, if the profits which might be made in the near future are not obtained, they (and perhaps a certain amount of permanent business) will be lost for good to a competitor, while delay in obtaining the more efficient machinery will affect the volume of output less and merely postpone the date when its costs will be lower. Closely connected with this will be the effect of the increasing uncertainty concerning the more distant future. Although the entrepreneur may expect the higher prices to continue indefinitely, he will be less certain that this will be so in the more distant future than in the near future. On the principle of "making hay while the sun shines," provision for the profits to be made in the near future will take the precedence.

Second, there is the fact that, since *in the short run* the more capitalistic methods will require *more* labor for any given increase of output than the less capitalistic methods, the rising supply price of labor will make itself felt more with the former than with the latter, i.e., the attempt to procure the machinery necessary for a given increase of output will meet with a rise in the price of the machinery comparatively greater than the rise in wages which would be caused by employing the number of men required to produce the same amount by less capitalistic methods.

Third, there is the point that, in so far as the producers of commodities increase their output in the first instance, not without any additional machinery but by the use of a cheaper kind of machinery, the need for the more elaborate machinery will arise only after the machinery provisionally installed wears out, and that therefore the demand for the more elaborate kind of machinery may for a time cease completely.

Finally, and perhaps most important, there will be the fact that so long as the producers of commodities do not succeed in actually increasing output quickly to the extent necessary to bring marginal returns down to a level they can expect to prevail in the long run, they will be uncertain which of the various elements in the picture will change so as to create a new equilibrium position. In other words, so long as profits on the quick methods do not actually fall and further endeavor appears to be needed to gather all the high profits that can be made immediately, the more elaborate preparations for future profits at a lower rate (though higher in the aggregate) and involving greater risk will not appear very attractive. But so long as people try to do both, to increase output quickly and to order more machinery, incomes and final demand will continue to run ahead of the expectations of the producers of consumers' goods. It will be only after investment has been considerably reduced that the cost of the expensive methods will catch up with prices and that thus the more capitalistic methods will once more appear attractive.

I am fully aware that all this is not very satisfactory and that a clearer picture of the precise process by which competition brings about this result would be very desirable. But I am not sure whether this is possible. We are dealing with a position of disequilibrium in which developments depend on the precise order in which the various changes follow one another in time and where the situation at any moment is likely to be, as we learned to say during the war, "confused." We cannot say precisely when entrepreneurs will abandon the self-defeating attempts at the same time to build up elaborate equipment and to increase production quickly. All we can say is that, the longer the effect with which we are concerned is delayed, the stronger must become the forces tending to bring it about (i.e., the longer increases in final demand are allowed to bring about proportionally larger increases in investment, the greater must become the rise of prices of final goods relative to costs), and that therefore they are bound sooner or later to become the dominating element in the picture.

7

Any attempt to discover from the available statistical information whether the Ricardo effect does in fact operate as these considerations suggest encounters considerable difficulties. We can do no more here than show what are these difficulties of an attempt at verification and why the evidence so far available does not seem to allow any definite conclusions.

In the first instance it must be pointed out that, although the phrase "real wages" is sometimes used in this connection, the relation between wages and product prices with which we are concerned has no close connection with "real wages" in the sense in which this term is commonly used. While in most contexts when real wages are discussed what is meant is the relation between wages as received by the worker and the prices of the commodities on which he spends these wages, we are concerned with the cost of labor to the entrepreneur and their relation to the prices of the products he produces. We shall merely mention that even the wages paid to the workers and the cost of labor to the entrepreneur may sometimes move differently.[29] The more important difference is, however, that between the prices of the goods on which the workers spend their wages and the prices of the goods in the production of which the labor is used. The following are the main sources of this difference:

1. While the "cost of living" is affected largely by the prices of agricultural products, it is for our purpose mainly the prices of manufactured articles that are of importance. More generally, the importance for our purpose of the change in price of any particular product varies with the relative amount of capital used in its production (which is relatively low in agriculture and relatively high in manufacture). The significance of this will be seen when it is remembered that for our purposes a mere shift in demand from articles requiring comparatively little capital in their production to articles requiring a great deal would have the same effect as an increase in total demand. Any statistical investigation would probably do well to confine itself in the first instance to the effect of changes in the relation between the prices of the product and wages in any given industry on investment in that industry. In so far as a more general investigation is attempted, prices ought probably to be weighted according to the proportional amount of capital used in the production of the different goods. Where we

29. In consequence of changes in taxation, social insurance charges, and legislative or trade-union regulations affecting conditions of work. I remember having once seen detailed comparative statistics of the "real wages" of linotype operators in Sweden and Austria, which seemed to show conclusively that, while the purchasing power of the wages to the workers was much lower in Austria, they meant a much larger real cost of labor to the manufacturer.

have to deal with an "open system," as will regularly be the case in statistical investigations, we shall have further to distinguish between prices of home-produced and of imported commodities.

2. While from the"cost of living" point of view it will be retail prices that will be relevant, for our purpose it will be prices received by the manufacturers that will count; and it is in general true that, for reasons into which we need not go here, the latter (or at least wholesale prices) fluctuate more than retail prices.

3. While from the "cost of living" point of view it is the relation between wages and the price of a fixed quantity of commodities which is relevant, we are here concerned with the relations between the costs of labor and the marginal product of that labor. This marginal product, however, is itself not a constant but a variable, and either may vary as a consequence of the effect with which we are concerned or may by its change become the cause of this effect. In other words, changes in the marginal product may appear either as dependent variables, when they are the consequence of a change in the proportional combination of capital and labor, or as independent variables, when they are brought about by changes in the "data," particularly by changes in technological knowledge. Technological change, at least when it is rapid and general, may here cause serious difficulties.

So long as technological knowledge remains constant, the relations between the cost of labor and the price of its product which are relevant for our purpose will generally be the same as the relations between the costs of a fixed amount of labor and the price of a fixed amount of the product—although, when we have to deal with an "open" system, changes in the price of an important raw material may disturb even this simple relationship. But, once changes in technical knowledge have to be taken into account, the problem becomes very much more complex. It is evident, to take an extreme case, that if an advance in knowledge enabled us to produce with exactly the same machinery and other outlay 20 per cent more than before, the immediate effect would be very similar to that of a rise in the price of the product. So long as such a change occurs in isolation, there is no special difficulty about it. But, when it is combined with price changes, a problem arises for which it is difficult to see a practicable solution. To judge the significance of any price change occurring together with technological change, we should have to know which price relationship now "corresponds" to the price relationship which existed before, that is, which relation between the cost of labor and the price of the product will now make investment no more and no less attractive than the price relationship which existed before the technological change. At the moment I have no solution of this difficulty to offer.

XII. The Economic Conditions of Interstate Federalism*

1

IT IS rightly regarded as one of the great advantages of interstate federation that it would do away with the impediments as to the movement of men, goods, and capital between the states and that it would render possible the creation of common rules of law, a uniform monetary system, and common control of communications. The material benefits that would spring from the creation of so large an economic area can hardly be overestimated, and it appears to be taken for granted that economic union and political union would be combined as a matter of course. But, since it will have to be argued here that the establishment of economic union will set very definite limitations to the realization of widely cherished ambitions, we must begin by showing why the abolition of economic barriers between the members of the federation is not only a welcome concomitant but also an indispensable condition for the achievement of the main purpose of federation.

Unquestionably, the main purpose of interstate federation is to secure peace: to prevent war between the parts of the federation by eliminating causes of friction between them and by providing effective machinery for the settlement of any disputes which may arise between them and to prevent war between the federation and any independent states by making the former so strong as to eliminate any danger of attack from without. If this aim could be achieved by mere political union not extended to the economic sphere, many would probably be content to halt at the creation of a common government for the pur-

* Reprinted from the *New Commonwealth Quarterly*, V, No. 2 (September, 1939), 131–49.

pose of defense and the conduct of a common foreign policy, when a more far-reaching unification might impede the achievement of other ideals.

There are, however, very good reasons why all plans for interstate federation include economic union and even regard it as one of its main objectives and why there is no historical example of countries successfully combining in a common foreign policy and common defense without a common economic regime.[1] Although there are instances of countries concluding customs unions without providing machinery for a common foreign policy and common defense, the decision of several countries to rely upon a common foreign policy and a common defense force, as was the case with the parts of the dual monarchy of Austria-Hungary, has inevitably been combined with a common administration of matters of tariffs, money, and finance.

The relations of the Union with the outside world provide some important reasons for this, since a common representation in foreign countries and a common foreign policy is hardly conceivable without a common fiscal and monetary policy. If international treaties are to be concluded only by the Union, it follows that the Union must have sole power over all foreign relations, including the control of exports and imports, etc. If the Union government is to be responsible for the maintenance of peace, the Union and not its parts must be responsible for all decisions which will harm or benefit other countries.

No less important are the requirements of a common policy for defense. Not only would any interstate barriers to commerce prevent the best utilization of the available resources and weaken the strength of the union but the regional interests created by any sort of regional protectionism would inevitably raise obstacles to an effective defense policy. It would be difficult enough to subordinate sectional to Union interests; but should the component states remain separate communities of interest, whose inhabitants gain and suffer together because they are segregated from the rest of the Union by various kinds of barriers,

1. To what extent the British Commonwealth of Nations since the Statutes of Westminster constitutes an exception to this statement remains yet to be seen.

it would be impossible to conduct a defense policy without being hampered at every stage by considerations of local interests. This, however, is only a facet of the wider problem which we must next consider.

The most compelling reasons for extending the union to the economic sphere are provided by the necessity to preserve the internal coherence of the Union. The existence of any measure of economic seclusion or isolation on the part of an individual state produces a solidarity of interests among all its inhabitants and conflicts between their interests and those of the inhabitants of other states which—although we have become so accustomed to such conflicts as to take them for granted—is by no means a natural or inevitable thing. There is no valid reason why any change which affects a particular industry in a certain territory should impinge more heavily upon all or most of the inhabitants of that territory than upon people elsewhere. This would hold good equally for the territories which now constitute sovereign states and for any other arbitrarily delimited region, if it were not for custom barriers, separate monetary organizations, and all the other impediments to the free movement of men and goods. It is only because of these barriers that the incidence of the various benefits and damages affecting in the first instance a particular group of people will be mainly confined to the inhabitants of a given state and extend to almost all the people living within its frontiers. Such economic frontiers create communities of interest on a regional basis and of a most intimate character: they bring it about that all conflicts of interests tend to become conflicts between the same groups of people, instead of conflicts between groups of constantly varying composition, and that there will in consequence be perpetual conflicts between the inhabitants of a state as such instead of between the various individuals finding themselves arrayed, sometimes with one group of people against another, and at other times on another issue with the second group against the first. We need not stress here the extreme but nevertheless important case that national restriction will lead to considerable changes in the standard of life of the population of one integral state composed with that of another.[2] The mere fact that everybody will find again and again that their interests are closely bound up with those of one constant group of people and antagonistic to that of another group is bound to set up severe frictions between the groups as such. That there will always be communities of interest which will be similarly affected by a particular event or a particular measure is unavoidable. But it is clearly in the interest of unity of the larger whole that these groupings should not be permanent and, more particularly, that the various communities of interest should overlap territorially and never become lastingly identified with the inhabitants of a particular region.

We shall later examine how in existing federal states, even though the states are denied the grosser instruments of protectionism such as tariffs and independent currencies, the more concealed forms of protectionism tend to cause increasing friction, cumulative retaliation, and even the use of force between the individual states. And it is not difficult to imagine what forms this would take if the individual states were free to use the whole armory of protectionism. It seems fairly certain that political union between erstwhile sovereign states would not last long unless accompanied by economic union.

2

The absence of tariff walls and the free movements of men and capital between the states of the federation has certain important consequences which are frequently overlooked. They limit to a great extent the scope of the economic policy of the individual states. If goods, men, and money can move freely over the interstate frontiers, it becomes clearly impossible to affect the prices of the different products through action by the individual state. The Union becomes one single market, and prices in its different parts will differ only by the costs of

2. It is only because, in consequence of these conditions, the standard of life of all the people in a country will tend to move in the same direction that concepts such as the standard of living or the price level of a country cease to be mere statistical abstractions and become very concrete realities.

transport. Any change in any part of the Union in the conditions of production of any commodity which can be transported to other parts will affect prices everywhere. Similarly, any change in the opportunities for investment, or the remuneration of labor in any part of the Union, will, more or less promptly, affect the supply and the price of capital and labor in all other parts of the Union.

Now nearly all contemporary economic policy intended to assist particular industries tries to do so by influencing prices. Whether this is done by marketing boards or restriction schemes, by compulsory "reorganization" or the destruction of excess capacity of particular industries, the aim is always to limit supply and thus to raise prices. All this will clearly become impossible for the individual states within the Union. The whole armory of marketing boards and other forms of monopolistic organizations of individual industries will cease to be at the disposal of state governments. If they still want to assist particular groups of producers, they will have to do so by direct subsidies from funds raised by ordinary taxation. But the methods by which, for example, in England, the producers of sugar and milk, bacon and potatoes, cotton yarn, coal, and iron have all been protected in recent years against "ruinous competition," from within and without, will not be available.

It will also be clear that the states within the Union will not be able to pursue an independent monetary policy. With a common monetary unit, the latitude given to the national central banks will be restricted at least as much as it was under a rigid gold standard—and possibly rather more since, even under the traditional gold standard, the fluctuations in exchanges between countries were greater than those between different parts of a single state, or than would be desirable to allow within the Union.[3] Indeed, it appears doubtful whether, in a Union with a universal monetary system, independent national central banks would continue to exist; they would probably have to be organized into a sort of Federal Reserve System. But, in any case, a

3. On the questions arising in this connection compare the author's *Monetary Nationalism and International Stability* (London, 1937).

national monetary policy which was predominantly guided by the economic and financial conditions of the individual state would inevitably lead to the disruption of the universal monetary system. Clearly, therefore, all monetary policy would have to be a federal and not a state matter.

But even with respect to less thoroughgoing interference with economic life than the regulation of money and prices entails, the possibilities open to the individual states would be severely limited. While the states could, of course, exercise control of the qualities of goods and the methods of production employed, it must not be overlooked that, provided the state could not exclude commodities produced in other parts of the Union, any burden placed on a particular industry by state legislation would put it at a serious disadvantage as opposed to similar industries in other parts of the Union. As has been shown by experience in existing federations, even such legislation as the restriction of child labor or of working hours becomes difficult to carry out for the individual state.

Also, in the purely financial sphere, the methods of raising revenue would be somewhat restricted for the individual states. Not only would the greater mobility between the states make it necessary to avoid all sorts of taxation which would drive capital or labor elsewhere, but there would also be considerable difficulties with many kinds of indirect taxation. In particular if, as would undoubtedly be desirable, the waste of frontier controls between the states were to be avoided, it would prove difficult to tax any commodities which could easily be imported. This would preclude not only such forms of state taxation as, for instance, a tobacco monopoly but probably many excise taxes.

It is not intended here to deal more fully with these limitations which federation would impose upon the economic policy of the individual states. The general effect in this direction has probably been sufficiently illustrated by what has already been said. It is in fact likely that, in order to prevent evasions of the fundamental provisions securing free movement of men, goods, and capital, the restrictions it would be desirable for the constitution of the federation to impose on the freedom of the individual states would have to be even greater than we have hitherto assumed and that their power of independent action would have to be limited still further. We shall have to revert later to this point.

Here it need only be added that these limitations will apply not only to state economic policy but also to economic policy conducted by trade and professional organizations extending over the territory of the state. Once frontiers cease to be closed and free movement is secured, all these national organizations, whether trade-unions, cartels, or professional associations, will lose their monopolistic position and thus, qua national organizations, their power to control the supply of their services or products.

3

The reader who has followed the argument so far will probably conclude that if, in a federation, the economic powers of the individual states will be thus limited, the federal government will have to take over the functions which the states can no longer perform and will have to do all the planning and regulating which the states cannot do. But, at this point, new difficulties present themselves. It will be advisable in this short survey to discuss these problems chiefly in connection with the best established form of government intervention in economic life, that is, tariffs. In the main, our remarks on tariffs pertain equally to other forms of restrictive or protective measures. A few references to particular kinds of government regulation will be added later.

In the first instance, protection for the whole of a particular industry within the Union may be of little use to those who now profit from protection, because the producers against whose competition they will desire protection will then be within the Union. The English wheat farmer will have little profit from a tariff which includes him and the Canadian and perhaps also the Argentinean wheat producer in the same free-trade area. The British motorcar manufacturer will have little advantage from a tariff wall which incloses at the same time the American producers. This point need hardly be labored any further.

261

Individualism and Economic Order

But even where, outside the federation, there should be important producers against whose competition a particular industry as a whole wants to be protected, there will arise special difficulties which are not present, to the same extent, within a national tariff system.

It should, perhaps, be pointed out, first, that, in order that a particular industry should benefit from a tariff, it is necessary that the tariff on its products should be higher than the tariffs on the commodities which the producers in that industry consume. A flat tariff at a uniform rate on all imports merely benefits all industries competing with imports at the expense of all others; but the incidence of these benefits is entirely indiscriminate, and they are not likely to assist where help is intended. Although such a tariff would tend to decrease the material wealth of everybody in the Union, it would probably be used to strengthen the political coherence between the members of the federation. There appear, therefore, to be no particular difficulties connected with it.

Difficulties arise only when a tariff is used to assist a particular industry to grow more rapidly than it would do without it or to protect it against adverse influence which would make it decline. In these cases, in order to subsidize one particular group of people, a sacrifice is inevitably imposed on all the other producers and consumers.

In the national state current ideologies make it comparatively easy to persuade the rest of the community that it is in their interest to protect "their" iron industry or "their" wheat production or whatever it be. An element of national pride in "their" industry and considerations of national strength in case of war generally induce people to consent to the sacrifice. The decisive consideration is that their sacrifice benefits compatriots whose position is familiar to them. Will the same motives operate in favor of other members of the Union? Is it likely that the French peasant will be willing to pay more for his fertilizer to help the British chemical industry? Will the Swedish workman be ready to pay more for his oranges to assist the Californian grower? Or the clerk in the city of London be ready to pay more for his shoes or his bicycle to help American or Belgian workmen? Or the South African miner prepared to pay more for his sardines to help the Norwegian fishermen?

It seems clear that, in a federation, the problem of agreeing on a common tariff will raise problems different in kind from those that arise in a national state. It would lack the support of the strong nationalist ideologies, the sympathies with the neighbor; and even the argument of defense would lose much of its power of conviction if the Union were really strong enough to have little to fear. It is difficult to visualize how, in a federation, agreement could be reached on the use of tariffs for the protection of particular industries. The same applies to all other forms of protection. Provided that there is great diversity of conditions among the various countries, as will inevitably be the case in a federation, the obsolescent or declining industry clamoring for assistance will almost invariably encounter, in the same field and within the federation, progressive industries which demand freedom of development. It will be much harder to retard progress in one part of the federation in order to maintain standards of life in another part than to do the same thing in a national state.

But even where it is not simply a question of "regulating" (i.e., curbing) the progress of one group in order to protect another group from competition, the diversity of conditions and the different stages of economic development reached by the various parts of the federation will raise serious obstacles to federal legislation. Many forms of state interference, welcome in one stage of economic progress, are regarded in another as a great impediment. Even such legislation as the limitation of working hours or compulsory unemployment insurance, or the protection of amenities, will be viewed in a different light in poor and in rich regions and may in the former actually harm and rouse violent opposition from the kind of people who in the richer regions demand it and profit from it. Such legislation will, on the whole, have to be confined to the extent to which it can be applied locally without at the same time imposing any restrictions on mobility, such as a law of settlements.

These problems are, of course, not unfamiliar in national states as we know them. But they are made less difficult by the comparative homogeneity, the common convictions and ideals, and the whole common tradition of the people of a national state. In fact, the existing sovereign national states are mostly of such dimensions and composition as to render possible agreement on an amount of state interference which they would not suffer if they were either much smaller or much larger. In the former instance (and what matters is not merely size in terms of numbers of inhabitants or area but size relative to the existing groups, which are at the same time more or less homogeneous and comparatively self-supporting), the attempts to make the national state self-supporting would be out of the question. If counties, or even smaller districts, were the sovereign units, there would be comparatively few industries in every such unit which would be protected. All the regions which did not possess, and could not create, a particular industry would constitute free markets for the produce of that industry. If, on the other hand, the sovereign units were much larger than they are today, it would be much more difficult to place a burden on the inhabitants of one region in order to assist the inhabitants of a very distant region who might differ from the former not only in language but also in almost every other respect.

Planning, or central direction of economic activity, presupposes the existence of common ideals and common values; and the degree to which planning can be carried is limited to the extent to which agreement on such a common scale of values can be obtained or enforced.[4] It is clear that such agreement will be limited in inverse proportion to the homogeneity and the similarity in outlook and tradition possessed by the inhabitants of an area. Although, in the national state, the submission to the will of a majority will be facilitated by the myth of nationality, it must be clear that people will be reluctant to submit to any interference in their daily affairs when the majority which directs the government is composed of people of different nationalities and different traditions. It is, after all, only common

4. Cf. on this and the following the present author's *Freedom and the Economic System* ("Public Policy Pamphlets," No. 29 [Chicago, 1939], and, more recently, *The Road to Serfdom* (Chicago: University of Chicago Press, 1944).

sense that the central government in a federation composed of many different people will have to be restricted in scope if it is to avoid meeting an increasing resistance on the part of the various groups which it includes. But what could interfere more thoroughly with the intimate life of the people than the central direction of economic life, with its inevitable discrimination between groups? There seems to be little possible doubt that the scope for the regulation of economic life will be much narrower for the central government of a federation than for national states. And since, as we have seen, the power of the states which comprise the federation will be yet more limited, much of the interference with economic life to which we have become accustomed will be altogether impracticable under a federal organization.

The point can be best illustrated if we consider for a moment the problems raised by the most developed form of planning, socialism. Let us first take the question of whether a socialist state, for example, the U.S.S.R., could enter a federation with the Atlantic democratic states. The answer is decisively in the negative—not because the other states would be unwilling to admit Russia but because the U.S.S.R. could never submit to the conditions which federation would impose and permit the free movement of goods, men, and money across her frontiers while, at the same time, retaining her socialist economy.

If, on the other hand, we consider the possibility of a socialist regime for the federation as a whole, including Russia, the impracticability of such a scheme is at once obvious. With the differences in the standard of life, in tradition and education, which would exist in such a federation, it would certainly be impossible to get a democratic solution of the central problems which socialist planning would raise. But even if we consider a federation composed merely of the present democratic states, such as that proposed by Clarence Streit, the difficulties of introducing a common socialist regime would scarcely be smaller. That Englishmen or Frenchmen should intrust the safeguarding of their lives, liberty, and property—in short, the functions of the liberal state—to a suprastate organization is conceivable. But that they should be willing to give the government of a federation the power to regulate their economic life, to decide what they should produce and consume, seems neither probable nor desirable. Yet, at the same time, in a federation these powers could not be left to the national states; therefore, federation would appear to mean that neither government could have powers for socialist planning of economic life.

4

The conclusion that, in a federation, certain economic powers, which are now generally wielded by the national states, could be exercised neither by the federation nor by the individual states, implies that there would have to be less government all round if federation is to be practicable. Certain forms of economic policy will have to be conducted by the federation or by nobody at all. Whether the federation will exercise these powers will depend on the possibility of reaching true agreement, not only on *whether* these powers are to be used, but on *how* they are to be used. The main point is that, in many cases in which it will prove impossible to reach such agreement, we shall have to resign ourselves rather to have no legislation in a particular field than the state legislation which would break up the economic unity of the federation. Indeed, this readiness to have no legislation at all on some subjects rather than state legislation will be the acid test of whether we are intellectually mature for the achievement of suprastate organization.

This is a point on which, in existing federations, difficulties have constantly arisen and on which, it must be admitted, the "progressive" movements have generally sided with the powers of darkness. In the United States, in particular, there has been a strong tendency on the part of all progressives to favor state legislation in all cases where union legislation could not be achieved, irrespective of whether such state legislation was compatible with the preservation of the economic unity of the union. In consequence, in the United States and similarly in Switzerland, the separate economic policies of the individual states have already gone far in the direction of bringing about a gradual disintegration of the common economic area.[5]

The experience in these federations makes it appear that, to prevent such trends, it is scarcely sufficient to prohibit tariffs and similar obvious impediments to interstate commerce. Evasion of such rules by an individual state which has embarked upon a course of national planning by means of administrative regulations has proved so easy that all the effects of protection can be achieved by means of such provisions as sanitary regulations, requirements of inspection, and the charging of fees for these and other administrative controls. In view of the inventiveness shown by state legislators in this respect, it seems clear that no specific prohibitions in the constitution of the federation would suffice to prevent such developments; the federal government would probably have to be given general restraining powers to this end. This means that the federation will have to possess the negative power of preventing individual states from interfering with economic activity in certain ways, although it may not have the positive power of acting in their stead. In the United States the various clauses of the Constitution safeguarding property and freedom of contract, and particularly the "due process" clauses of the Fifth and Fourteenth amendments, have, to some extent, fulfilled this function and contributed probably more than is generally realized to prevent an even more rapid disintegration into many separate economic areas; but they have in consequence been the object of persistent attack on the part of all those who demand more rapid extension of state control of economic life.

There will, of course, always be certain kinds of government activity which will be done most efficiently for areas corresponding to the present national states and which, at the same time, can be exercised nationally without endangering the economic unity of the federation. But, on the whole, it is likely that in a federation the weakening of

5. For the United States cf. R. L. Buell, *Death by Tariff: Protectionism in State and Federal Legislation* ("Public Policy Pamphlets," No. 27 [Chicago, 1939]), and F. E. Melder, *Barriers to Inter-state Commerce in the United States* (Orono, Me., 1937).

the economic powers of the individual states would and should gradually be carried much further than will at first be evident. Not only will their powers be decreased by the functions taken over by the federation, and by those which cannot be exercised by either federation or states but must be left free from legislative control, but there will probably also be a great deal of devolution of powers from the states to smaller units. There are many activities which are today intrusted to the sovereign states merely in order to strengthen the states as such, but which could really be carried out much more efficiently locally, or, at any rate, by smaller units. In a federation all the arguments for centralization which are based on the desire to make the sovereign national states as such as strong as possible disappear—in fact, the converse seems to apply. Not only could most of the desirable forms of planning be conducted by comparatively small territorial units, but the competition between them, together with the impossibility of erecting barriers, would at the same time form a salutary check on their activities and, while leaving the door open for desirable experimentation, would keep it roughly within the appropriate limits.

It should, perhaps, be emphasized that all this does not imply that there will not be ample scope for economic policy in a federation and that there is no need for extreme laissez faire in economic matters. It means only that planning in a federation cannot assume the forms which today are pre-eminently known under this term; that there must be no substitution of day-to-day interference and regulation for the impersonal forces of the market; and, in particular, that there must be no trace of that "national development by controlled monopolies" to which, as has recently been pointed out in an influential weekly journal, "British leaders are growing accustomed."[6] In a federation economic policy will have to take the form of providing a rational permanent framework within which individual initiative will have the largest possible scope and will be made to work as beneficently as possible; and it will have to supplement the working of the

6. *Spectator*, March 3, 1939.

Interstate Federalism

competitive mechanism where, in the nature of the case, certain services cannot be brought forth and be regulated by the price system. But it will, at least in so far as the policy of the federation as such is concerned, essentially have to be a long-term policy, in which the fact that "in the long run we are all dead" is a decided advantage; and it must not be used, as is often the case today, as a pretext for acting on the principle *après nous le déluge;* for the long-term character of the decisions to be taken makes it practically impossible to foresee the incidence of their effects upon individuals and groups and thus prevents the issue from being decided by a struggle between the most powerful "interests."

It does not come within the scope of a short article to consider in any detail the positive tasks of the liberal economic policy which a federation would have to pursue. Nor is it even possible to give here further consideration to such important problems as those of monetary or colonial policy which will, of course, continue to exist in a federation. On the last point it may, however, be added that the question which probably would be raised first, i.e., whether colonies ought to be administered by the states or by the federation, would be of comparatively minor importance. With a real open-door policy for all members of the federation, the economic advantages derived from the possession of colonies, whether the colonies were administered federally or nationally, would be approximately the same to all the members of the federation. But, in general, it would undoubtedly be preferable that their. administration should be a federal and not a state matter.

5

Since it has been argued so far that an essentially liberal economic regime is a necessary condition for the success of any interstate federation, it may be added, in conclusion, that the converse is no less true: the abrogation of national sovereignties and the creation of an effective international order of law is a necessary complement and the logical consummation of the liberal program. In a recent discussion of international liberalism, it has been rightly contended that it was one of the main deficiencies of nineteenth-century liberalism that its advocates did not sufficiently realize that the achievement of the recognized harmony of interests between the inhabitants of the different states was only possible within the framework of international security.[7] The conclusions which Professor Robbins drew from his considerations of these problems and which are summed up in the statement that "there must be neither alliance nor complete unification; neither *Staatenbund* nor *Einheitsstaat* but *Bundesstaat*,"[8] are essentially the same as those which have recently been elaborated by Clarence Streit in greater detail in their political aspects.

That nineteenth-century liberalism did not succeed more fully is due largely to its failure to develop in this direction; and the cause is mainly that, because of historical accidents, it successively joined forces first with nationalism and later with socialism, both forces being equally incompatible with its main principle.[9] That liberalism became first allied with nationalism was due to the historical coincidence that, during the nineteenth century, it was nationalism which in Ireland, Greece, Belgium, and Poland and later in Italy and Austro-Hungary fought against the same sort of oppression which liberalism opposed. It later became allied with socialism because agreement as to some of the ultimate ends for a time obscured the utter incompatibility of the methods by which the two movements tried to reach their goal. But now when nationalism and socialism have

7. L. C. Robbins, *Economic Planning and International Order* (1937), p. 240.
8. *Ibid.*, p. 245.
9. This trend can be well observed in John Stuart Mill. His gradual movement toward socialism is, of course, well known, but he also accepted more of the nationalist doctrines than is compatible with his wholly liberal program. In *Considerations of Representative Government* (p. 298) he states: "It is in general a necessary condition of free institutions that the boundaries of government should coincide in the main with those of nationalities." Against this view, Lord Acton argued that "the combination of different nations in one State is as necessary a condition of civilised life as the combination of men in society" and that "this diversity in the same State is a firm barrier against the intention of the Government beyond the political sphere which is common to all into the social department which escapes legislation and is ruled by spontaneous laws" (*History of Freedom and Other Essays* [1909], p. 290).

combined—not only in name—into a powerful organization which threatens the liberal democracies, and when, even within these democracies, the socialists are becoming steadily more nationalist and the nationalists steadily more socialist, is it too much to hope for a rebirth of real liberalism, true to its ideal of freedom and internationalism and returned from its temporary aberrations into the nationalist and the socialist camps? The idea of interstate federation as the consistent development of the liberal point of view should be able to provide a new *point d' appui* for all those liberals who have despaired of and deserted their creed during the periods of wandering.

This liberalism of which we speak is, of course, not a party matter; it is a view which, before World War I, provided a common ground for nearly all the citizens of the Western democracies and which is the basis of democratic government. If one party has perhaps preserved slightly more of this liberal spirit than the others, they have nevertheless all strayed from the fold, some in one direction and some in another. But the realization of the ideal of an international democratic order demands a resuscitation of the ideal in its true form. Government by agreement is only possible provided that we do not require the government to act in fields other than those in which we can obtain true agreement. If, in the international sphere, democratic government should only prove to be possible if the tasks of the international government are limited to an essentially liberal program, it would no more than confirm the experience in the national sphere, in which it is daily becoming more obvious that democracy will work only if we do not overload it and if the majorities do not abuse their power of interfering with individual freedom. Yet, if the price we have to pay for an international democratic government is the restriction of the power and scope of government, it is surely not too high a price, and all those who genuinely believe in democracy ought to be prepared to pay it. The democratic principle of "counting heads in order to save breaking them" is, after all, the only method of peaceful change yet invented which has been tried and has not been found wanting. Whatever one may think about the desirability of other

271

aims of government, surely the prevention of war or civil strife ought to take precedence, and, if achievement lies only in limiting government to this and a few other main purposes, these other ideals will have to give place.

I make no apology for pointing out obstacles in the way of a goal in whose value I profoundly believe. I am convinced that these difficulties are genuine and that, if we do not admit them from the beginning, they may at a later date form the rock on which all the hopes for international organization may founder. The sooner we recognize these difficulties, the sooner we can hope to overcome them. If, as it appears to me, ideals shared by many can be realized only by means which few at present favor, neither academic impartiality nor considerations of expediency should prevent one from saying what one recognizes to be the right means for the given end—even if these means should happen to be those favored by a political party.